Water Drops from
Women Writers

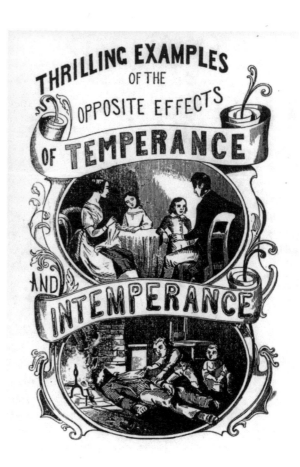

Water Drops from Women Writers

A TEMPERANCE READER

Edited by Carol Mattingly

Southern Illinois University Press
Carbondale and Edwardsville

Frontispiece: From *The Fountain and the Bottle: Comprising Thrilling Examples of the Opposite Effects of Temperance and Intemperance,* edited by a son of temperance, frontispiece. Boston: H. Wentworth, 1850.

Library of Congress Cataloging-in-Publication Data
Water drops from women writers : a temperance reader / edited by Carol Mattingly.
   p. cm.
Includes bibliographical references.
    1. Alcoholics—Family relationships—Fiction. 2. Drinking of alcoholic beverages—Fiction. 3. Alcoholics—Rehabilitation—Fiction. 4. Alcoholics—Fiction. 5. Temperance—Fiction. 6. American fiction—Women authors. 7. American fiction—19th century. I. Mattingly, Carol, 1945–

PS648.A42 W38 2001
813'.309355—dc21
ISBN 0-8093-2399-0 (alk. paper)   00-068021

for Maggie

CONTENTS

ILLUSTRATIONS

PREFACE

The abuse of alcohol in the nineteenth century and its subsequent effect on women led many to write in support of temperance. My title reflects the tendency of these women to speak of their temperance writing as "water drops" because they promoted the drinking of water in place of alcohol. In most of the fiction that follows, I have remained true to the original text, maintaining nineteenth-century conventions for spelling and punctuation. Occasionally, however, in cases that might create confusion for today's readers, such as spacing within contractions, I have silently emended text.

Compiling this anthology has been a pleasure, partly because of the fascinating authors and stories but also because of the support of colleagues, friends, and family. During the early stages of this project, Angeletta Gourdine and Robin Roberts, my colleagues at Louisiana State University, read headnotes and stories and offered suggestions. As I completed the manuscript, Karen Chandler, Ben Hefbauer, and Susan Ryan, my colleagues at the University of Louisville, gave invaluable advice.

Janine Conant provided a variety of assistance and support as I compiled the manuscript, as did the staff at the microfilm reading room at LSU. Claire Schlect helped to proof stories and gave suggestions about their inclusion, and Judi Kemerait and Irv Peckham kindly retrieved copies of illustrations for me.

I appreciate as well suggestions from two outside readers for Southern Illinois University Press, Jamie Barlowe and Shirley Samuels, and for continuous support and guidance from Karl Kageff, acquisitions editor at SIUP. I also wish to thank Liz Brymer and Carol Burns for suggestions regarding this manuscript and Julie Bush for her careful copyediting.

Finally, as always, I want to express my appreciation for my daughters, Amy and Maggie, and for my siblings, who bring so much joy to my life.

INTRODUCTION

Temperance was the largest single organizing force for women in U.S. history, moving women to take public action in unprecedented numbers and providing a topic of concern for the best writers of the nineteenth century. The cultural contexts written into women's temperance fiction reveal the radical nature of that activism. Taken together, the many works written by women on this subject provide an understanding of nineteenth-century society and culture that repudiates beliefs about temperance women and about nineteenth-century women in general—that they were "conservative," uninteresting, and often complicit in their own oppression. Such prejudices have encouraged neglect of a powerful, ongoing conversation by and about women that serves to demonstrate that large numbers of nineteenth-century women were dissatisfied, and often angry, about the unequal position to which they had been relegated. Feeling a communion with other women, they worked together to create change.

Women's temperance fiction is always about women. It provides the earliest examples of American fiction that address many of the issues that remain a concern for twenty-first-century women. Protagonists are women, and while temperance provides the frame, writers present worthy role models for readers and dwell primarily on legal, social, and economic conditions that place women in jeopardy. Authors demonstrate the universal nature of such problems for women by depicting seemingly implausible victims: protagonists who come from "good" families, who are popular and respected, and with whom the reader might readily identify. The author's focus is usually a well-loved daughter and friend with bright prospects whose happy dreams for the future fade quickly as her promising husband or successful father becomes increasingly involved with drink and the ills that accompany it—gaming, violence, and subsequent economic vulnerability. As the husband or father moves closer and closer to destruction, so does his family, and the primary attention focuses on women's difficulties in protecting themselves and their children because of economic, social, and legal roadblocks.

Temperance fiction written by nineteenth-century women both reinforces and discredits stereotypes that have developed around such work. Temperance fiction *is* often formulaic, even though it makes use of many and diverse formulas. It *does,* to some degree, always deal with the evils of alcohol. However, such features do not prevent much of women's temperance fiction from being genuinely engaging, poignant, and well crafted. That such fiction serves an agenda does not, in itself, diminish its value. As with any genre, women's temperance fiction exhibits varying degrees of literary quality.

Temperance, a major reform arena in the United States during the nineteenth century, represented the most important and far-reaching issue for most women during that period; more women united around the temperance issue than any other, and discussions of intemperance permitted a treatment of women's injustices in forums that large audiences attended and numerous readers examined. Audiences willingly listened to and considered women's unfair treatment when directly connected with problems of intemperance.

Intemperance, or overindulgence in alcohol, was rampant in America during the nineteenth century, and temperance forces attempted to abolish the manufacture and sale of liquor. Women formed and joined temperance organizations in large numbers in an effort to promote such reform. By the end of the century, more than 200,000 women had joined the largest single organization for temperance women, the Woman's Christian Temperance Union (WCTU), and numerous others belonged to other temperance organizations.

Even though some nineteenth-century women drank alcohol in large quantity, men in that century drank far more. According to Rorabaugh, two-thirds of all the distilled spirits drunk were consumed by 50 percent of adult men, who comprised only one-eighth of the total population (11). As the century progressed, women drank even less proportionally because of cultural restrictions on their consumption. Therefore, intemperance came to be accepted as a problem of men, rather than of women, providing an ideal forum for demanding more just and equitable treatment for women.

Vast numbers of women spoke on and wrote about the dangers of intemperance, but the subject permitted them to address the wrongs women felt generally. In fact, many women saw temperance and woman's rights as one and the same issue. In an 1854 letter to *The Lily,* for example, Frances D. Gage clearly suggests such a connection: "I gave twenty-five lectures on the two great subjects of reform, Temperance and Woman's Rights (which indeed seem but one, so closely are all the interests united)" (104). And in the preface explaining the need for her novel *The Present Problem,* Sarah K. Bolton tells her reader:

> Intemperance and immorality are on every side. We have tacitly countenanced them in one sex, while we have condemned them in the other. The women of America are beginning to feel the magnitude of the evils they are called upon to meet, and the greatness of the work God has laid upon them.

Such authors believed that by addressing temperance, they could impress audiences with the need for overall reforms on behalf of women. Others came to accept the importance of woman's rights issues through their support of the temperance reform. In seeking to change laws governing alcohol, they became increasingly aware of legal inequities between the sexes; often experiencing firsthand the disdain and disrespect heaped upon women, they devoted themselves to changing legal as well as social and economic systems. Both because of the large numbers of women involved in the movement and because of its appeal to a broad spectrum of women, the temperance movement was essential to women generally coming to consciousness about, and ultimately insisting upon a change in, sexual inequalities in the nineteenth- and early-twentieth-century United States.

Politically astute and effective, temperance women were instrumental in achieving numerous local and state political gains with regard to women's issues: raising the legal age of sexual consent for girls in nearly every state (age of consent in some states had been as young as seven), changing property laws that prevented married women from controlling their own income and property, requiring the presence of matrons in jails and prisons where women were brought and housed, and opening homes for unwed mothers. Temperance women achieved success at the national level, securing passage of the Eighteenth Amendment to the U.S. Constitution, prohibiting the manufacture and sale of alcohol. In addition, they effectively convinced the "average woman," the woman somewhat hesitant to join public reform efforts, of the need for woman's suffrage, leading to passage of the Nineteenth Amendment to the Constitution.[1] It is no mere coincidence that the woman's suffrage amendment became part of the Constitution in 1920, one year after Prohibition.[2]

Beginning in the 1820s, women made up a substantial portion of membership in temperance organizations,[3] and from as early as the 1830s, they published fiction presenting temperance as an overwhelming concern for women. From the 1840s, women organized in independent, exclusively women's organizations to fight for temperance, publishing their proceedings and resolutions in state and local newspapers. By the early 1850s, numerous women began to speak publicly in support of temperance; others confronted retail dealers, sometimes destroying their wares.

Between December 1873 and November 1874, a movement of women labeled the Woman's Crusade widely protested the manufacture and sale of alcohol. These protests represent the largest public demonstration by women in the nineteenth century: between 57,000 and 143,000 women participated in at least 911 crusades throughout the United States.[4] Crusaders' participation differed from location to location. Most often, women protested the sale of liquor by marching and praying, inside or in front of saloons; sometimes they destroyed the saloons' products. Such public participation required great courage of women, given the extent to which they were ridiculed, both in the streets and in the press. They often braved physical harm as well and sometimes were jailed.[5] Following the demonstrations, in 1874, crusade leaders organized the Woman's Christian Temperance Union, which became the largest organization of women in the century.

While women became members as well as officers in some organizations open to both men and women, such as the Good Templars, they constituted the *only* officers in the WCTU. Men might be honorary members, but the organization was composed of and administered by women. And the WCTU afforded numerous opportunities for leadership roles. A massively networked and layered system composed of approximately forty departments, the union required scores of officers at the national, state, district, county, and local levels, necessitating that the members become publicly active speakers and writers. Departments at every level were numerous. For example, at the national WCTU meeting held in Detroit in 1888, President Frances E. Willard announced that Ohio alone had five hundred local unions. Meetings and conventions held at each level required astute skills in organization, leadership, and speaking.

Women's temperance fiction, produced in impressive quantity, provided effective support for women's political involvement. By 1875, John Newton Stearns, who had been agent and editor for the National Temperance Publication Association for thirty years, declared women to be the primary writers of temperance fiction, writing at least three-fourths of temperance tracts and books (*Minutes* 49). Such fiction sanctioned a remarkably candid presentation of injustices toward women, allowing for criticism of the entire cultural pattern of women's dependence on men; concomitantly, it allowed for insistence upon a greater equality between the sexes.

Much has been written about nineteenth-century women's ability to express personal dissatisfaction and doubt in subversive and sublimated texts that lurk beneath their surface writing, but women temperance writers were able to represent more openly than other writers nineteenth-century women's dissatisfaction with their assigned roles. They broached otherwise proscribed topics, subjects writers of fiction generally and male writers of temperance fiction dared not address: not only general inequality between the sexes and violence against women but also prejudicial societal attitudes towards victims of male assault and abuse, a woman's right to her own body, marital infidelity, and the imperative for women to focus on their own needs.

Women temperance writers' primary subject is women, and much fiction labeled temperance or published in temperance collections actually addresses intemperance only superficially, focusing instead on other issues of importance to women. Authors provide advice to women, afford strong role models, and interrogate the dichotomous systems that treat women unfairly. As early as 1836, Sarah J. Hale proclaimed the need for women's perspective on intemperance in her preface to *My Cousin Mary: or The Inebriate*:

It may, at first, seem an unnecessary labor, for a new writer of moral stories to attempt depicting the evils of intemperance, while the popular author of "My Mother's Gold Ring" is still in the field.[6] But a little reflection will show those who have read the interesting and instructive series of "Temperance Tales," put forth by Mr. Sargent, that, notwithstanding all he has done, there is still room for others, in this great work of national reformation. He has, as he naturally would do, addressed his lessons to men, rather than to women, and thus spoke to the heart and mind of the active bustling world, rather than to the feelings of the romantic and fashionable.

But the evils of intemperance reach all classes, and often involve the helpless and innocent female in deeper sufferings, than the hardier sex ever endure. Many a fair, delicate girl, reared in the lap of indulgence, and surrounded by all those pleasures and advantages which make youth appear like the opening scene of a sweet romance, which is sure to end in love and happiness, many such have found their dreams of bliss rudely dissipated, while awakening to the reality of wretchedness, which the wife of an intemperate man, in any station in life, must endure. (3–4)

By mid-century, the New York state women's temperance society was sponsoring "$10 premiums" for the best fictional temperance tracts by women because men's writings were "dwelling on the surface of things, instead of going down to the great foundation principles on which this cause rests" ("$10 Premiums").[7] Those "foundational principles" were the social, legal, and judicial inequities that imperiled women's lives and livelihoods.

Women appear in men's temperance fiction, but they are nearly always pathetic victims as opposed to the usually strong characters in women's temperance fiction. Men's temperance fiction more often focuses on the drunkard or on a male narrator, whose perspective distances him from the perils associated with alcohol, often in a voyeuristic manner. While men do often call for reform of the laws governing the manufacture and sale of alcohol, they almost never seek changes in laws that specifically pertain to women— those associated with married women's property rights and suffrage, for example. Nor do they examine the broader economic and social concerns so important to women.

Women writers of temperance fiction deliberately sought to raise the self-esteem of women, and they did not hesitate to take male writers of temperance fiction to task for sending women the wrong messages. For example, Amelia Bloomer, editor and publisher of the first temperance and woman's rights newspaper, *The Lily,* publicly condemned "Ruling a Wife," a short story by the popular temperance writer T. S. Arthur, for "the manner in which it treated poor Mrs. Lane and her sex at large" (86). Arthur had depicted Mrs. Lane's leaving her abusive husband but portrayed her grateful return to her repentant "protector" after suffering a series of overwhelming, precarious incursions in her attempt to support herself and her infant. The last of these perils involved an effort to force Mrs. Lane into prostitution; she was rescued by her estranged husband while being dragged, babe in arms, upstairs to the bedrooms of a house of ill repute. Bloomer reprimanded Arthur for showing that women are "weak and helpless—incapable of taking care of ourselves or keeping out of harm's way." She suggested that Arthur, in future, show woman "equal to the emergency" by permitting her the dignity of supporting herself, "teaching her to respect" herself rather than humbling her. Bloomer's suggestions to Arthur demonstrate a major difference between temperance fiction by men and women authors.

As women became the major writers of temperance fiction, their publications proliferated in ways that assured their availability to large numbers of readers. Not only was their fiction published inexpensively by temperance and Sunday school publication houses and by tract societies but it was often included in popular periodicals and gift books.[8] Perhaps most importantly, Sunday school libraries, the only free, publicly accessible distribution sources for the majority of the population, circulated temperance fiction.[9] Temperance women's ideas, therefore, not only reached a large and diverse variety of women but did so with general acceptance because of implied support of religious institutions. Temperance fiction by women was, thus, widely read and highly effective in communicating messages about the dangers of intemperance and about other reform efforts for women.

Because of the brutalities and injustices suffered by women at the hands of intemperate men, and because of subsequent economic and social hardships falling to women and children, nearly all women could agree upon the need to promote temperance, even if they opposed strict prohibition. References in temperance fiction to women's clothing being sold or locked away by husbands, to wives and children being forced outside in the dark of night, often in the dead of winter, and to wives being beaten, even killed, may seem exaggerated to twenty-first-century readers; however, nineteenth-century newspapers abound in reports of just such happenings. Because of widespread attention to such brutalities, and since intemperance highlighted so many inequities for women, the topic provided an ideal forum for women to address a broad spectrum of related issues.

The fiction included here demonstrates the far-reaching appeal of the temperance topic for women and provides a representative sample of the abundant temperance fiction written by women. However, most of the protagonists—as most of the authors represented here—are white and middle class. The majority of women who answered the temperance call fit this description. By the final quarter of the century, however, the diversity of these organizations increased, especially that of the WCTU. Still, even as part of the WCTU, non-Anglo groups were sometimes marginalized. The state unions created departments to recruit and/or perform missionary work among groups perceived to have special needs. In the upper Midwest, Germans were often targeted because of their association with the brewing industry; a large Irish presence in Massachusetts convinced leaders there of the need to promote temperance among those immigrants. At the national level, the WCTU had a specific Work among Colored People department for varying periods of time; other special departments targeted Native Americans and Mormons. The union also had a Work among Southerners department until southern white women protested that such special designation for them be eliminated.

None of these special charges created a national scandal, however, except the separate treatment of African American women within the union. In the 1890s, Ida B. Wells leveled charges of racism against Frances E. Willard and the WCTU, initiating a controversy that raged for years. Despite such charges, however, black women joined the WCTU in large numbers, most often creating separate unions in the South, which allowed black leaders membership to the national executive committee and other prestigious boards.[10]

Although many women other than white, middle-class women became active in temperance reform, I have found temperance fiction by only one, the accomplished author Frances Ellen Watkins Harper. Although a noted writer even during her own time, much of Watkins Harper's fiction is published in places where research-ers have not traditionally sought literature. For example, *Sowing and Reaping,* excerpted here, was made available to general read-ers only recently when Frances Smith Foster located some of Watkins Harper's fiction in the *Christian Recorder,* the journal of the African Methodist Episcopal Church. We may learn of addi-tional temperance fiction written by marginalized groups as schol-ars continue to search in places not traditionally considered sources for literature.

Despite this limitation, readers familiar with nineteenth-century women authors and activists will appreciate the inclusion here of many of the best-loved writers of the day. I have classified fiction according to what I see as the three primary themes in women's temperance fiction: family relationships, legislative shortcomings, and reexamination of gender roles. These categories are broad, and women's temperance fiction varies within the divisions. Because much fiction addresses multiple concerns, a great deal of overlap often exists between categories; many features of one category ap-pear in works placed within another. However, I have grouped pieces according to what I consider the principal feature of each work in order to provide as clear a picture as possible of the over-all nature of women's temperance fiction.

Fiction in parts 1 and 2 exposes women's anxiety about and anger toward a social, economic, and legal system that failed to shelter them. The primary argument against changes in the eco-nomic and legal systems was that men already provided adequate protection for women. Men's intemperance served uniquely to re-pudiate such assurances, and women's temperance fiction often debunks such conventional fallacies. To the contrary, such fiction demonstrates that men themselves pose the chief danger for women through physical force and legal privilege.

Part 1 includes temperance stories characteristic of the most prevalent type written by women. Since "woman's sphere" was in the home, the direction of women's lives was determined primarily in relation to family, and the majority of temperance fiction exam-ines women's position within family structures. The largest portion of such stories exposes the precarious nature of marriage. Authors caution young women that marriage is a dangerous gamble. This dictum dispels the romantic ideology of the domestic sphere and suggests instead that women cautiously evaluate suitors with an eye to their own safety. Authors often suggest that women may improve their odds, however, by carefully considering suitors' past behavior, and they make examples of characters who fail to heed such warnings.

These stories most often begin with the marriage of the protagonist—a departure from other women's fiction during the century, which usually ends with the happy wedding day—and depict the hardships endured by women when husbands become irresponsible or abusive. The narratives thus emphasize the perilous position of women who are expected, or find it necessary, to marry but whose welfare, along with that of their children, becomes entirely dependent upon their husbands. The first three selections in part 1 typify temperance fiction dealing primarily with the hardships of wives in intemperate relationships. Caroline H. Butler's "Emma Alton" begins with the protagonist's wedding. Emma typifies women protagonists in her double victimization: she becomes destitute because her husband squanders their resources; she is also victimized by a social system that, although she is the "innocent sufferer for her husband's vices," in turn neglects and treats her with derision. In "The Intemperate," Lydia Sigourney, one of the best-loved authors of her day, demonstrates, as does Butler, the falsehood behind the joy and promises of the wedding day. Sigourney depicts the hardships of Jane Harwood, who, in her efforts to remove her husband from temptation, migrates from family and friends. Jane thus increases her own isolation and further endangers herself and her children.

In their discussions of marriage and its hazards for women, some authors also address the related issue of marital rape. Although they do not address such forced intimacy explicitly (nineteenth-century women had not yet named such an abuse), readers would have recognized the meaning behind the constant birthing of children in a situation where the husband has become an alcoholic. Ann Douglas has noted the tendency among American women in the nineteenth century to control their number of pregnancies, and Linda Gordon notes the two methods that adherents of "voluntary motherhood" promoted: a couple's mutual decision to abstain (which Gordon suggests was in actuality the husband's self-imposed celibacy) and "the right of the wife unilaterally to refuse her husband" (103). The wife of a drunkard could hardly have depended on a husband's complicity in either context, and some authors make clear that wives of drunkards retain no "rights" of refusal.[11] The first of Frances D. Gage's "Tales of Truth" suggests the inability of women to retain control over their own bodies in marital situations with alcoholic men. Gage indicts a social and legal system that not only neglects to protect women but also gives their husbands all rights to their bodies. Her protagonist, Mary Cadwallader, longs to leave her husband and specifically wishes for no more children; still, three children, including twins, are born to her subsequent to her expressing such desires.

The following two selections also concern the marital relationship but, written later in the century, demonstrate the growing concern over psychological ramifications implicated in intemperance. Elizabeth Stuart Phelps's *Jack the Fisherman* and Mary Dwinell Chellis's *Our Homes* depict the environmental conditions that encourage replication of abusive and alcoholic behavior, making it difficult for female victims to escape and for male victims to reform. Phelps suggests the need for breaking cycles of intemperance and violence, and Chellis, the most prolific author of temperance fiction, suggests that women with greater self-esteem are less likely to remain in abusive situations.

In addition to dangers related to the marital contract, authors expose dangers women face in other family relationships—as daughters and sisters. Daughters and sisters suffer more deeply than sons and brothers because of their particular vulnerability in such matters as reduced marital prospects, absence of presumed physical protection, lack of economic options, and legal inequities. Caroline Lee Hentz's protagonist in "The Drunkard's Daughter" demonstrates amazing physical and emotional strength. Still, Hentz points to both the grown daughter's shame and embarrassment at the public exposure of her father's drunkenness and the demeaning attitudes she, though innocent, must endure because of his addictions. Hentz's narrative also illustrates the many ways women's temperance fiction addresses issues still unresolved today: the conspiracy of silence surrounding addiction, notions of disease and heredity implicated in alcoholism, and the idea that addiction crosses class borders, claiming the distinguished and respected as well as the poor and downtrodden. Similarly, Julia Perkins Ballard's "Only a Drunkard's Daughter" represents the typical change in societal attitudes toward wives and daughters when husbands and fathers become drunkards. As economic disaster approaches, social standing and, therefore, treatment by former friends become drastically altered.

Corra Lynn's *Durham Village; A Temperance Tale* depicts sibling relationships to further demonstrate that it is men from whom women need protection, again belying the notion that men ensure safety for the women in their lives. Precisely because of their relationship to their brother, William, Edith and Julia Lundley are threatened with rape, humiliation, and blackmail. Both women demonstrate that their only security comes from their own composure and intelligence rather than from men.

Many authors explicitly address the need to remedy legal injustices with regards to women. In their fiction, they unqualifiedly insist upon greater rights for women, especially married women. Coverture, the traditional common law that united women's legal rights with those of their husbands, existed to varying degrees in every state. When women married, their personal property and, to differing extents, their real property (real estate, cattle, and the like), as well as their persons, their labor, and their children, came under ownership of their husbands, were subject to his disposal, and could be confiscated by his creditors. While a woman's property might be misused or squandered by any husband, chances of loss became greater when husbands became alcohol abusers. Women's inability to protect themselves or their children from abusive, irresponsible husbands who drank thus provided an effective means for speakers and writers to point out women's precarious position with regards to law.

In part 2, authors address unfair and unequal legal treatment of women, most often as related to marriage but in other arenas as well, and summarily deny that men adequately protect women. They scrutinize legislation that creates hardships for women—divorce and custody laws, married women's property laws, husbands' and fathers' legal ownership of wives' and children's wages, and single women's taxation without representation. Humor provides an effective means of presenting women's wrongs, and many women writing temperance fiction included wit in their stories. In one of the more effective humorous treatments of intemperance, Marietta Holley highlights the numerous legal inequalities for women. Excerpts from Holley's novel *Sweet Cicely or Josiah Allen as a Politician* introduce part 2 because Holley so skillfully illustrates in a few pages nearly every complaint temperance women made against the unfair legal and judicial systems.

Selections by Elizabeth Cady Stanton and Frances Ellen Watkins

Harper follow, demonstrating the need to educate children about the unfair legal system. In "Henry Neil and His Mother," Stanton establishes a series of conversations between a young man and his mother in order to answer opponents' arguments against banning the manufacture and sale of alcohol. Watkins Harper's *Sowing and Reaping* illustrates the wisdom of Belle Gordon, who breaks her engagement to an intemperate young man. Her cousin Jeanette scoffs at Belle for breaking her engagement, but her own subsequent unhappy marital circumstances provide an opportunity for Mrs. Gladstone to discuss such matters with her daughter Mary and Mary's friend Annette. Deliberation about temperance matters leads Mrs. Gladstone to address legal issues with respect to women, including that of suffrage. Under the guise of explaining injustices to children, the authors also educate readers, of course, and provide them with scripts for their own arguments in favor of changes in the laws.

Many authors proclaimed the need for laws that would permit divorce for wives of inebriates and for societal acceptance under such conditions. Chellis, in *Wealth and Wine,* calls for societal acceptance of divorce for women married to alcoholics and demands women's legal right to protect their children. The gentle authority figure, Dr. Saunders, encourages the divorced protagonist, Jane Warland, to live her life with vigor, disregarding her past bad experience with marriage.

Throughout the century, women angry at the failure of the legal system to protect them took matters into their own hands. The final two selections in part 2, written at mid-century when women across the country were destroying the wares of those who sold alcohol, extol such activity. In Sophia Little's *The Reveille: or, Our Music at Dawn,* the fearless Mary Woodliffe, exasperated with the failure of the legal system to prohibit the manufacture and sale of alcohol as well as of the refusal of saloon keepers to voluntarily limit the sale of alcohol to drunkards, becomes an "avenging angel." She destroys the wares of Hal Wood, a local saloon keeper, as an astonished and respectful crowd of townsmen look on. Mrs. E. N. Gladding's "Minnie—A Temperance Tale" demonstrates the positive outcomes that result from such tactics. The narrator appears to question the propriety and morality of Minnie's activities, but Minnie is nonetheless rewarded handsomely for her actions. Both Minnie and Mary Woodliffe become tributes to the many women who, although they broke the law by destroying saloons, were nonetheless honored as courageous heroes.

Stories included in part 3 examine "woman's sphere," critiquing and redefining gender roles. All stories present strong role models. At a time when popular consensus held that public concerns should be of no concern to women—were outside "woman's sphere"—one major purpose of authors was to justify and promote women's participation in reform and other public causes. While they vary greatly, many works both at mid-century and at century's end deliberately attempted to draw women into the temperance movement. Some fiction promoted acceptance of women's public work on behalf of reform but suggested that role should come primarily through efforts to influence men rather than from public activity, especially for younger women. These works are represented here by Harriet Beecher Stowe's "The Coral Ring" and Louisa May Alcott's "Silver Pitchers." Stowe's Florence Elmore has "bewitched wise men into doing foolish things" but learns to use her powers of influence for good. Alcott questions the notion that "young men will be young men" or that it is acceptable for men to "sow wild oats"; she also appropriates much territory for women as they labor to protect their "sphere." Both women writers promote the notion of intemperance as a problem of men and the idea that women have a more important social role than mere ornamentation and entertainment, and both suggest women's "duty" in promoting reform, helping to remove fears about women's activity in public causes.

The question of whether or not women should leave intemperate husbands was hotly contested through much of the century. Stowe's protagonists never deserted their husbands, using their influence instead to change their husbands' behavior. Elizabeth F. Ellet's "A Country Recollection, or, The Reformed Inebriate" also portrays women's power to influence; however, without explicitly mentioning divorce, Ellet permits her protagonist to leave an abusive husband and father while he remains a victim to alcohol. The husband's eventual imprisonment, on charges unrelated to his family, emphasizes the nature of a system that punishes for crimes committed against strangers but not for those perpetrated on one's own family. The story also intimates positive possibilities when abusive husbands are imprisoned. Ellet suggests a wife's ability to influence her alcoholic husband, but only after she and her children are removed from danger. Ellet's story, written during a period of intense debate over women's right to divorce, or at least to abandon, alcoholic husbands and amidst fears of women's "going out of their sphere," responds to standard arguments whose purpose was to confine women's activity.

While women writers occasionally portray women alcoholics, protagonists in women's temperance fiction are nearly always strong, admirable women, but the protagonists in much fiction by women break the mold of what is considered "appropriate" for nineteenth-century women. The second of Frances D. Gage's "Tales of Truth" represents such fiction. Gage's protagonist typifies the beautiful and promising young woman whose marriage rapidly deteriorates because of her husband's use of alcohol. Gage offers advice to women who find themselves so situated. Ignoring societal derision, Polly Dean Wells takes measures to ensure that her husband ends his wasteful dissipation.

Writers often combined arguments for temperance reform with other causes. The final selection, Caroline H. Butler's "Amy," presents one such example. Butler illustrates women's vulnerability in relation to poor employment options, men's laws, and intemperance, but she suggests that women should take responsibility for supporting other women; she demonstrates the negative repercussions when women neglect such duty and illustrates the beneficial impact when they take these obligations seriously.

Although women's temperance fiction depicts women as innocent "victims" to an unjust legal, social, and economic system, the protagonists are nearly always women—strong, admirable, even heroic models who endure and struggle to cope with and change the system that oppresses them. Women's temperance fiction exposes reasons for women's concern about alcohol abuse and complicates our notions of women's thinking during the nineteenth century by indicating less passivity and suggesting a greater degree of unhappiness and dissatisfaction among "traditional" women than previously assumed; women whom we have regarded as very accepting and conservative wrote and read literature that openly challenged women's restricted role and unjust treatment. Within the appropriate topic of temperance, their narratives encouraged women to become active and to work to improve the material conditions of their lives.

NOTES

1. Frances E. Willard, believing that major reform for women would come only when large numbers of women demanded change, delivered several speeches entitled "The Average Woman" in which she urged other women activists not to alienate the average woman. Willard insisted,

> If we are going to win, there is one individual we have got to win—she is the key to our position—the average woman. For the abstract principle of justice on which the woman question is really based, the average woman does not care a farthing; though for the sake of justice in the concrete she often plays the part of a heroine. If she thinks she ought to want the ballot she will seek it with persevering zeal; but she honestly believes that it is more womanly to cry out against than for it. She has been told this from press and pulpit since her earliest recollection, and she has learned the same doctrine from her husband at home. (623)

2. For comparison, late in the second decade of the twentieth century, official membership in the WCTU numbered more than 346,000 while that of the National American Woman's Suffrage Association was listed at just over 70,000 (Mattingly 303). Official numbers are generally low, since many individual women as well as local organizations refused or were unable to pay dues, the means by which official membership was determined. In 1893, Susan B. Anthony reported that the WCTU "can report a half-million members; I will tell you frankly and honestly that all we [National American Woman's Suffrage Association] number is seven thousand" (quoted in DuBois 178).

3. Blocker *(American Temperance Movements)* and Tyrell estimate women's membership during the 1820s and 1830s at one-third to one-half of total membership. According to Rorabaugh, women dominated temperance societies as early as the 1830s (257).

4. The most complete study of the Woman's Crusade is Jack S. Blocker Jr.'s *"Give to the Winds Thy Fears": The Women's Temperance Crusade, 1873–1874.* Numbers that I use are based substantially on Blocker's work.

5. In her history of the crusades, Eliza Stewart attests to the physical exhaustion women experienced (365), to their being jostled and spit upon (379), to their being doused with dirty water and beer in the cold of winter (150), even to how one woman, a seventy-five-year-old president of the Temperance League of Bucyrus, Ohio, was dragged through the streets and had her arm lacerated to the bone (351). Jack Blocker documents newspaper reports of further violence toward women: some were drenched with paint; accosted with water from force pumps and hoses; pelted with rotten eggs, stones, old boots, and even bricks; threatened by mobs so large and violent that police protection was inadequate; and forced by husbands

to leave the streets. One spouse even publicly horsewhipped his wife for her participation (*"Give to the Winds"* 76–77).

6. Lucius Marcellus Sargent was probably the most popular writer of temperance fiction in the nineteenth century. He was best known for his *Temperance Tales,* a collection that, according to Mark Edward Lender, saw 130 editions and was translated into a number of foreign languages. "My Mother's Gold Ring," perhaps the best loved of his short works, was anthologized in *Tales,* under its own cover, and in other compilations.

7. The first $10 premium contest asked for a story entitled "The Duty of the Drunkard's Wife." The winner was Clarina Howard Nichols, early woman activist and editor of the Brattleboro, Vermont, *Wyndham County Democrat.* The length of the story was to be four or eight pages, appropriate lengths for inexpensive tracts. I have been unable to locate an extant copy of the tract, but most certainly it illustrated the duty of the drunkard's wife to leave and/or divorce her husband. Nichols often spoke on this topic.

8. Gift books, usually lavishly bound volumes, were very popular during the nineteenth century. Intended to be given as gifts, the works generally collected short stories by popular authors, often addressing a single theme, for example, Christmas or temperance.

9. For example, a typical promotion directed to "Sunday-School Libraries" by the National Temperance Society and Publication House assures librarians and readers of the value of its publications based on approval by religious authorities:

> The National Temperance Society and Publication House have published one hundred and twenty volumes, written by some of the best authors in the land. These have been carefully examined and approved by the Publication Committee of the Society, representing the various religious denominations and temperance organizations of the country. These volumes have been cordially commended by leading clergymen of all denominations, and by various National and State bodies all over the land. (Chellis, appendix)

10. Association with the widely respected WCTU afforded an avenue for many black women to move safely around the country as lecturers and organizers and as representatives of their unions to the national and international conventions. The safe and economic means of travel permitted them to promote other concerns as well. For further exploration of black women's involvement in the WCTU, charges of racism, and benefits for black women, see Mattingly, chapter 4.

11. For such a discussion about Mary Todd Lincoln, Elizabeth Cady Stanton, and Harriet Beecher Stowe, see Sklar.

Part 1

FAMILY RELATIONSHIPS

CAROLINE HYDE BUTLER (LAING)
1804–1892

Like that of many early American women writers, most of Caroline H. Butler's life remains a mystery. Butler wrote at least eight novels, several of which enjoyed at least three or four printings. She also wrote stories for periodicals, such as *Godey's Lady's Book*. Her most popular books included *The Little Messenger Birds, or, The Chimes of the Silver Bells,* printed repeatedly between 1850 and 1853, and *Child's History of Rome,* with at least four printings between 1872 and 1875. Butler apparently married around 1850 or 1851. Stories and novels published before that date list Caroline H. Butler as author. Later publications include the name Laing.

Two of Butler's short stories are included in this volume. "Amy," a story of intemperance and poor working conditions for women, appears in part 3. This section includes "Emma Alton," published in a popular temperance gift book edited by "A Son of Temperance," *The Fountain and the Bottle: Comprising Thrilling Examples of the Opposite Effects of Temperance and Intemperance* (Boston: H. Wentworth, 1850).

"Emma Alton" provides a good example of many temperance short stories and novels written in the 1840s and 1850s and intended primarily as cautionary tales for young women. "Emma" warns of two traditional concerns for young women contemplating marriage: the dangers associated with moving away from fam-

ily and friends, who provide protection for women who must relinquish all legal rights with marriage, and the perilous nature of
naive notions about love and marriage.

Many works by temperance women during this period begin
with the idyllic marriage of the protagonist and end with her dismal unhappiness or death resulting from her union to an intemperate man. Some protagonists fare better than others, either because
they tenaciously hold onto their own earnings despite the law and
their husbands' insistence on his right to them, or because they leave
the drunkard, fleeing to a distant geographic location where he has
no influence over them. In either case, however, life is often difficult for the women who find few or no good options for supporting themselves and their children. "Emma Alton" is an example of
such a story. Butler castigates a society that further punishes the
victims of the intemperate by treating wives and children associated
with alcoholics with prejudicial disdain.

Emma Alton

It was Emma's bridal morn. I saw her standing at the door of her
father's cottage, a simple wreath of the pure lily of the valley en-
twined amid the rich braids of her auburn hair—the image of innocence and happiness. That morning, fair Emma Alton had given her
hand where long her young affections had been treasured; and to
those who then saw the fine handsome countenance of Reuben Fairfield, and the pride and love with which he regarded the fair being
at his side, it seemed impossible that aught but happiness could
follow the solemn rites the cottage had that morning witnessed.

The dwelling of my friend to whose rural quiet I had escaped
from the heat and turmoil of the city, was directly opposite the neat
little cottage of Emma's parents, and as I sat at my chamber window, my eye was of course attracted by the happy scene before me.
The morning was truly delightful—scarce a cloud floated o'er the
blue vault of heaven—now and then a soft breeze came whispering through the fragrant locust blossoms and proud catalpas, then
stooping to kiss the dewy grass, sped far off in fantastic shadows
over the rich wheat and clover fields. All seemed in unison with the
happiness so apparent at the cottage—the birds sang—butterflies
sported on golden wing—bees hummed busily. Many of Emma's
youthful companions had come to witness the ceremony, and to bid
adieu to their beloved associate, for as soon as the holy rites were

concluded, Reuben was to bear his fair bride to a distant village, where already a beautiful cottage was prepared, over which she was to preside the charming mistress.

There is always, I believe, a feeling of sadness commingled with the pleasure with which we regard the young and trusting bride, and as I now looked upon Emma standing in the little portico surrounded by the bright and happy faces of her companions, her own still more radiant, I involuntarily sighed as I thought of what her future lot might be. *Was my sigh prophetic?* Presently the chaise which was to convey the new-married pair to their future home, drove gaily to the gate of the cottage. I saw Emma bid adieu to her young friends as they all gathered around her. I saw her fair arms thrown around the neck of her weeping mother, and then, supported by her father and Reuben, she was borne to the carriage. Long was she pressed to her father's heart, ere he resigned her forever to her husband.

"God bless you, my child!" at length said the old man; but no sound escaped Emma's lips—she threw herself back in the chaise, and drew her veil hastily over her face—Reuben sprang to her side—waved his hand to the now weeping assemblage at the cottage door, and the chaise drove rapidly away.

I soon after left the village, and heard no more of the youthful pair. Three years elapsed ere I again visited that pleasant spot, and the morning after my arrival, as I took my favourite seat, and looked over upon the little dwelling opposite, the blithe scene I had there witnessed, recurred to me, and I marvelled if all which promised so fair on the bridal morn had been realized. To my eye the cottage did not look as cheerful, the air of neatness and comfort which before distinguished it seemed lessened. I noticed the walk was now overgrown with grass, and the little flower plot, about which I had so often seen Emma employed, was now rank with weeds. The blinds were all closely shut, and every thing about the cottage looked comfortless and desolate. Presently the door opened, and a female appeared, bearing in her hand a small basket which she proceeded to fill with vegetables growing sparsely among the weeds and tall tangled grass. Her step was feeble, and she seemed hardly capable of pursuing her employment. As she turned her face toward me I started with surprise—I looked at her again more earnestly—is it possible—can that be Emma, thought I—can that pale, wretched looking girl be her whom I last saw a happy, blooming bride?

Yes, it was Emma! Alas! how soon are the bright visions of

youth dispelled; like those beautiful images which flit around the couch of dreams, they can never be realized.

The history of Emma is one which has often been written by the pen of truth—a tearful record of *man's* ingratitude and folly— of *woman's* all-enduring love, sufferance, and constancy.

The first few months of Emma's married life flew by in unalloyed happiness. Reuben lived but in her smiles, and life to the young affectionate girl, seemed but a joyous holiday, and she the most joyous participant. Too soon the scene was changed. Reuben Fairfield was of a gay and reckless nature, fond of conviviality, of the jest and song, he was consequently a great favourite with the young men of the village, and there had been rumours that even before his marriage he had been too free a partaker of the wine- cup. If this were the case, months certainly passed on after that event, when Reuben seemed indifferent to any society but that of his young wife. Little by little his old habits returned upon him, so insensibly too that even he himself could not probably have defined the time when he again found pleasure away from the home of love and Emma. In the only tavern of the village, a room was devoted exclusively to the revels of a band of reckless, dissolute young men, with whom Reuben had at one time been intimate, and it needed but the slightest appearance on the part of the latter to tolerate once more their idle carousals, than with one consent they all united to bring back the Benedict to his old habits. They thought not of the misery which would follow the success of their fiendish plot; of the broken heart of the young being who looked up to their victim as her only hope and happiness.

It was the gay spring-time, when Reuben Fairfield bore his bride away from the arms of her aged parents; but what became of the solemn vows he then uttered, to protect and cherish their beloved daughter? For when next the forest trees unfolded their tender leaves, and the orchards were white with fragrant blossoms, misery and despair had fallen as a blight upon poor Emma! The heart of affection is the last to acknowledge the errors of a beloved object, so it was with Emma; but her cheek grew pale, and her mild blue eyes dimmed beneath their wo-charged lids.

Reuben now almost entirely neglected his patient, still loving wife. In vain she reasoned, entreated, implored, yet *never reproached*. He was alike regardless; daily he gave himself up more and more to the insatiate destroyer, until destruction, both of soul and body, followed. And loud rang the laugh, and the glasses rattled, and the voice of the *Inebriate* shouted forth its loathsome jargon from the *Tempter's Hell!* There were times, it is true, when he would pause in his reckless career; and then hope once more buoyed up the sinking heart of Emma; and when for the first time he pressed their babe to his bosom, while a tear fell on its innocent cheek, it is no wonder that the young mother felt her sorrows ended. That tear, the tear as she thought, of repentance, had washed them all away. But when vice once gets the ascendancy, it reigns like a despot, and too soon the holy feelings of the *father* were lost in the intoxicating bowl.

Poverty, with all its attendant ills, now came upon the wretched wife. One by one the articles of her *menage* were taken from her by Reuben, to satisfy the cravings of *appetite,* and with her babe she was at last forced to leave the cottage where her early days of married life so blissfully flew by, and seek shelter from the winds of heaven in a miserable hut, which only misery might tenant. The unfortunate find few friends, and over the threshold of poverty new ones seldom pass, and therefore it was that Emma was soon neglected and forgotten. There were some, it is true, who regarded her with pity and kindness, but there were also very many who pointed the finger of derision at the *drunkard's-wife*—innocent sufferer for her husband's vices! At length the babe fell ill. It died, and poor, poor Emma, pale, disconsolate, knelt by the little cradle *alone;* no sympathizing hand wiped the tear from her eye; no kind word soothed her lacerated bosom; the earthly friend that should have sustained her under this grievous trial was not at her side, but revelling in scenes of low debauchery.

That night was marked by a storm of terrific violence. The rain poured in torrents; dreadful thunder rent the heavens, the whirlwinds uplifted even the largest trees, while the incessant flashing of the lightning only added tenfold horrors to the scene. But the bereaved mother, the forsaken wife heeded it not; with her cheek pressed against the scarce colder one of her dead babe, she remained for hours totally unconscious of the wild war of the elements—for more complete desolation reigned in her heart. At length the door opened and Reuben entered. With an oath, he was about to throw himself upon the straw pallet, when his eye casually fell upon the pale, marble-like face of the little babe. His senses, stupefied as they were, aroused at the sight.

"What ails the child?" he muttered.

"Reuben, our darling babe is *dead!*" replied Emma, lifting her pallid features to the bloated gaze of her husband. Then rising from her knees, she approached him and led him to look upon the placid countenance of their first born.

We will not dwell upon the scene; remorse and grief stirred the heart of Reuben almost to madness. On his knees he implored forgiveness of his much injured wife; he swore a solemn oath, that never again would he swerve from the path of sobriety, but that years of penitence and affection should atone for his past abuse of life and love.

The day came for the funeral. Reuben had promised his wife that he would not again leave the house until the remains of their babe had been given to the earth; he intended to keep his promise, but as the day wore on the insatiable cries of habit tempted him away. Only *one glass*, he thought—*but another followed*—and then another, until alike forgetful of himself and his unhappy wife, he soon became grossly intoxicated.

The death of the first-born. From Caroline H. Butler, "Emma Alton," in *The Fountain and the Bottle: Comprising Thrilling Examples of the Opposite Effects of Temperance and Intemperance,* edited by a son of temperance. Boston: H. Wentworth, 1850, p. 55.

In the meanwhile a few of the neighbours had assembled; the clergyman, too, had arrived, and the funeral rites were only delayed by the absence of Reuben. Minutes wore on.

"He will not come," whispered one. "Ah, it is easy to guess where he is," added another, and looks of pity were turned upon the heart-stricken mother, as with her head bowed upon the little coffin she hid her grief and shame. The clergyman at length approaching the mourner, in a low tone demanded if the ceremony should proceed.

"Has *he* come?" eagerly inquired Emma.

The clergyman shook his head.

"O wait, wait, he will be here, he promised me. O yes he will come!"

But another half hour rolled on, and still Reuben came not. The neighbours now moved to depart, when rising from her seat, her pallid countenance betokening the agony of her heart, Emma signified her assent that the solemn rites should proceed. But suddenly in the midst of that earnest prayer for comfort and support to the afflicted mother, a loud shout was heard, and Reuben was seen staggering towards the hut. With a brutal oath he burst into the room, but happily for poor Emma, she saw him not, the first sound of his voice had deprived her of consciousness, and she was placed fainting on the bed. Reuben was overpowered and dragged from the hut—the funeral service ended, and leaving the unconscious mother in the care of a few compassionate neighbours, the little procession wound its way to the church-yard.

It was nearly a year after this sad scene, that one evening a stranger alighted from the stage at the Inn, announcing his intention to remain there for the night. Entering the bar-room (for it was before the health-establishment of the temperance law) he ordered a glass of brandy, which he was about to carry to his lips, when his eye encountered the wistful gaze of Reuben Fairfield who now without the means to allay the death-worm upon his vitals, was stretched upon a bench at one end of the room.

"I say, neighbour, you look thirsty," ejaculated the stranger in a gay tone. "Here, take this, for faith *thou hast a lean and hungry look.*"

Eagerly seizing it, Reuben drained the contents of the glass to the bottom, and for a moment the worm was appeased! The stranger now made some casual remark to which Reuben replied in language so well chosen, and evidently so far above his apparent station in life, that the former was astonished, and by degrees a lively conversation took place between them, during which Reuben more than once partook of the young man's mistaken kindness. While conversing, the stranger several times drew from his pocket a handsome gold watch, and the chink of silver fell upon the famished ears of Reuben with startling clearness. Apparently with that feeling of *ennui* which so often seizes upon the solitary traveller, the stranger now strolled from the bar-room into the hall, a door leading into a room opposite was open, and sounds of loud merriment attracted his eyes in that direction. A company of young men were playing at cards—without ceremony he entered, and, advancing to the table, appeared to watch the game with some interest. He was invited to join them, and, after some hesitation accepted.

Reuben had followed the young man into the room, and now eagerly watched the pile of silver, and an occasional bank note, which rather ostentatiously, it would seem, the stranger displayed. The evening wore away, and with a promise from Reuben that he would awaken him betimes to visit a singular cave in the neighbourhood, the stranger retired to rest. Not so Reuben. A fiendish plot entered his brain—*that money must be his*—and even at that moment when robbery, perhaps murder, was at his heart, he dared to think of the pure-minded, innocent Emma as a sharer of his ill-gotten wealth! All night he paced the dark forest contiguous to his abode, where long after midnight the feeble lamp shone upon the haggard features of the once lovely girl as she strove with trembling fingers to render the apparel of the *inebriate* decent for the morrow.

As the day was breaking, Reuben passed softly into the cottage, for he knew that Emma now slept, approaching the bedside, something like a shade of pity stole over his countenance. She smiled in her sleep and called upon his name—this was too much for the miserable man. Hastily opening a table drawer, he drew forth a sharp knife which he concealed beneath his coat, muttering as he did so—"I may need it," and then without daring to cast his eye again toward the bed, left the house and proceeded to the inn, where the stranger already awaited his arrival.

With each point of view as they proceeded on their route the latter expressed himself delighted, particularly as his guide, too, endeavoured to give interest to every scene by the relation of some anecdote or history attached. At length they reached the neighbourhood of the cavern. Here the river which before had rolled so gently along, reflecting the varied hues of autumn in its translucent depths, now suddenly changed its course; and leaping over a precipice some thirty feet in height, pursued its way for some distance between huge masses of shelving rocks crowned on either side by dark, gloomy forests. After a laborious descent they arrived at the mouth of the cave, situated about mid-way down the bank. Reuben entered first, and the stranger was about to follow, when turning suddenly upon him with a blow of giant strength, hurled him from the precipice, and he fell senseless upon the jagged rocks below! Leaping quickly down, Reuben now rifled the pockets of the unfortunate man of both money and watch, and then drew him, still breathing, up the ragged cliff and far into the cave. More than once as he saw life yet stirred in the limbs of his victim, his hand was upon the knife—but *he drew it not forth!*

Covering the body with fragments of rock and under-wood, he left the hapless man to his fate, certain that even if consciousness returned, his efforts to extricate himself from the mass would be unavailing, and as he had taken the precaution also to closely bind his mouth, he could utter no cry for assistance.

Returning now to the village, he boldly entered the inn, and stating to the landlord that the stranger had been tempted by the fineness of the morning to pursue his journey a few miles on foot, proceeded to hand him a sum of money which he said he had charged him to deliver as equivalent to the amount due for supper and lodging. This all appeared very reasonable and no questions were asked. But ere the day was over, some boys who had strayed in the vicinity of the cave, came running home pale and frightened, declaring they had heard dreadful groans issue thence, and that many of the rocks around were stained with blood! Immediately every eye was turned to the spot where a moment before Reuben Fairfield had been standing, and although no one spoke, probably the same terrible conviction flashed through the mind of each; but *guilt* is always cowardly. Reuben had already disappeared.

A party of villagers immediately set forth to search the cave. The result may be imagined—the stranger was discovered still alive, although but for this timely aid, a few hours would doubtless have determined his fate. Reuben attempted to make his escape, but was soon overtaken and delivered up to justice—found guilty, and sentenced to *ten years' hard labour in the State Prison!*

This sad history I learned from my friend; and now poor Emma had come back *to die!* Come back to that home she had left with so many bright visions of happiness before her, a heart-broken, wretched being. It was not long ere from the same little gate, whence but a few years before I had seen her led a happy blooming bride, I saw her coffin borne to the still graveyard!

"Ah!" thought I, as the hot tears gathered, "thou art but another victim at the shrine of Intemperance!" Rest thee in peace, poor Emma!

LYDIA HOWARD HUNTLEY SIGOURNEY
1791–1865

L ydia Sigourney, a prolific and popular nineteenth-century author, was perhaps the best-known poet of the century; she is most often recognized today for her consolation literature. Possibly because three of her five children died in infancy, Sigourney wrote many poems and short stories about death, focusing most often on mortality among small children. Sigourney published regularly in *Godey's Lady's Book*, *Sartain's*, and other popular nineteenth-century periodicals. She also contributed to and edited gift books.

Sigourney published many pieces about intemperance. Her poems can be found in temperance speakers, collections provided for children and adults as ready means of performance at temperance functions. Her 1848 *Waterdrops* included both poetry and prose related to the temperance topic.

"The Intemperate" demonstrates the popularity and facility for publishing that temperance offered writers. First published anonymously in 1833 as *The Intemperate and The Reformed; Showing the Awful Consequences of Intemperance, and the Blessed Effects of the Temperance Reform*, a companion piece with Gerrit Smith's positive letter to Edward C. Delavan about an inebriate's redemption (Boston: S. Bliss, 1833), the story also appeared in numerous other guises. In 1834, "The Intemperate" was included in a gift book, *Religious Souvenir*, and as a companion piece to Grenville Mellen's "The First Glass" in *The First Glass by Grenville Mellen. And The Intemperate by Mrs. Sigourney*. Sigourney included the piece in her 1848 *Waterdrops* and again in the 1854 *The Young Lady's Offering*.

In "The Intemperate," Sigourney demonstrates several themes representative of women's temperance fiction. Jane Harwood had been a happy, well-loved young woman looking forward to a bright future, but her life, inextricably intertwined with that of her husband, becomes a nightmare. Sigourney highlights the young wife's danger, as well as that of her children, at the hands of an intemperate husband. As does Butler in "Emma Alton," Sigourney suggests the particular danger for married women who increase their dependence on their husbands by moving away from family and friends, the only source of protection and support for many women who by law had no rights: "He felt that she had no friend to protect her from insolence, and was entirely in his own power; and she was compelled to realize that it was a power without generosity, and that there is no tyranny so perfect as that of a capricious and alienated husband." Sigourney evades any discussion of divorce, but readers must have questioned Jane's wisdom in remaining with a husband who abuses both her and her feeble child, contributing to the early death of their son.

The Intemperate

"Reserving woes for age, their prime they spend,—
Then wretched, hopeless, in the evil days,
With sorrow to the verge of life they tend,
Griev'd with the present.—of the past asham'd,—
They live and are despised; they die, nor more are nam'd"

—Lowth

Where the lofty forests of Ohio, towering in unshorn majesty, cast a solemn shadow over the deep verdure of beautiful and ample vales, a small family of emigrants were seen pursuing their solitary way. They travelled on foot, but not with the aspect of mendicants, though care and suffering were variably depicted on their countenances. The man walked first, apparently in an unkind, uncompromising mood. The woman carried in her arms an infant, and aided the progress of a feeble boy, who seemed sinking with exhaustion. An eye accustomed to scan the never-resting tide of emigration, might discern that these pilgrims were inhabitants of the Eastern States, probably retreating from some species of adversity, to one of those imaginary El Dorados, among the shades of the far West, where it is fabled that the evils of mortality have found no place.

James Harwood, the leader of that humble group, who claimed from him the charities of husband and of father, halted at the report of a musket, and while he entered a thicket, to discover whence it proceeded, the weary and sad-hearted mother sat down upon the grass. Bitter were her reflections during that interval of rest among the wilds of Ohio. The pleasant New-England village from which she had just emigrated, and the peaceful home of her birth, rose up to her view—where, but a few years before, she had given her hand to one, whose unkindness now strewed her path with thorns. By constant and endearing attentions, he had won her youthful love, and the two first years of their union promised happiness. Both were industrious and affectionate, and the smiles of their infant in his evening sports or slumbers, more than repaid the labors of the day.

But a change became visible. The husband grew inattentive to his business, and indifferent to his fireside. He permitted debts to accumulate, in spite of the economy of his wife, and became morose and offended at her remonstrances. She strove to hide, even from her own heart, the vice that was gaining the ascendancy over him, and redoubled her exertions to render his home agreeable. But too frequently her efforts were of no avail, or contemptuously rejected. The death of her beloved mother, and the birth of a second infant, convinced her that neither in sorrow nor in sickness could she expect sympathy from him, to whom she had given her heart, in the simple faith of confiding affection. They became miserably poor, and the cause was evident to every observer. In this distress, a letter was received from a brother, who had been for several years a resident in Ohio, mentioning that he was induced to remove further westward, and offering them the use of a tenement which his family would leave vacant, and a small portion of cleared land, until they might be able to become purchasers.

Poor Jane listened to this proposal with gratitude. She thought she saw in it the salvation of her husband. She believed that if he were divided from his intemperate companions, he would return to his early habits of industry and virtue. The trial of leaving native and endeared scenes, from which she would once have shrunk, seemed as nothing in comparison with the prospect of his reformation and returning happiness. Yet, when all their few effects were converted into the wagon and horse which were to convey them to a far land, and the scant and humble necessaries which were to sustain them on their way thither; when she took leave of her brother and sisters, with their households; when she shook hands with the friends whom she had loved from her cradle, and remembered that it might be for the last time; and when the hills that encircled her native village faded into the faint, blue outline of the horizon, there came over her such a desolation of spirit, such a foreboding of evil, as she had never before experienced. She blamed herself for these feelings, and repressed their indulgence.

The journey was slow and toilsome. The autumnal rains and the state of the roads were against them. The few utensils and comforts which they carried with them, were gradually abstracted and sold. The object of this traffic could not be doubted. The effects were but too visible in his conduct. She reasoned—she endeavored to persuade him to a different course. But anger was the only result. When he was not too far stupified to comprehend her remarks, his deportment was exceedingly overbearing and arbitrary. He felt that she had no friend to protect her from insolence, and was entirely in his own power; and she was compelled to realize that it was a power without generosity, and that there is no tyranny so perfect as that of a capricious and alienated husband.

As they approached the close of their distressing journey, the roads became worse, but their horse utterly failed. He had been but scantily provided for, as the intemperance of his owner had taxed and impoverished every thing for his own support. Jane wept as she looked upon the dying animal, and remembered his laborious and ill-repaid services.

The unfeeling exclamation with which her husband abandoned him to his fate, fell painfully upon her heart, adding another proof of the extinction of his sensibilities, in the loss of that pitying kindness for the animal creation, which exercises a silent and salutary guardianship over our higher and better sympathies. They were now approaching within a short distance of the termination of their journey, and their directions had been very clear and precise. But his mind became so bewildered and his heart so perverse, that he persisted in choosing by-paths of underwood and tangled weeds, under the pretence of seeking a shorter route. This increased and prolonged their fatigue; but no entreaty of his wearied wife was regarded. Indeed, so exasperated was he at her expostulations, that she sought safety in silence. The little boy of four years old, whose constitution had been feeble from his infancy, became so feverish and distressed, as to be unable to proceed. The mother, after in vain soliciting aid and compassion from her husband, took him in her arms, while the youngest, whom she had previously carried, and who was unable to walk, clung to her shoulders. Thus burdened, her progress was tedious and painful. Still she was enabled to go on; for the strength that nerves a mother's frame, toiling for her sick child, is from God. She even endeavored to press on more rapidly than usual, fearing that if she fell behind, her husband would tear the sufferer from her arms, in some paroxysm of his savage intemperance.

Their road during the day, though approaching the small settlement where they were to reside, lay through a solitary part of the country. The children were faint and hungry; and as the exhausted mother sat upon the grass, trying to nurse her infant, she drew from her bosom the last piece of bread, and held it to the parched lips of the feeble child. But he turned away his head, and with a scarcely audible moan, asked for water. Feelingly might she sympathize in the distress of the poor outcast from the tent of Abraham, who laid her famishing son among the shrubs, and sat down a good way off, saying,—"Let me not see the death of the child." But this Christian mother was not in the desert, nor in despair. She looked upward to Him who is the refuge of the forsaken, and the comforter of those whose spirits are cast down.

The sun was drawing towards the west, as the voice of James Harwood was heard, issuing from the forest, attended by another man with a gun, and some birds at his girdle.

"Wife, will you get up now, and come along? We are not a mile from home. Here is John Williams, who went from our part of the country, and says he is our next-door neighbor."

Jane received his hearty welcome with a thankful spirit, and rose to accompany them. The kind neighbor took the sick boy in his arms, saying,—

"Harwood, take the baby from your wife; we do not let our women bear all the burdens, here in Ohio."

James was ashamed to refuse, and reached his hands towards the child. But, accustomed to his neglect or unkindness, it hid its face, crying, in the maternal bosom.

"You see how it is. She makes the children so cross, that I never have any comfort of them. She chooses to carry them herself, and always will have her own way in everything."

"You have come to a new settled country, friends," said John Williams; "but it is a good country to get a living in. Crops of corn and wheat are such as you never saw in New-England. Our cattle live in clover, and the cows give us cream instead of milk. There is plenty of game to employ our leisure, and venison and wild turkey do not come amiss now and then on a farmer's table. Here is a short cut I can show you, though there is a fence or two to climb. James Harwood, I shall like well to talk with you about old times and old friends down east. But why don't you help your wife over the fence with her baby?"

"So I would, but she is so sulky. She has not spoke a word to me all day. I always say, let such folks take care of themselves till their mad fit is over."

A cluster of log cabins now met their view through an opening in the forest. They were pleasantly situated in the midst of an area of cultivated land. A fine river, surmounted by a rustic bridge of the trunks of trees, cast a sparkling line through the deep, unchanged autumnal verdure.

"Here we live," said their guide, "a hard-working, contented people. That is your house which has no smoke curling up from the chimney. It may not be quite so genteel as some you have left behind in the old states, but it is about as good as any in the neighborhood. I'll go and call my wife to welcome you; right glad will she be to see you, for she sets great store by folks from New-England."

The inside of a log cabin, to those not habituated to it, presents but a cheerless aspect. The eye needs time to accustom itself to the rude walls and floors, the absence of glass windows, and doors loosely hung upon leathern hinges. The exhausted woman entered, and sank down with her babe. There was no chair to receive her. In the corner of the room stood a rough board table, and a low frame resembling a bedstead. Other furniture there was none. Glad, kind voices of her own sex, recalled her from her stupor. Three or four matrons, and several blooming young faces, welcomed her with smiles. The warmth of reception in a new colony, and the substantial services by which it is manifested, put to shame the ceremonious and heartless professions, which in a more artificial state of society are dignified with the name of friendship.

As if by magic, what had seemed almost a prison, assumed a different aspect, under the ministry of active benevolence. A cheerful flame rose from the ample fire-place; several chairs and a bench for children appeared; a bed with comfortable coverings concealed the shapelessness of the bedstead, and viands to which they had long been strangers were heaped upon the board. An old lady held the sick boy tenderly in her arms, who seemed to revive as he saw his mother's face brighten; and the infant after a draught of fresh milk, fell into a sweet and profound slumber. One by one the neighbors departed, that the wearied ones might have an opportunity of repose. John Williams, who was the last to bid goodnight, lingered a moment as he closed the door, and said,—

"Friend Harwood, here is a fine, gentle cow, feeding at your door; and for old acquaintance sake, you and your family are welcome to the use of her for the present, or until you can make out better."

When they were left alone, Jane poured out her gratitude to her Almighty Protector in a flood of joyful tears. Kindness to which she had recently been a stranger, fell as balm of Gilead upon her wounded spirit.

"Husband," she exclaimed, in the fullness of her heart, "we may yet be happy."

He answered not, and she perceived that he heard not. He had thrown himself upon the bed, and in a deep and stupid sleep was dispelling the fumes of intoxication.

This new family of emigrants, though in the midst of poverty, were sensible of a degree of satisfaction to which they had long been strangers. The difficulty of procuring ardent spirits in this small and isolated community, promised to be the means of establishing their peace. The mother busied herself in making their humble tenement neat and comfortable, while her husband, as if ambitious to earn in a new residence the reputation he had forfeited in the old, labored diligently to assist his neighbors in gathering of their harvest, receiving in payment such articles as were needed for the subsistence of his household. Jane continually gave thanks in her prayers for this great blessing; and the hope she permitted herself to indulge of his permanent reformation, imparted unwonted cheerfulness to her brow and demeanor. The invalid boy seemed also to gather healing from his mother's smiles; for so great was her power over him, since sickness had rendered his dependence complete, that his comfort, and even his countenance, were a faithful reflection of her own. Perceiving the degree of her influence, she endeavored to use it, as every religious parent should, for his spiritual benefit. She supplicated that the pencil which was to write upon his soul, might be guided from above. She spoke to him in the tenderest manner of his Father in Heaven, and of His will respecting little children. She pointed out his goodness in the daily gifts that sustain life; in the glorious sun, as it came forth rejoicing in the east, in the gently-falling rain, the frail plant, and the dews that nourish it. She reasoned with him of the changes of nature, till he loved even the storm, and the lofty thunder, because they came from God. She repeated to him passages of scripture, with which her memory was stored; and sang hymns, until she perceived that if he was in pain, he complained not, if he might but hear her voice. She made him acquainted with the life of the compassionate Redeemer, and how he called young children to his arms, though the disciples forbade them. And it seemed as if a voice from heaven urged her never to desist from cherishing this tender and deep-rooted piety; because, like the flower of grass, he must soon fade away. Yet, though it was evident that the seeds of disease were in his system; his health at intervals seemed to be improving, and the little household partook, for a time, the blessings of tranquillity and content.

But let none flatter himself that the dominion of vice is suddenly or easily broken. It may seem to relax its grasp, and to slumber; but the victim who has long worn its chain, if he would utterly escape, and triumph at last, must do so in the strength of Omnipotence. This, James Harwood never sought. He had begun to experience that prostration of spirits which attends the abstraction of an habitual stimulant. His resolution to recover his lost character was not proof against this physical inconvenience. He determined at all hazards to gratify his depraved appetite. He laid his plans deliberately, and with the pretext of making some arrangements about the wagon, which had been left broken on the road, departed from his home. His stay was protracted beyond the appointed limit, and at his return, his sin was written on his brow, in characters too strong to be mistaken. That he had also brought with him some hoard of intoxicating poison, to which to resort, there remained no room to doubt. Day after day did his shrinking household witness the alternations of causeless anger and brutal tyranny. To lay waste the comfort of his wife, seemed to be his prominent object. By constant contradiction and misconstruction, he strove to distress her, and then visited her sensibilities upon her as sins. Had she been more obtuse by nature, or more indifferent to his welfare, she might with greater ease have borne the cross. But her youth was nurtured in tenderness, and education had refined her susceptibilities, both of pleasure and pain. She could not forget the love he had once manifested for her, nor prevent the chilling contrast from filling her with anguish. She could not resign the hope that the being who had early evinced correct feelings and noble principles of action, might yet be won back to that virtue which had rendered him worthy of her affections. Still, this hope deferred was sickness and sorrow to the heart. She found the necessity of deriving consolation, and the power of endurance, wholly from above. The tender invitation by the mouth of a prophet, was as balm to her wounded soul,—"As a woman forsaken and grieved in spirit, and as a wife of youth, when thou wast refused, have I called thee, saith thy God."

So faithful was she in the discharge of the difficult duties that devolved upon her—so careful not to irritate her husband by reproach or gloom—that to a casual observer she might have appeared to be confirming the doctrine of the ancient philosopher, that happiness is in exact proportion to virtue. Had he asserted, that virtue is the source of all that happiness which *depends upon ourselves,* none could have controverted his position. But, to a woman, a wife, a mother, how small is the portion of independent happiness! She has woven the tendrils of her soul around many props. Each revolving year renders their support more necessary. They cannot waver, or warp, or break, but she must tremble and bleed.

There was one modification of her husband's persecutions which the fullest measure of her piety could not enable her to bear unmoved. This was unkindness to her feeble and suffering boy. It was at first commenced as the surest mode of distressing her. It opened a direct avenue to her heart-strings.—What began in perverseness seemed to end in hatred, as evil habits sometimes create perverted principles. The wasted and wild-eyed invalid shrank from his father's glance and footstep, as from the approach of a foe. More than once had he taken him from the little bed which maternal care had provided for him, and forced him to go forth in the cold of the winter storm.

"I mean to harden him," said he. "All the neighbors know that you make such a fool of him that he will never be able to get a living. For my part, I wish I had never been called to the trial of supporting a useless boy, who pretends to be sick only that he may be coaxed by a silly mother."

On such occasions, it was in vain that the mother attempted to protect her child. She might neither shelter him in her bosom, nor control the frantic violence of the father. Harshness, and the agitation of fear, deepened a disease which might else have yielded. The timid boy, in terror of his natural protector, withered away like a blighted flower. It was of no avail that friends remonstrated with the unfeeling parent, or that hoary-headed men warned him solemnly of his sins. Intemperance had destroyed his respect for man, and his fear of God.

Spring at length emerged from the shades of that heavy and bitter winter. But its smile brought no gladness to the declining child. Consumption fed upon his vitals, and his nights were restless and full of pain.

"Mother, I wish I could smell the violets that grew upon the green bank by our old, dear home."

"It is too early for violets, my child. But the grass is beautifully green around us, and the birds sing sweetly, as if their hearts were full of praise."

"In my dreams last night, I saw the clear waters of the brook that ran by the bottom of my little garden. I wish I could taste them once more. And I heard such music, too, as used to come from that white church among the trees, where every Sunday the happy people meet to worship God."

The mother saw that the hectic fever had been long increasing, and knew there was such an unearthly brightness in his eye, that she feared his intellect wandered. She seated herself on his low bed, and bent over him to soothe and compose him. He lay silent for some time.

"Do you think my father will come?"

Dreading the agonizing agitation which, in his paroxysms of coughing and pain, he evinced at the sound of his father's well-known footstep, she answered,—

"I think not, love. You had better try to sleep."

"Mother, I wish he would come. I do not feel afraid now. Perhaps he would let me lay my cheek to his once more, as he used to do when I was a babe in my grandmother's arms. I should be glad to say good bye to him, before I go to my Saviour."

Gazing intently in his face, she saw the work of the destroyer, in lines too plain to be mistaken.

"My son—my dear son—say, Lord Jesus receive my spirit."

"Mother," he replied, with a sweet smile upon his ghastly features, "he is ready. I desire to go to him. Hold the baby to me, that I may kiss her. That is all. Now sing to me, and, oh! wrap me close in your arms, for I shiver with cold."

He clung with a death grasp, to that bosom which had long been his sole earthly refuge.

"Sing louder, dear mother,—a little louder.—I cannot hear you."

A tremulous tone, as of a broken harp, rose above her grief, to comfort the dying child. One sigh of icy breath was upon her cheek, as she joined it to his—one shudder—and all was over. She held the body long in her arms, as if fondly hoping to warm and revivify it with her breath. Then she stretched it upon its bed, and kneeling beside it, hid her face in that grief which none but mothers feel. It was a deep and sacred solitude, along with the dead. Nothing save the soft breathing of the sleeping babe fell upon that solemn pause. Then the silence was broken by a wail of piercing sorrow. It ceased, and a voice arose,—a voice of supplication for strength to endure, as "seeing Him who is invisible." Faith closed what was begun in weakness. It became a prayer of thanksgiving to Him who had released the dove-like spirit from the prison-house of pain, that it might taste the peace and mingle in the melody of heaven.

She arose from the orison, and bent calmly over her dead. The thin, placid features wore a smile, as when he had spoken of Jesus. She composed the shining locks around the pure forehead, and gazed long on what was to her so beautiful. Tears had vanished from her eyes, and in their stead was an expression almost sublime, as of one who had given an angel back to God.

The father entered carelessly. She pointed to the pallid, immovable brow. "See, he suffers no longer." He drew near, and looked on the dead with surprise and sadness. A few natural tears forced their way, and fell on the face of the first-born, who was once his pride. The memories of that moment were bitter. He spoke tenderly to the emaciated mother; and she, who a short time before was raised above the sway of grief, wept like an infant as those few affectionate tones touched the sealed fountains of other years.

Neighbors and friends visited them, desirous to console their sorrow, and attended them when they committed the body to the

earth. There was a shady and secluded spot, which they had con-
secrated by the burial of their few dead. Thither that whole little
colony were gathered, and seated on the fresh springing grass, listening to the holy, healing words of the inspired volume. It was read
by the oldest man in the colony, who had himself often mourned.
As he bent reverently over the sacred page, there was that on his
brow which seemed to say,—"This has been my comfort in my affliction." Silver hairs thinly covered his temples, and his low voice
was modulated by feeling, as he read of the frailty of man, withering like the flower of grass, before it groweth up; and of His majesty in whose sight "a thousand years are as yesterday when it is
past, and as a watch in the night." He selected from the words of
that compassionate One, who "gathereth the lambs with his arm,
and carrieth them in his bosom," who, pointing out as an example
the humility of little children, said,—"Except ye become as one of
these, ye cannot enter the kingdom of heaven," and who calleth all
the weary and heavy-laden to come unto him, that he may give them
rest. The scene called forth sympathy, even from manly bosoms. The
mother, worn with watching and weariness, bowed her head down
to the clay that concealed her child. And it was observed with gratitude by that friendly group, that the husband supported her in his
arms, and mingled his tears with hers.

He returned from this funeral in much mental distress. His sins
were brought to remembrance, and reflection was misery. For many
nights, sleep was disturbed by visions of his neglected boy.—Sometimes he imagined that he heard him coughing from his low bed,
and felt constrained to go to him, in a strange disposition of kindness, but his limbs were unable to obey the dictates of his will.
Then he would see him pointing with a thin dead hand, to the dark
grave, or beckoning him to follow to the unseen world. Conscience
haunted him with terrors, and many prayers from pious hearts
arose, that he might now be led to repentance. The venerable man
who had read the Bible at the burial of his boy, counselled and
entreated him, with the earnestness of a father, to yield to the warning voice from above, and to "break off his sins by righteousness,
and his inequities by turning unto the Lord."

There was a change in his habits and conversation, and his
friends trusted it would be permanent. She who, above all others,
was interested in the result, spared no exertion to win him back to
the way of truth, and to soothe his heart into peace with itself, and

obedience to his Maker. Yet was she doomed to witness the full force of grief and of remorse upon intemperance, only to see them utterly overthrown at last. The reviving virtue, with whose indications she had solaced herself, and even given thanks that her beloved son had not died in vain, was transient as the morning dew. Habits of industry, which had begun to spring up, proved themselves to be without root. The dead, and his cruelty to the dead, were alike forgotten. Disaffection to the chastened being, who against hope still hoped for his salvation, resumed its dominion. The friends who had alternately reproved and encouraged him, were convinced that their efforts had been of no avail. Intemperance, "like the strong man armed," took possession of a soul that lifted no cry for aid to the Holy Spirit, and girded on no weapon to resist the destroyer.

Summer passed away, and the anniversary of their arrival at the colony returned. It was to Jane Harwood a period of sad and solemn retrospection. The joys of early days, and the sorrows of maturity, passed in review before her, and while she wept, she questioned her heart, what had been its gain from a father's discipline, or whether it had sustained that greatest of all losses—*the loss of its afflictions.*

She was alone at this season of self-communion. The absences of her husband had become more frequent and protracted. A storm, which feelingly reminded her of those which had often beat upon them when homeless and weary travellers, had been raging for nearly two days. To this cause she imputed the unusually long stay of her husband. Through the third night of his absence she lay sleepless, listening for his steps. Sometimes she fancied she heard shouts of laughter, for the mood in which he returned from his revels was various. But it was only the shriek of the tempest. Then she thought some ebullition of his frenzied anger rang in her ears. It was the roar of the hoarse wind through the forest. All night long she listened to these sounds, and hushed and sang to her affrighted babe. Unrefreshed she arose and resumed her morning labors.

Suddenly her eye was attracted by a group of neighbors, coming up slowly from the river. A dark and terrible foreboding oppressed her. She hastened out to meet them. Coming towards her house was a female friend, agitated and tearful, who passing her arm around her, would have spoken.

"Oh, you come to bring me evil tidings! I pray you let me know the worst."

The object was indeed to prepare her mind for a fearful calamity. The body of her husband had been found drowned, as was supposed, during the darkness of the preceding night, in attempting to cross the bridge of logs, which had been partially broken by the swollen waters. Utter prostration of spirit came over the desolate mourner. Her energies were broken and her heart withered. She had sustained the privations of poverty and emigration, and the burdens of unceasing labor and unrequited care, without murmuring. She had lain her first-born in the grave with resignation, for faith had heard her Saviour saying,—"Suffer the little child to come unto me." She had seen him, in whom her heart's young affections were garnered up, become a "persecutor and injurious," a prey to vice the most disgusting and destructive. Yet she had borne up under all. One hope remained with her as an "anchor of the soul,"—the hope that he might yet repent and be reclaimed. She had persevered in her complicated and self-denying duties with that charity which "beareth all things,—believeth all things,—endureth all things."

But now, he had died in his sin. The deadly leprosy which had stolen over his heart, could no more be "purged by sacrifice or offering for ever." She knew not that a single prayer for mercy had preceded the soul on its passage to the High Judge's bar. There were bitter dregs in this grief, which she had never before wrung out.

Again the sad-hearted community assembled in their humble cemetery. A funeral in an infant colony awakens sympathies of an almost exclusive character. It is as if a large family suffered. One is smitten down whom every eye knew, every voice saluted. To bear along the corpse of the strong man, through the fields which he had sown, and to cover motionless in the grave that arm which trusted to have reaped the ripening harvest, awakens a thrill deep and startling in the breast of those who wrought by his side during the burden and heat of the day. To lay the mother on her pillow of clay, whose last struggle with life was, perchance, to resign the hope of one more brief visit to the land of her fathers,—whose heart's last pulsation might have been a prayer that her children should return and grow up within the shadow of the school-house and the church of God, is a grief in which none save emigrants may participate. To consign to their narrow, noteless abode, both young and old, the infant and him of hoary hairs, without the solemn knell, the sable train, the hallowed voice of the man of God, giving back, in the name of his fellow-Christians, the most precious roses of their pilgrim path, and speaking with divine authority of Him who is the "resurrection and the life," adds desolation to that weeping with which man goeth downward to his dust.

But with heaviness of an unspoken and peculiar nature was this victim of vice borne from the home that he troubled, and laid by the side of his son to whose tender years he had been an unnatural enemy. There was sorrow among all who stood around his grave, and it bore features of that sorrow which is without hope.

The widowed mourner was not able to raise her head from the bed, when the bloated remains of her unfortunate husband were committed to the earth. Long and severe sickness ensued, and in her convalescence a letter was received from her brother, inviting her and her child to an asylum under his roof and appointing a period to come and conduct them on their homeward journey.

With her little daughter, the sole remnant of her wrecked heart's wealth, she returned to her kindred. It was with emotions of deep and painful gratitude that she bade farewell to the inhabitants of that infant settlement, whose kindness through all her adversities had never failed. And when they remembered the example of uniform patience and piety which she had exhibited, and the saint-like manner in which she had sustained her burdens, and cherished their sympathies, they felt as if a tutelary spirit had departed from among them.

In the home of her brother, she educated her daughter in industry, and that contentment which virtue teaches. Restored to those friends with whom the morning of life had passed, she shared with humble cheerfulness the comfort that earth had yet in store for her; but in the cherished sadness of her perpetual widowhood, in the bursting sighs of her nightly orison, might be traced a sacred and deep-rooted sorrow—the memory of her erring husband, and the miseries of unreclaimed intemperance.

FRANCES DANA GAGE
1808–1880

Frances D. Gage was born into a reform family, her parents active participants in the abolitionist cause. Gage herself worked in numerous political reforms, including abolition, woman's rights, and temperance. She believed the temperance cause to be vital in protecting women and furthering their rights. As did many nineteenth-century women, Gage saw temperance and woman's rights as essentially the same reform: "I gave twenty-five lectures on the two great subjects of reform, Temperance and Woman's Rights (which indeed seem but one, so closely are all the interests united)" (Letter to *The Lily*).

Gage is probably best known today as an early woman's rights activist and contributor to the Ohio chapter in volume 1 of *History of Woman's Suffrage*. It is here that Gage details Sojourner Truth's famous "Ain't I a Woman" speech, delivered to the 1851 woman's rights convention in Akron, Ohio.

Gage wrote under her own name as well as under the pseudonym Aunt Fanny. Most of her stories and letters to women's newspapers, such as Amelia Bloomer's *The Lily* and Jane Grey Swisshelm's *Saturday Visiter,* appeared under this pseudonym. The pen name was not intended to obscure her identity. In fact, Bloomer and Swisshelm often prefaced letters and stories written by Aunt Fanny by announcing another addition from Mrs. Gage. The appellation was one Gage apparently enjoyed using in recognition of the series she wrote for children under that name: *Pop-guns. One Serious and*

One Funny (1864); *Fanny at School* (1866); *Fanny's Birth-Day* (1866); *Fanny's Journey* (1866); and *Funny Pop-Guns* (1866).

Like many women writers of temperance works, Gage wrote a variety of genres and published with both commercial and nonprofit publishing houses. In addition to her temperance works and children's stories, she published a volume of short stories, *Aunt Fanny's Christmas Stories* (1849), and verse, *Poems* (1867). Her temperance novels include *The Man in the Well* (1850), *Elsie Magoon, or the Old Still-House in the Hollow* (1867), *Gertie's Sacrifice, or, Glimpses at Two Lives* (1870), and *Steps Upward* (1870).

Two of Gage's short stories are included in this volume—both from a series of "Tales of Truth" addressed in conversational style to Amelia Bloomer, editor of *The Lily*. In this "Tale of Truth" (January 1852: 2–3), Gage depicts the difficulties of the most popular and smartest girl in L., Mary Cadwallader—typically one we would not expect to become the wife of a drunkard—after her propitious marriage to Edward Harris. She exposes the treachery and danger behind the seemingly supportive conventional advice given to women who wish to escape abusive husbands; such wisdom suggests the victim is at fault and might remedy matters if only she were more gentle, more loving. Gage also exposes men's control over women's bodies in marriage. Edward's "hellish appetites" manifest themselves in various ways, but particular evidence surfaces in the births of three unwanted children, even while "every feeling of [Mary's] soul revolted at the idea of living with a drunkard." Mary would not have had these children had she "yielded to the suggestions of her heart." Gage also touches on issues of infidelity, Edward having broken his marriage vow in his failure to "leav[e] all others, [and] cleave only unto her."

Tales of Truth (No. 1)

"Will you please, ma'am, to let my mother have some milk?" said a pale-faced, slender little girl, of about ten years.

"Which will you have, Jenny, sweet or sour, this morning?"

"Mother said it was no difference which, we can eat either; and mother says beggars must not be choosers."

"How is your mother, now, Jenny—any better than she was last week?"

"Yes, I guess she is. She has been out washing every day this week—though she says her breast hurts her all the time."

"She ought to keep quiet till her breast gets well. You tell her, Jenny, that I said so; if she don't she will be entirely laid up, and then she will lose more than she gains by hurrying out."

"So Mrs. Keys said to her the other day.—But mother said it was no use for people to talk so—she could not lie by; if she did she must starve, for she had not got her winter's wood, or flour, or meal, nor any shoes for Kate or Edward. The day that she went out first after she was sick, she cried hard before she started. We had not a mite of bread in the house, and mother said she was afraid she should get clear down again—but what could she do?"

"True enough," said Mrs. Marcy, musing, after Jenny was gone, "what can she do? How heartless it is for us to tell one like Mary Harris to keep still; how wrong it is too, to do it, without we open our hands to help her hard needs. No, she cannot rest and get well, with her children crying for food; and we, reveling in luxury, forget her poverty, her sorrow and her pain, till she is forced to do what we heartlessly, coldly tell her she must not do."

"Mother," said Helen, "what made Mrs. Harris so poor?"

"Listen, and I will tell you—and you, George, may give heed, for it is a talk that may teach you a deep and impressive lesson. Yes, my son, though you feel strong in the fresh vigor of your manhood to resist evil, you may still be overtaken; and when I saw you yesterday smoking that cigar, and laughing over it in your glee, I felt a sad presentiment creeping into my heart. Yes, George, this thought stung me like the bite of an adder—MY BOY, TOO, MAY FALL! But to my story."

Mary Cadwallader was, twelve years ago, one of the brightest and smartest girls in L. Her father was a farmer and well to do; and Mary was better educated than the common run of farmer's daughters. She was not taught what the world calls accomplishments; but she was accomplished in the principles of honest industry, careful frugality, and earnest truth, which, if we can have but the one, are far better than the outward garnishings of genteel life. Mary was considered a great beauty; but beauty did not spoil her heart, though it worked out for her a sad and fearful destiny.

In one of her visits to the village, she met Edward Harris—then a young lawyer just commencing practice. He was considered far above mediocrity, for talent and manliness, and every one thought when he offered himself to Mary, that he was almost stooping from his high elevation; for he might have married among the gay, the wealthy, and fashionable. But he chose Mary. Her father gave her a good setting out, and Mr. Harris' prosperous business enabled them to live pleasantly and comfortable, and bid fair to soon provide for them an ample independence. Mary seemed as happy as her good heart deserved to be, and all went on quietly and peaceable for two or three years. But Edward was often from home, and in his association with "gentlemen of the Bar"—men, educated, intelligent, and influential—men to whom the young and less favored mentally look up as patterns—he learned to be a drinker of ardent spirits,—*genteelly*, at first—and when Mary cautiously and kindly remonstrated, and spoke of danger, he laughed rudely at her fears, and pointed to Judge G., who took his dram half-a-dozen times a day, and had done so for twenty years without hurting him. Oh! ye moderate drinkers—ye who stand in high places in society, how fearful is your responsibility! How many thousand noble souls ye have led to perdition! how many thousand hearts ye have broken! how many thousand wives ye have widowed! how many thousand children ye have beggared and orphaned! Oh, George! trust not thy own strength. Where one man has self-control and self-denial to tamper with the accursed stimulant, and yet be saved, thousands fail.

But as I was saying, Edward laughed at the fears of his gentle wife; but too soon, Oh, all too soon, her fears were realized. The bloated countenance, the dull eye, the morose temper, told the stricken wife their fearful tale.—Things grew worse and worse. Clients forsook him, and business left his hands. His unkindness almost prompted Mary to leave him and try to take care of herself. She consulted with a few friends, upon whose counsel she felt she could rely; but they told her the old tale of woman's patient kindness and endearing love, bade her be gentle, smiling—aye, and *loving*,—as if woman could love and fondle the man who with every passing hour is giving himself up to his hellish appetites, and becoming in thought, word, and deed—a *fiend*. But they bade her be kind, and try it awhile longer. If she left him he would be totally lost—she was his wife, and she must not violate her marriage vow. He was not so bad yet as Mr. Jones, who often beat his wife, and took her hard earnings to buy his liquor.—Besides, Edward would never let her have any peace—he was a lawyer and would try to get the children—every body would blame her, &c., &c. With such arguments was she kept at his side, while every feeling of her soul revolted at the idea of living with a drunkard. Edward Harris had broken, in the sight of God and man, *his* marriage vow. The compact entered into, *he* had made null and void. He did neither *love, cherish* nor *protect,* nor did he, *"leaving all others, cleave only unto her."* Religiously, sacredly had she lived up to every requirement of duty, while he recklessly, boldly set every duty aside; and yet the world said she must live with him—live, bear, and suffer on. And she did live and suffer on for two years more, and then a pair of twins—two little girls—were added to her heart trials. This was what she had dreaded—that she should, by living with him, add to the number of those whom his hourly self-indulgence was bringing down to wretchedness and woe. Had she yielded to the suggestions of her heart, there would have been but two to have born the name of "drunken Harris' children."

About the time her babes were born his house, and all his effects that the law would allow to be taken, went through the sheriff's hands at public auction, and the proceeds into the pockets of the tavern keeper of the village—a very *good man*—so the world said, for he was a member of the most popular church, never drank a drop himself, gave largely to benevolent societies, and was *very liberal to the poor.*

Mary and her four children, (the oldest our little Jenny, not five years old,) were obliged, while she was yet weak, to move into a hovel in the outskirts of the town; and Edward, driven to desperation, drank more freely than ever. He pawned his own clothes for drink, and finally stole away some trinkets, which had been Mary's in her better days, and sold them for one-half their value. With this money he got liquor, and for days lay drunk around the bar-room doors. In this state he was laid on a sled and brought home to his poor, despairing wife. She, pale, trembling, with her wailing infants not yet four weeks old, received him—aye, received him—what can I say more? A fit of delirium tremens followed, and the poor, suffering woman seemed to have strength given her to live and bear, still—to nurse him and comfort him, for his horrid agony stirred her sympathies to their lowest depths. You will wonder where Mary's father was all this time. He was dead—the brothers had sold the homestead, and with their widowed mother and sister gone to the far west; leaving Mary four years before, prosperous and happy. The small estate, though it made a comfortable living for them while the managing, energetic father lived, made but a small stipend when divided among eight children. They had not prospered, and were not in condition to help Mary.

By degrees Edward Harris recovered from his dreadful disease, but too weak to go out and obtain again the poisonous draught, and for once in years, he became duly sober. Conscience seemed to be awakened as he gained strength. He seemed to feel, more and more acutely, his terrible situation. He knew his name and fame bore a brand that in his old haunts could never be expunged; and he urged Mary to pack up their few effects and go with him to a new country. He promised her, faithfully and solemnly, to reform, and become a good father and husband. Mary consented; and by selling everything that would bring money, and by the assistance of a few friends who loved her, she gathered together enough to pay their way upon a steamer's deck to a far-off western village.—Edward kept sober till they arrived there; and here they were set down by the captain without one dollar. They found a vacant room, into which they moved, and Edward, with a humbled pride and an aching heart, went to hunt work, that they might again live. He found a job of sawing wood, and at night took home three-quarters of a dollar. Mary fixed up their straw bed in the corner of the room, and made things just as comfortable as possible, and then she went out, feeble as she was, to hunt work also. This she soon found, in the shape of washing. By borrowing a tub, a kettle, and some other things, which her lady-like manners and her pleasant pale face insured to her for the asking, she, too, had earned fifty cents ere nightfall; and as they gathered round the poor, broken hearth, and ate the scant, but wholesome meal of their own earning, Mary's heart swelled with hope—aye, earnest hope, that the husband of her early love, the father of her children, might yet be a man; and she laid her head upon his shoulder and wept tears of hopeful joy.

A little meal, and a little flour were procured, and with the surplus of their day's labor, Mary bought a wash-tub; and as their house was on the bank of the stream, where water was handy, and she could still have the kettle a few days, she went on with her work rejoicing. For a week all went well. Edward's fine manners and education attracted attention, and his resolution to help himself, made others willing to help him. Many little comforts were furnished, and Mary's renewed hopes seemed to give renewed strength. But, at the expiration of a week, all her bright prospects banished! Edward came home one evening evidently excited with liquor, and told her that he had found permanent business—that the tavern-keeper of the village had offered him the place of bar keeper, till he could get acquainted and set up his profession again. Mary warned, begged, prayed, but all in vain. He had already tasted, and the demon was within. Down, down, down he went. Mary toiled, toiled, toiled, as he went down. She was a good sewer, but she knew that she could not support herself at that slow work, neither would it secure her health.—Everybody pitied, everybody loved her that knew her. But she was too proud—loved independence too well, to beg.

At length the scarlet-fever swept through the neighborhood, and her little twins, now two years old, died. Mary clasped her hands in mute anguish over the little, unadorned coffin that held them both, and hardly knew, amid her soul's deep tortures, whether to weep or rejoice that they were taken from life's sufferings. Subdued and chastened, was her sorrow over that humble mound in the rural churchyard, compared with the soul-sickening conviction that another was soon to be added to share her trials—another, whose ushering into life would deprive her of the power of ministering to the wants of those who had only a mother's care to shield them.—Edward Harris was often found drunk in the muddy streets, rooted about by the hogs, and picked up by some one more humane than his fellows, and brought home to his own wretched door, to get sober on his own wretched bed, and to pour out his hideous curses and imprecations in the ears of his own wretched wife and children.

Mary's fifth child was born, and kind neighbors (for where are there not kind neighbors?) helped her through her day of trial; and she was soon well enough to resume her labors, little by little. Two years more—two terrible wearisome years, passed over her with no change for the better in Edward. At length, one stormy, dreary, cold spring morning, he was found, half-way between his home and the tavern—DEAD. He had fallen, on his way the night before, with his face in a pool of water, and was too drunk to get out; and there he had strangled—his face to the earth, and the ice frozen about his head. Oh! horrible death! But yet, was it more horrible than his life? No, nothing can be more horrible than the life of a drunkard!

This happened two years ago. Since then Mary has got into a better cabin, and still works and washes round for those who need her, because she can thus earn more than in any other way. Little Jenny and Edward do go to school, and she takes her baby with her to her work.—She was doing pretty well till she took that cold a few days ago, and her sickness exhausted her little means.

Now you know, my children, how Mrs. Harris came to be so poor. George, you are just entering life with a fair prospect before you. But not fairer or clearer is your sky, than was Edward Harris' when he married Mary Cadwallader. Had there been no fashionable drinking—had there been no licensed bar-rooms—had there been no strong, proud men to have winked at his first steppings aside from duty, he might now be standing among the great, the wealthy, and the good. His wife would not have been a washerwoman, toiling with an aching breast and heart, nor his children begging at this neighbor's door for a little milk. George, my child, BEWARE!

ELIZABETH STUART PHELPS (WARD)
1844–1911

Elizabeth Stuart Phelps was born Mary Gray Phelps; at eight years of age, after the death of her mother, also a writer, Mary assumed her mother's name. Phelps published more than twenty-five novels, the most popular being *The Gates Ajar* (1868) and two sequels.

Phelps's works often deal with the psychological and sociological influences she observed in the areas where she actively supported reform. Many of her novels examine the unjust and unequal treatment of women; she often published articles on women's rights in women's reform newspapers, such as the *Woman's Journal*. Her 1871 novel, *A Silent Partner,* portrays the difficult life of young women who worked in the mills.

Phelps participated in temperance causes, contributing to the formation and continuation of a temperance organization in Gloucester and living among and befriending members of a community with numerous alcoholics. She wrote two specifically temperance works, *A Singular Life* (1894) and *Jack the Fisherman,* a novella (Boston: Houghton, Mifflin, 1887). Like many other women temperance writers, Phelps tries to make readers aware of the prejudicial treatment directed toward victims of the alcoholic.

In *Jack the Fisherman,* Phelps examines a number of issues present in much of women's temperance fiction, including the pervasiveness of physical abuse and the hereditary nature of alcoholism. But Phelps also explores social and psychological conditions that contribute to the continuation of the cycle of intemperance—and violence. Even though Jack and his wife, Teen, struggle to create a better life, they are products of a society whose attitudes and behaviors entrap the couple. Rather than looking only to changes in the legal system, Phelps suggests that hope for breaking the cycles of substance addiction and spousal abuse lies in social and economic improvements, here represented in the benevolence of temperance workers, especially Mother Mary, who actually live among and understand the environment of the alcoholic—not reformers who separate themselves from those they would help.

Jack the Fisherman

I

Jack was a Fairharbor boy. This might be to say any of several things; but it is at least sure to say one,—he was a fisherman, and the son of a fisherman.

When people of another sort than Jack's have told their earthly story through, the biography, the memorial, the obituary remains. Our poet, preacher, healer, politician, and the rest pass on to this polite sequel which society has ordained for human existence. When Jack dies, he stops. We find the fisherman squeezed into some corner of the accident column: "Washed overboard," or "Lost in the fog," and that is the whole of it. He ends just there. There is no more Jack. No fellow-members in the Society for Something-or-Nothing pass resolutions to his credit and the consolation of his family. No funeral discourse is preached over him and privately printed at the request of the parishioners. The columns of the religious weekly to which he did not subscribe contain no obituary sketches signed by the initials of friends not thought to be too afflicted to speak a good word for a dead man. From the press of the neighboring city no thin memorial volume sacred to his virtues and stone-blind to his defects shall ever issue. Jack needs a biographer. Such the writer of this sketch would fain aspire to be.

Jack was born at sea. His father was bringing his mother home from a visit at a half-sister's in Nova Scotia, for Jack's mother was one of those homesick, clannish people who pine without their relations as much as some of us pine with them; and even a half-sister was worth more to her in her fanciful and feeble condition than a whole one is apt to be to bolder souls.

She had made her visit at her half-sister's, and they had talked over receipts, and compared yeast, and cut out baby things, and turned dresses, and dyed flannel, and gone to prayer-meetings together; and Jack's mother was coming home, partly because Jack's father came for her, and partly because he happened to come sober, which was a great point, and partly because the schooner had to sail, which was another,—she was coming home, at all events, when a gale struck them. It was an ugly blow. The little two-masted vessel swamped, in short, at midnight of a moonlit night, off the coast, just the other side of seeing Cape Ann light. The crew were picked up by a three-master, and taken home. Aboard the three-master, in fright and chill and storm, the little boy was born. They always put it that he was born in Fairharbor. In fact, he was born rounding Eastern Point. "The toughest place to be borned in, this side o' Torment," Jack's father said. But Jack's mother said nothing at all.

Jack's father kept sober till he got the mother and the child safely into the little crumbling, gray cottage in half of whose meagre dimensions the family kept up the illusion which they called home. Then, for truth compels me, I must state that Jack's father went straightway out upon what, in even less obscure circles than his, it is customary to call "a tear." There seems to be something in the savage, incisive fitness of this word which has over-ridden all mere distinctions of class or culture, and must ultimately make it a classic in the language. "I've stood it long as I ken stand, and I'm goin' on a tear,—I'm agoin' on a *netarnal* tear," said Jack's father to his oldest dory-mate, a fellow he had a feeling for, much as you would for an oar you had handled a good many years; or perhaps a sail that you were used to, and had patched and watched, and knew the cracks in it, and the color of it, and when it was likely to give way, and whereabouts it would hold.

In fact, that proved to be, in deed and truth, an eternal tear for Jack's father. Drunk as a fisherman could be,—and that is saying a good deal,—he reshipped that night, knowing not whither nor why, nor indeed knowing that the deed was done; and when he came to himself he was twelve hours out, on his way to the Banks of Newfoundland; and the young mother, with her baby on her arm, looked out of the frosty window over the foot of her old bedstead, and watched for him to come, and did not like to tell the neighbors that she was short of fuel.

She was used to waiting—women are; Fairharbor women always are. But she had never waited so long before. And when, at the end of her waiting, the old dory-mate came in one night and told her that it happened falling from the mast because he was not sober enough to be up there, Jack's mother said she had always expected it. But she had not expected it, all the same. We never expect trouble, we only fear it. And she had put the baby on the edge of the bed and got upon her knees upon the floor, and laid her face on the baby, and tried to say her prayers,—for she was a pious little woman, not knowing any better,—but found she could not pray, she cried so. And the old dory-mate told her not to try, but to cry as hard as she could. And she told him he was very kind; and so she did. For she was fond of her husband although he got drunk; because he got drunk, one is tempted to say. Her heart had gone the way of the hearts of drunkards' wives: she loved in proportion to her misery, and gave on equation with what she lost. All the woman in her mothered her husband when she could no longer wifely worship him. When he died she felt as if she had lost her eldest child. So, as I say, she kneeled with her face on the baby, and cried as if she had been the blessedest of wives. Afterward she thought of this with self-reproach. She said one day to the old dory-mate:

"When my trouble came, I did not pray to God. I'd ought to have. But I only cried at Him."

Jack had come into the world in a storm, and he began it stormily. He was a big, roaring baby, and he became a restless boy. His mother's gentle and unmodified femininity was helpless before the problem of this wholly masculine little being. She said Jack needed a man to manage him. He smoked at six; he lived in the stables and on the wharves at eight; he came when he got ready, and went when he pleased; he obeyed when he felt like it, and when he was punished, he kicked. Once, in an imaginative moment, he bit her.

She sent him to pack mackerel, for they were put to it to keep soul and body together, and he brought home such habits of speech as even the Fairharbor woman had never heard. From her little boy, her baby,—not yet old enough to be out of short trousers, and scarcely out of little sacks, had he been *yours,* my Lady, at the pretty age when one still fastens lace collars round their necks, and has them under shelter by dark, and hears their prayers, and challenges the breath of heaven lest it blow too rudely on some delicate forming fibre of soul or body,—from her little boy, at eight years old, the mother first learned the abysses of vulgarity in a seaport town.

It must be admitted that her education in this respect had been defective. She had always been one of the women in whose presence her neighbors did not speak too carelessly.

But Jack's mother had the kind of eyes which do not see mire,—the meek, religious, deep-blue eye which even growing sons respect while they strike the tears from it. At his worst Jack regarded her as a species of sacred fact, much like heaven or a hymn. Sometimes on Sunday nights he stayed at home with her; he liked to hear her song. She sang Rock of Ages in her best black alpaca with her work-worn hands crossed upon the gingham apron which she put on to save the dress.

But ah, she said, Jack needed a man to manage him. And one day when she said this, in spite of her gentle unconsciousness, or because of it, the old dory-mate to whom she said it said he thought so too, and that if she had no objections he would like to be that man.

And the Fairharbor widow, who had never thought of such a thing, said she didn't know as she had; for nobody knew, she said, how near to starving they had come; and it was something to have a sober man. So, on this reasonable basis, Jack acquired a step-father, and his step-father sent him straightway to the Grand Banks.

He meant it well enough, and perhaps it made no difference in the end. But Jack was a little fellow to go fishing,—only ten. His first voyage was hard: it was a March voyage; he got badly frost-bitten, and the skipper was rough. He was knocked about a good deal, and had the measles by himself in his berth; and the men said they didn't know they had brought a baby to the Banks, for they were very busy; and Jack lay and cried a little, and thought about his mother, and wished he hadn't kicked her, but forgot it when he got well. So he swaggered about among the men, as a boy does when he is the only one in a crew, and aped their talk, and shared their grog, and did their hard work, and learned their songs, and came home with the early stages of moral ossification as well set in upon his little heart as a ten-year-old heart allows.

The next voyage did not mend the matter; nor the next. And though the old dory-mate was an honest fellow, he had been more successful as a dory-mate than he was as a step-father. He and Jack did not "get on." Sometimes Jack's mother wondered if he *had* needed a man to manage him; but she never said so. She was a good wife, and she had fuel enough, now; she only kissed Jack and said she meant it for the best, and then she went away and sang Rock of Ages to the tune of Martyn, very slow, and quite on the wrong key. It seemed to make her feel better, poor thing. Jack sometimes wondered why.

When he was twelve years old he came home from a winter voyage one night, and got his pay for his share,—boy's pay, yet, for a boy's share; but bigger than it used to be,—and did not go home first, but went rollicking off with a crowd of Portuguese. It was a Sunday night, and his mother was expecting him, for she knew the boat was in. His step-father expected him too,—and his money; and Jack knew that. His mother had been sick, but Jack did not know that; she had been very sick, and had asked for him a great deal. There had been a baby,—born dead while its father was offshore after cod,—and it had been very cold weather; and something had gone wrong.

At midnight of that night some one knocked at the door of the crumbling cottage. The step-father opened it; he looked pale and agitated. Some boys were there in a confused group; they bore what seemed to be a lifeless body on a drag, or bob-sled; it was Jack, dead drunk.

It was the first time,—he was only twelve,—and one of the Fairharbor boys took the pipe from his mouth to explain.

"He was trapped by a Portygee, and they've stole every cent of him, 'n kicked him out, 'n lef' him, stranded like a monk-fish, so me and the other fellers we borryed a sled and brung him home, for we thought his mother'd rather. He ain't dead, but he's just as drunk as if he was sixty!"

The Fairharbor boy mentioned this circumstance with a kind of abnormal pride, as if such superior maturity were a point for a comrade to make note of. But Jack's step-father went out softly, and shut the door, and said:

"Look here, boys,—help me in with him, will you? Not *that* way. His mother's in there. She died an hour ago."

II

And so the curse of his heredity came upon him. She never knew, thank Heaven. Her knowledge would have been a kind of terrible fore-omniscience, if she had. She would have had no hope of him from that hour. Her experience would have left her no illusions. The drunkard's wife would have educated the drunkard's mother too "liberally" for that. She would have taken in the whole scope and detail of the future in one midnight moment's breadth, as a problem in the high mathematics may rest upon the width of a geometrical point. But she did not know. We say—I mean, it is our fashion of saying—that she did not know. God was merciful. She had asked for Jack, it seemed, over and over, but did not complain of him for not coming; she never complained of Jack. She said the poor boy must have stayed somewhere to have a pleasant time; and she said they were to give her love to him, if he came in while she was asleep. And then she asked her husband to sing Rock of Ages for her, because she did not feel very strong. He couldn't sing,—more than a halibut, poor fellow; but he did not like to disappoint her, for he thought she looked what he called "miser'ble"; so he sat down by the bed and raised his hoarse, weather-beaten voice to the tune of Martyn, as best he could, and mixed up two verses inextricably with a line from "Billy's on the bright blue sea," which he added because he saw he must have something to fill out, and it was all he could think of—but she thanked him very gently, and said he sang quite well; and said once more that he was to give her love to Jack; and went to sleep afterward; and by and by, they could not wake her to see her boy of twelve brought to her drunk. . . .

He was a happy-go-lucky fellow. Life sat airily on him. He had his mother's handsome eyes dashed with his father's fun (for she couldn't take a joke, to save her); he told a good story; he did a kind deed; he was generous with his money, when he had any, and never in the least disturbed when he hadn't. He was popular to the dangerous extent that makes one's vices seem a kind of social introduction, and not in Jack's circle alone, be it said. Every crew wanted him. Drunk or sober, as a shipmate he was at par. It was usually easy for him to borrow. The fellows made up his fines for him, there was always somebody to go bail for him when he got before the police court. Arrested perhaps a half dozen times a year, in his maddest years, he never was sent to the House in his life. There were always people enough who thought it a pity to let such a good fellow go to prison. He had—I was going to say as a matter of course he had—curly hair. One should not omit to notice that he was splendidly tattooed. He was proud, as seamen are, of his brawny arms dashed from wrist to shoulder with the decorative ingenuity of his class. Jack had aesthetic views of his own, indeed, about his personal allowance of indigo. He had objected to the customary medley of anchors, stars, and crescents, and exhibited a certain reserve of taste, which was rather interesting. On his left arm he bore a very crooked lighthouse rising from a heavy sea; he was, in fact, quite flooded along the bicipital muscle with waves and billows, but nothing else interfered with the massive proportions of the effect. This was considered a masterly design, and Jack was often called upon to push up his sleeve and explain how he came by the inspiration.

Upon the other arm he wore a crucifix, ten inches long; this was touched with blood-red ink; the dead Christ hung upon it, lean and pitiful. Jack said he took the crucifix against his drowning. It was an uncommonly large and ornate crucifix.

Jack was a steady drinker at nineteen. At twenty-five he was what either an inexperienced or a deeply experienced temperance missionary would have called incurable. The intermediate grades would have confidently expected to save him.

Of course he reformed. He would not have been interesting if he had not. The unmitigated sot has few attractions even for sea-faring society. It is the foil and flash, the by-play and side-light of character, that "lead us on." Jack was always reforming. After that night when he was brought home on the bob-sled, the little boy was as steady and as miserable as he knew how to be for a long time; he drew the unfortunate inference that the one involved the other. By the time his mother's grave was green with the scanty Fairharbor church-yard grass,—for even the sea-wind seems to have a grudge against the very dead for choosing dry graves in Fairharbor, and scants them in their natural covering,—that time rank weeds had overgrown the sorrow of the homeless boy. He and his step-father "got on" less than ever now, as was to be expected; and when one day Jack announced with characteristic candor that he was going to get drunk, if he went to Torment for it, the two parted company; and the crumbling cottage knew Jack no more. By and by, when his step-father was drowned at Georges', Jack borrowed the money for some black gloves and a hat-band. He had the reputation of being a polite fellow; the fishermen spelled it t-o-n-y. Truth to tell, the old dory-mate had wondered sometimes on Sunday afternoons if he *had* been the man to manage Jack; and felt that the main object of his second marriage had been defeated.

Jack, as I say, was always reforming. Every temperance society in the city had a hand at him. They were of the old-fashioned, easy type which took their responsibilities comfortably. They held him out on a pair of moral tongs, and tried to toast his misdemeanors out of him, before a quick fire of pledges and badges; and when he tumbled out of the tongs, and asked the president and treasurer why they didn't bow to him in the street when he was drunk, or why, if he was good enough for them in the lodge-room, he wasn't good enough to shake hands with before folks on the post-office steps, or propounded any of those ingenious posers with which his kind are in the habit of disturbing the benevolent spirit, they snapped the tongs to, and turned him over to the churches.

These touched him gingerly. They invited him into the free pews,—a dismal little row in the gallery,—sent him a tract or two, and asked him a few well-meant and very confusing religious questions, to which Jack's replies were far from satisfactory. One ardent person, a recent convert, coaxed him into a weekly prayer-meeting. It was a very good, honest, uninteresting prayer-meeting, and there were people sitting there beside him with clean lives and clear faces whose motives Jack was not worthy to understand, and he knew enough to know it. But it happened to be a foreign mission prayer-meeting, devoted to the Burmese field; which was, therefore, be it said, not so much an argument against foreign missions, as a deficient means of grace to the fisherman. Jack was terribly bored. He ran his hands through his curls, and felt for his tobacco, and whispered to the young convert to know if there weren't any waits in the play so a man could get out without hurting anybody's feelings. But just then the young convert struck up a hymn, and Jack stayed.

He liked the singing. His restless, handsome face took on a change such as a windy day takes on toward dusk, when the breeze dies down. When he found they were singing Rock of Ages, he tried to sing it too,—for he was a famous tenor on deck. But when he had sung a line or two,—flash! down in one of the empty pews in front, he saw a thin old lady with blue eyes, sitting in a black alpaca dress with her hands clasped on her gingham apron.

"That's my mother. Have I got the jim-jams?" asked this unaccustomed worshiper of himself. But then he remembered that he was sober. He could sing no longer after this, but bowed his head and looked into his old felt hat, and wondered if he were going to cry, or get religion. In point of fact, he did neither of these things, because a very old church-member arose just then, and said he saw a poor castaway in our midst tonight, and he besought the prayers of the meeting for his soul. Jack stopped crying. He looked hard at the old church member. He knew him; had always known him. The fisherman waited till that prayer was through,—it was rather a long prayer,—and then he too sprang to his feet. He looked all around the decorous place; his face was white with the swift passion of the drinking man.

"I never spoke in meetin' in my life," said Jack in an unsteady voice. "I ain't religious. I drink. But I'm sober to-night, and I've got something to say to you. I heard what that man said. I know him. He's old Jim Crownoby. I've always knowed Jim Crownoby. He owns a sight of property in this town. He's a rich man. He owns that block on Black street. You know he does. You can't deny it. Nor he can't neither. All I want to say is, I've got drunk in one of them places of his, time and again; and if there ain't anybody but *him* to pray for my soul, I'd rather go to the devil."

Jack stopped short, jammed on his hat, and left the meeting. In the shocked rustle that followed, some one had the tact to start "Rescue the perishing," as the fisherman strode down the broad aisle. He did not go again. The poor young convert followed him up for a week or two, and gave him an expensive Testament, bought out of an almost invisible personal income, in vain.

"I've no objections to you," said Jack candidly; "I'm much obliged to ye for yer politeness, sir. But them churches that sub-leases to a rum-seller, I don't think they onderstand a drinkin' man. Hey? Well, ain't he their biggest rooster, now? Don't he do the heft of the payin', and the tallest of their crowin', consequent? Thought so. Better leave me go, sir. I ain't a pious man; I'm a fisherman.

"Fishes," said Jack, "is not fools."

He gave voice to this remark one day in Boston, when he was twenty-five years old. He was trying to entertain a Boston girl; she was not familiar with Fairharbor or with the scenery of his calling; he wanted to interest her; he liked the girl. He had liked a good many girls, it need not be said; but this one had laid upon the fisherman—she knew not how, he knew not why, and what man or woman of us could have told him?—the power that comes not of reason, or of time, or of trying, or of wisdom, or of rightness, but of the mystery to which, when we are not speaking of Jack, we give the name of love. It seems a sacrilege, admit, to write it here, and of these two. But there, again, it would be easy to be wrong. The study of the relativity of human feeling is a delicate science; it calls for a fine moral equipment. If this were the high-water mark of nature for Jack—and who shall say?—the tide shall have its sacred due, even down among those weeds and in that mud. He liked that girl, among them all, and her he thought of gently. He had known her a long time; as much as three months. When the vessel came into Boston to sell halibut, he had a few days there, drifting about as seamen do, homeless and reckless; dashing out the wages just paid off, in ways that sometimes he remembered and sometimes he forgot, and that usually left him without a dollar toward his next fine when he should be welcomed by the police court of his native city on returning home.

Jack thought, I say, gravely of this girl. He never once took her name in vain among the fellows; and she had not been a very good girl either. But Jack reflected that he was not very good himself, if you came to that. His downright, honest nature stood him in stead in this moral distinction; there was always a broad streak of generosity in him at his worst; it goes with the temperament, we say, and perhaps we say it too often to give him half the credit of it.

She was a pretty girl, and she was very young. She had told Jack her story, as they strolled about the bright Boston streets on comfortable winter evenings; when he took her to the variety show, or to the oyster-shop, and they talked together. Jack pitied her. Perhaps she deserved it; it was a sad little story—and she was so very young! She had a gentle way, with Jack; for some reason, God knows why, she had trusted him from the first, and he had never once been known to disturb her trust. That was the pleasant part of it.

On this evening that we speak of, Jack was sober. He was often sober when he had an evening to spend with the Boston girl; not always—no; truth must be told. She looked as pretty as was in her that night; she had black eyes and a kind of yellow hair that Jack had never seen crinkled low on the forehead above black eyes before; he thought her as fine to look at as any actress he ever saw; for the stage was Jack's standard of the magnificent, as it is to so many of his sort. The girl's name was Teen. Probably she had been called Christine once, in her country home; she even told Jack she had been baptized.

"I wasn't, myself," said Jack; "I roared so, they darsen't do it. My mother got me to church, for she was a pious woman, and I pummeled the parson in the face with both fists, and she said she come away, for she was ashamed of me. She always said that christenin' wasn't never legal. It disappointed her, too. I was an awful baby."

"I should think likely," said Teen with candor. "Do you set much by your mother?"

"She's dead," said Jack in a subdued voice. Teen looked at him; she had never heard him speak like that.

"I 'most wished mine was," said the girl; "she'd 'a' ben better off—along of me."

"That's so," said Jack.

The two took a turn in silence up and down the brightly lighted street; their thoughts looked out strangely from their marred young faces; they felt as if they were in a foreign country. Jack had meant to ask her to take a drink, but he gave it up; he couldn't, somehow.

"Was you always a fisherman?" asked Teen, feeling, with a woman's tact, that somebody must change the current of the subject.

"I was a fisherman three generations back," Jack answered her; "borned a fisherman, you bet! I couldn't 'a' ben nothin' else if I'd drownded for it. It's a smart business. You hev to keep your wits about you. Fishes is no fools."

"Ain't they?" asked the girl listlessly. She was conscious of failing in conversational brilliancy; but the truth was, she couldn't get over what they had been saying: it was always unfortunate when she remembered her mother. Jack began to talk to her about his business again, but Teen did not reply; and when he looked down at her to see what ailed her, there were real tears rolling over her pretty cheeks.

"Why, Teen!" said Jack.

"Leave go of me, Jack," said Teen, "and let me get off; I ain't good company to-night. I've got the dumps. I can't entertain ye, Jack. And, Jack—don't let's talk about mothers next time, will we? It spoils the evenin'. Leave go of me, and I'll go home by my own self. I'd rather."

"I won't leave go of you!" cried Jack with a sudden blazing purpose lighting up all the corners of his soul. It was a white light, not unholy; it seemed to shine through and through him with a soft glow like a candle on an altar. "I'll never leave go of you, Teen, if you'll say so. I'd rather marry you."

Jack asks Teen to marry him. From Elizabeth Stuart Phelps (Ward), *Jack the Fisherman*. Boston: Houghton, Mifflin, 1887, p. 20.

"Marry *me?*" said Teen.

"Yes, marry you. I'd a sight rather. There now! It's out with it. What do you say to that, Teen?"

With one slow finger-tip Teen wiped away the tears that fell for her mother. A ring on her finger glistened in the light as she did this. She saw the sparkle, tore off the ring and dashed it away; it fell into the mud, and was trodden out of sight instantly. Jack sprang gallantly to pick it up.

"Don't you touch it!" cried the girl. She put her bared hand back upon his arm. The ring had left a little mark upon her finger; she glanced at this, and looked up into Jack's handsome face: he looked very kind.

"Jack, dear," said Teen softly, "I ain't fit to marry ye."

"You're fitter 'n I be," answered Jack manfully. Teen sighed; she did not speak at once; other tears came now, but these were tears for herself and for Jack. Jack felt this, after his fashion; they gave him singular confusion of mind.

"I wouldn't cry about it, Teen. You needn't have me if you don't want to."

"But I *do* want to, Jack."

"Honest?"

"Honest it is, Jack."

"Will ye make a good wife, Teen?" asked Jack, after some unprecedented thought.

"I'll try, Jack."

"You'll never go back on me, nohow?"

"I ain't that sort!" cried the girl, drawing herself up a little. A new dignity sat upon her with a certain grace which was beautiful to see.

"Will you swear it, Teen?"

"If you'd rather, Jack."

"What'll you swear by, now?" asked Jack. "You must swear by all you hold holy."

"What *do* I hold holy?" mused Teen.

"Will you swear," continued Jack seriously, "will you swear to me by the Rock of Ages?"

"What's that?" asked the girl.

"It's a hymn-tune. I want you to swear me by the Rock of Ages that you'll be that you say you will, to me. Will you do it, Teen?"

"Oh yes," said Teen, "I'll do it. Where shall we come across one?"

"I guess I can find it," Jack replied. "I can find most anything I set out to."

So they started out at random, in their reckless fashion, in the great city, to find the Rock of Ages for the asking.

Jack led his companion hither and yon, peering into churches and vestries and missions, and wherever he saw signs of sacred things. Singing they heard abundantly in the gay town; songs merry, mad, and sad; but not the song for a girl to swear by, that she would be true wife to a man who trusted her.

Wandering thus, on the strange errand whose pathos was so far above their own dream of knowledge, they chanced at last upon the place and the little group of people known in that part of Boston as Mother Mary's meeting.

The girl said she had been there once, but that Mother Mary was too good for her; she was one of the real kind. Everybody knew Mother Mary and her husband; he was a parson. They were poor folks themselves, Teen said, and understood poor folks, and did for them all the year round, not clearing out, like rich ones, when it came hot weather, but stood by 'em, Teen said. They kept the little room open, and if you wanted a prayer you went in and got it, just as you'd call for a drink or a supper; it was always on hand for you, and a kind word sure to come with it, and you always knew where to go for 'em; and Mother Mary treated you like folks. She liked her, Teen said. If she'd been a different girl, she'd have gone there of a cold night all winter. But Teen said she felt ashamed.

"I guess she'll have what I'm after," said Jack. "She sounds like she would. Let's go in and see."

So they went into the quiet place among the praying people, and stood staring, for they felt embarrassed. Mother Mary looked very white and peaceful; she was a tall, fair woman; she wore a black dress with white about the bosom; it was a plain, old dress, much mended. Mother Mary did not look rich, as Teen had said. The room was filled with poor creatures gathered about her like her children, while she talked with them and taught them as she could. She crossed the room immediately to where the young man stood, with the girl beside him.

"We've come," said Jack, "to find the Rock of Ages." He drew Teen's hand through his arm, and held it for a moment; then, moved by some fine instinct mysterious to himself, he lifted and laid it in Mother Mary's own.

"Explain it to her, ma'am," he said; "tell her, won't you? I'm going to marry her, if she'll have me. I want her to swear by somethin' holy she'll be a true wife to me. She hadn't anything particularly holy herself, and the holiest thing I know of is the Rock of Ages. I've heard my mother sing it. She's dead. We've been huntin' Boston over to-night after the Rock of Ages."

Mother Mary was used to the pathos of her sober work, but the tears sprang now to her large and gentle eyes. She did not speak to Jack,—could not possibly, just then; but, delaying only for the moment till she could command herself, she flung her rich, maternal voice out upon the words of the old hymn. Her husband joined her, and all the people present swelled the chorus.

> "Rock of Ages, cleft for me!
> Let me hide myself in thee;
> . . . .
> Be of sin the double cure,
> Cleanse me from its guilt and power."

They sang it all through,—the three verses that everybody knows,— and Jack and Teen stood listening. Jack tried to sing himself; but Teen hid her face, and cried upon his arm.

"Thou must save," sang the praying people; "Thou must save, and thou alone!"

The strain died solemnly; the room was quiet; the minister yonder began to pray, and all the people bowed their heads. But Mother Mary stood quite still, with the girl's hand trembling in her own.

"Swear it, Teen!" Jack bent down his curly head and whispered; he would not shame his promised wife before these people. "Swear by *that*, you'll be true wife to me!"

"I swear it, Jack," sobbed Teen. "If *that's* the Rock of Ages, I swear by it, though I was to die for it, I'll be an honest wife to you.

"Come back when you've got your license," said Mother Mary, smiling through her tears, "and my husband will marry you if you want him to."

"We'll come to-morrow," Jack answered gravely.

"Jack," said Teen in her pretty way,—for she had a very pretty way,—"If I'm an honest wife to you, will you be *kind* to me?" She did not ask him to swear it by the Rock of Ages. She took his word for it, poor thing! Women do.

III

Mother Mary's husband married them next day at the Mission meeting; and Mother Mary sat down at the melodeon in the corner of the pleasant place, and played and sang Toplady's great hymn for them, as Jack had asked her. It was his wedding march. He was very sober and gentle,—almost like a better man. Teen thought him the handsomest man she had ever seen.

"Oh, I say, Teen," he nodded to her, as they walked away, "one thing I forgot to tell you,—I'm reformed."

"Are you, Jack?"

"If I ever drink a drop again, so help me"—But he stopped.

"So help you, Rock of Ages?" asked the new-made wife. But Jack winced; he was honest enough to hesitate at this.

"I don't know's I'd darst—*that*," he added ruefully. "But I'm reformed. I have lost all hanker for liquor. I shall never drink again. You'll see, Teen."

Teen did see, as was to be expected. She saw a great deal, poor thing! Jack did not drink—for a long time; it was nearly five months, for they kept close count. He took her to Fairharbor, and rented the old half of the crumbling cottage where his mother used to sit and watch for him on long, late evenings. The young wife did the watching now. They planted some cinnamon rose-bushes by the doorsteps of the cottage, and fostered them affectionately. Jack was as happy and sober as possible, to begin with. He picked the cinnamon roses and brought them in for his wife to wear. He was proud to have a home of his own; he had not expected to; in fact, he had never had one since that night when his mother said they were to give her love to him, if he came home while she was asleep. He had beaten about so, sleeping for the most part in his berth, and sailing again directly; he had never had any place, he said, to hang his winter clothes in; closets and bureaus seemed treasure-houses to him, and the kitchen fire a luxury greater than a less good-looking man would have deserved. When he came home, drenched and chilly, from a winter voyage, and Teen took the covers off, and the fiery heart of the coals leaped out to greet him, and she stood in the rich color, with her yellow hair, young and fair and sweet as any man's wife could look, and said she had missed him, and called him her dear husband, Jack even went so far as to feel that Teen was the luxury. He treated her accordingly; that was at first. He came straight home to her; he kept her in flour and fuel; she had the little things and the gentle words that women need. Teen was very fond of him. This was the first of it,—I was going to say this was the worst of it. All there was of Teen seemed to have gone into her love for Jack. A part of Jack had gone into his love for Teen. Teen was very happy, to begin with. The respectable neighbors came to see her, and said, "We're happy to make your acquaintance." Nobody knew that it had not always been so that Teen's acquaintance would have been a source of social happiness. And she wrote to her mother that she was married; and her mother came on to make her a little visit; and Teen cried her soul out for joy. She was very modest and home-keeping and loving; no wife in the land was truer than this girl he had chosen was to the fisherman who chose her. Jack knew that. He believed in her. She made him happy; and therefore she kept him right.

All this was at first. It did not last. Why should we expect that, when we see how little there is in the relation of man and woman which lasts? If happy birth and gentle rearing, and the forces of what we call education, and the silken webs of spun refinements, are so strained in the tie which requires two who cannot get away from each other to make each other happy, how should we ask, of the law of chances, the miracle for Teen and Jack?

There was no miracle. No transubstantiation of the common bread to holy flesh was wrought upon that poor altar. Their lot went the way of other lots, with the facts of their history dead against them. Trouble came, and poverty, and children, and care, and distaste. Jack took to his old ways, and his wife to the tears that they bring. The children died; they were poor sickly babies who wailed a little while in her arms, and slipped out because there wasn't enough to them to stay. And the gray house was damp. Some said it was diphtheria; but their mother said it was the will of God. She added: Might his will be done! On the whole she was not sorry. Their father struck her when he was in liquor. She thought if the babies lived they might get hurt. A month before the last one was born she showed to Jack's biographer a bruise across her shoulder, long and livid. She buttoned her dress over it with hasty repentance.

"Maybe I'd oughtn't to have told," she said. "But he said he'd be *kind* to me."

Jack was very sorry about this when he was sober. He kissed his wife, and bought a pair of pink kid shoes for the baby; which it never grew large enough to wear.

It grew comfortless beside the kitchen fire. From Elizabeth Stuart Phelps (Ward), *Jack the Fisherman*. Boston: Houghton, Mifflin, 1887, p. 31.

I am not writing a temperance story, only the biography of a fisherman, and a few words will say better than many how it was. Alcoholized brain-cells being one of the few bequests left to society which the heirs do not dispute, Jack went back to his habits with the ferocity that follows abstinence. Hard luck came. Teen was never much of a housekeeper; she had left her mother too early; had never been taught. Things were soggy, and not always clean; and she was so busy in being struck and scolded, and in bearing and burying babies, that it grew comfortless beside the kitchen fire. The last of the illusions which had taken the name of home within the walls of the crumbling half-cottage withered out of it, just as the cinnamon roses did the summer Jack watered them with whiskey by a little emotional mistake.

A worse thing had happened too. Some shipmate had "told" in the course of time; and Teen's prematrimonial story got set adrift upon the current—one of the cruelest currents of its kind—of Fairharbor gossip. The respectable neighbors made her feel it, as only respectable neighbors do such things. Jack, raging, overheard her name upon the wharves. Teen had been "that she said she would" to him. He knew it. No matron in the town had kept her life or heart more true. In all her sickness and trouble and slackness, and in going cold or hungry, and in her vivid beauty that none or all of these things could quench, Teen had carried a sweet dignity of her own as the racer in the old Promethean festival carried the torch while he ran against the wind. Jack knew,—oh yes, he knew. But he grew sullen, suspicious. When he was drunk he was always jealous; it began to take that form. When he was sober he still admired his wife; sometimes he went so far as to remember that he loved her. When this happened, Teen dried her eyes, and brushed her yellow hair, and washed up the kitchen floor, and made the coffee, and said to the grocer when she paid for the sugar:

"My husband has reformed."

IV

. . . He went aboard sober, and sober he stayed. He kept a good deal by himself and thought of many things. His face paled out and refined, as their faces do, from abstinence; the ghost of his good looks hovered about him; he mended up his clothes; he did a kind turn to a messmate now and then; he told some excellent clean stories, and raised the spirits of the crew; he lent a dollar to a fellow with the rheumatism who had an indebtedness to liquidate for St. Galen's Oil. When he had done this, he remembered that he had left his wife without money, and said aloud: "That's a ——— mean trick to play on a woman."

He had bad luck, however, that trip; his share was small; he made seven dollars and twenty-seven cents in three weeks. This was conceded by the crew of the fishing-schooner (her name was the *Destiny*) to be because Jack had "sworn off." It is a superstition among them. One unfamiliar with the lives of these men will hammer cold iron if he thinks to persuade them that rum and luck do not go together; or that to "reform" does not imply a reduction of personal income. You might as well try to put the fisherman's fist into a Honiton lace jumper, as the fisherman's mind into proportion upon this point. . . .

When Jack stepped off the *Destiny* at Zephaniah Salt & Co.'s wharf at Fairharbor, after that voyage, clean, pale, good-natured, and sober, thinking that he would get shaved before he hurried home to Teen, and wishing he could pay the grocer's bill upon the way, and thinking that, in default of this, he would start an account at the market, and carry her a chop or a sausage, in fact, thinking about her with an absorption which resembled consideration, if not affection,—suddenly he caught her name upon the wharves.

It may have been said of accident, or of the devil,—God knew; they may have been too drunk to notice Jack at first, or they may have seen and scented from afar the bad blood they stirred, like the hounds they were. It will never be told. The scandal of these places is incredibly barbarous, but it is less than the barbarity of drinking men to a man who strikes out from among themselves, and fights for his respectability.

The words were few,—they are not for us,—but they were enough to do the deed. Jack was quite sober. He understood. They assailed the honor of his home, the truth of his wife; they hurled her past at her and at himself; they derided the trust which he had in her in his absence; they sneered at the "reformed man" whose domestic prospects were—as they were; they exulted over him with the exultation in the sight of the havoc wrought, which is the most inexplicable impulse of evil.

Everybody knew how hot-blooded Jack was; and when the fury rushed red over his face painted gray by abstinence, there was a smart scattering upon the wharves.

They assailed the honor of his home. From Elizabeth Stuart Phelps (Ward), *Jack the Fisherman*, frontispiece. Boston: Houghton, Mifflin, 1887.

His hand clapped to his pockets; but his was an old, cheap, rusty pistol (he had swapped a Bible and his trawls for it once, upon a spree, and got cheated); it held but one cartridge, and his wrist shook. The shot went sputtering into the water, and no harm came of it. Jack jammed the pistol back into his pocket; he glared about him madly, but had his glare for his pains; the men were afraid of him; he was alone upon the wharf.

It can hardly be said that he hesitated. Would that it could. Raving to himself,—head down, hands clenched, feet stumbling like a blind man's,—the fisherman sank into the first open door he staggered by, as a seiner, pierced by an invisible swordfish, sinks into the sea. He had fifteen such places to pass before he reached his house. His chances were—as such chances go—at best.

He drank for half an hour—an hour—a half more—came out, and went straight home.

It was now night of a February day. It had not been a very cold day; a light, clean snow had fallen, which was thawing gently. Jack, looking dimly on through his craze, saw the light of his half of the gray cottage shining ahead; he perceived that the frost was melted from the windows. The warm color came quietly down to greet him across the fresh snow; it had to him in his delirium the look of a woman's eyes when they are true, and lean out of her love to greet a man. He did not put this to himself in these words, but only said:

"Them lamps look like she used to,—curse her!" and so went hurtling on.

He dashed up against the house, as a bowsprit dashes on the rocks, took one mad look through the unfrosted window, below the half-drawn curtain, and flung himself against the door, and in.

His wife sat there in the great rocking chair, leaning back; she had a pillow behind her and her feet on the salt-fish box which he had covered once to make a cricket for her, when they were first married. She looked pale and pretty—very pretty. She was talking to a visitor who sat upon the lounge beside her. It was a man. Now, Jack knew this man well; it was an old messmate; he had sworn off, a year ago, and they had gone different ways; he used to be a rough fellow; but people said now you wouldn't know him.

"I ain't so drunk but I see who you be, Jim," began the husband darkly; "I'll settle with *you* another day. I've got that to say to my wife I'd say better if we missed your company. Leave us by ourselves!"

"Look here, Jack," Jim flashed good-humoredly, "you're drunk, you know. She'll tell you what I come for. You ask her. Seein' she wasn't right smart—and there's them as says she lacked for vict-uals,—my wife sent me over with a bowl of cranberry sass, so help me Heaven!"

"I'll kill *you* some other evenin'. Leave us be!" cried Jack.

"We was settin' and talkin' about the Reform Club when you come in," objected Jim, with the patience of an old friend. "We was wonderin' if we couldn't get you to sign, Jack. Ask her if we wasn't. Come, now! I wouldn't make a fool of myself if I was you, Jack. See there. You've set her to cryin' already. And she ain't right smart."

"Clear out of my house!"* thundered Jack. "Leave us be by ourselves!"

"I don't know's I'd ought to," hesitated Jim.

"Leave us be! or I won't leave you be a d——minute longer! Ain't it my house? Get out of it!"

"It is, that's a fact," admitted the visitor, looking perplexed; "but I declare to Jupiter I don't know's I'd oughter leave it, the way things look. Have your senses, Jack, my boy! Have your senses! She ain't right smart."

But with this Jack sprang upon him, and the wife cried out between them, for the love of mercy, that murder would be done.

"Leave us be!" she pleaded, sobbing. "Nothin' else won't pacify him. Go, Jim, go, and shut the door, and thank her, for the cran-berry sarse was very kind of her, and for my husband's sake don't tell nobody he wasn't kind to me. There. That's right. There."

She sank back into the rocking-chair, for she was feeble still, and looked gently up into her husband's face. All the tones of her agitated voice had changed.

She spoke very low and calmly, as if she gathered her breath for the first stage of a struggle whose nature she solemnly understood. She had grown exceedingly pale.

"Jack, dear?" softly.

"I'll give ye time," he answered with an ominous quiet. "Tell yer story first. Out with it!"

"I haven't got nothin' to tell, Jack. He brought the cranberry sarse, for his wife took care of me, and she was very kind. And he

---

*Such peculiarities of Jack's pronunciation as were attributable to his condition will not be reproduced here.

set a little, and we was talkin' about the club, just as he says we was. It's Mother Mary's club, Jack. She's made Jim secretary, and she wanted you to join, for I told her you'd reformed. Oh, Jack, I told her you'd reformed!—Jack, Jack! Oh, Jack! What are you goin' to do to me! What makes you look like that?—Jack, Jack, Jack!"

"Stand up here!" he raved. He was past reason, and she saw it; he tore off his coat and pushed up his sleeves from his tattooed arms.

"You've played me false, I say! I trusted ye, and you've tricked me. I'll teach ye to be the talk upon the wharves another time when I get in from Georges'!"

She stood as he bade her, tottered and sank back; crawled up again, holding by the wooden arm of the rocking-chair, and stretched one hand out to him, feebly. She did not dare to touch him; if she had clung to him, he would have throttled her. When she saw him rolling up his sleeves, her heart stood still. But Teen thought: "I will not show him I'm afraid of him. It's the only chance I've got."

The poor girl looked up once into his face, and thought she smiled.

"Jack? Dear Jack!"

"I'll teach ye! I'll teach ye!"

"Oh, wait a moment, Jack. For the love of Heaven,—stop a minute! I've been that I said I'd be to you, since we was married. I've been an honest wife to you, my boy, and there's none on earth nor heaven as can look me in the eye and darst to say I haven't. I swore to ye upon the Rock of Ages, Mother Mary witnessin'—why, Jack!" her voice sank to infinite sweetness, "have ye forgotten? You ain't yourself, poor boy. You'll be so sorry. I ain't very strong, yet,— you'd feel bad if you should hit me—again. I'd hate to have you feel so bad. Jack dear, don't. Go look in the other room, before you strike again. Ye ain't seen it yet. Jack, for the love of mercy!— Jack! Jack!"

"Say you've played me false, and I'll stop. Own up, and I'll quit. Own up to me, I say!"

"I can't own up to you, for I swore you by the Rock of Ages; I swore ye I would be an honest wife. You may pummel me to death, but I'll not lie away them words I swore to ye . . . by that, . . . Jack, for the love of Heaven, don't ye, Jack! For the way you used to feel to me, dear, dear Jack! For the sake of the babies we had, . . . and you walked beside of me, to bury 'em! Oh, for God's sake . . . Jack!

. . . Oh, you said you'd be kind to me . . . Oh, ye'll be so sorry! For the love of pity! For the love of God! Not the pistol! Oh, for the Rock of"—

But there he struck her down. The butt end of the weapon was heavy enough to do the deed. He struck, and then flung it away.

Upon his bared arm, as it came crashing, the crucifix was spattered red.

V

He stood up stupidly and looked about the room. The covers were off the kitchen stove, and the heart of the coals blazed out. Her yellow hair had loosened as she fell, and shone upon the floor.

He remembered that she spoke about the other room, and said of something yonder, that he hadn't seen it yet. Confusedly he wondered what it was. He stumbled in and stared about the bedroom. It was not very light there, and it was some moments before he perceived the cradle, standing straight across his way.

The child waked as he hit the cradle, and began to cry, stretching out its hands.

He had forgotten all about the baby. There had been so many.

"You'd better get up, Teen," he said as he went out; "it's cryin' after you."

He shut the door and staggered down the steps. He hesitated once, and thought he would go back and say to her:

"What's the use of layin' there?"

But he thought better, or worse, of it, and went his way. He went out and reshipped at once, lingering only long enough to drink madly on the way, at a place he knew, where he was sure to be let alone. The men were afraid of Jack, when he was so far gone under as this. Nobody spoke to him. He went down to Salt Brothers' wharf, opposite Salt & Co.'s, and found the *Daredevil*, just about to weigh. She was short by one hand, and took him as he was.

He was surprised to find himself aboard when the next sun went down; he had turned in his bunk and was overheard to call for Teen, ordering her to do some service for him, testily enough.

"Oh," he muttered, "she ain't here, is she? Be blasted if I ain't on the *Daredevil*."

He was good for nothing for a matter of days, and silent or sullen for the trip. It had been a heavy spree. He fell to, when he came to himself, and fished desperately; his luck turned, and he made money; he made seventy-five dollars. They were gone three weeks. They had a bitter voyage, for it was March.

They struck a gale at Georges', and another coming home. It snowed a great deal, and the rigging froze. The crew were uncommonly cold. They kept the steward cooking briskly, and four or five hot meals a day were not enough to keep one's courage up. They were particular about their cooking, as fishermen are, and the steward of the *Daredevil* was famous in his calling. But it was conceded to be unusually cold, even for March, at Georges'. One must keep the blood racing, somehow, for life's sake.

Whiskey flowed fast between meals. Jack was observed not to limit himself. "It was for luck," he said. Take it through, it was a hard trip. The sober men—there were some—looked grim and pinched; the drinkers ugly.

"It's a hound's life," said a dory-mate of Jack's one day. His name was Rowe—Rowe Salt; he was a half-brother of Jim's. But Jim was at home. And Teen, of course, was at home. Jack had not spoken of her; he had thought of her,—he had thought of nothing else. God knows what those thoughts had been. When Rowe spoke to him in this fashion, Jack looked hard at him.

"I've been thinkin' ef it disobligated a feller," he said.

"Hey?" asked Rowe.

"If you was treated like folks, but you ain't. You're froze. You're soaked. You're wrecked. Your nets is stole. You're drove off in the fog. You're drownded, and you lose your trawls. If you swear off, you miss your luck. It's dirty aboard. Folks don't like the looks of you. There's alwers a hanker in the pit o' your stomick. When you get upon a tear you don't know what you—do to—folks."

Jack stopped himself abruptly, and leaned upon his oar; they were trawling, and the weather grew thick.

"Rowe," he said, staring off into the fog, "did ye ever think we was like fishes, us Fairharbor folks?"

"I don't know's I hev," said the dory-mate, staring too.

"Well, we be, I think. We live in it and we're drownded in it, and we can't get out on 't,—we cant *get* out. We look like 'em, too. I've thought about that. Some of us look like haddock. You've got the halibut look yourself. Skipper, he's got the jib of a monk-fish,—you ken see it for yourself. There's a man I messed with, once, reminded me of a sculpin. I guess I'd pass for a lobster, myself,—for color, anyhow. We take it out someways, each on us. Don't ye know the look the women folks have when they get old and have gone hungry? You can tell by the build of a boy which way he'll turn out,—halibut way, or hake, or mebbe mackerel if he's sleek and little. It's a kind of a birth-mark, I shouldn't wonder. There's no gettin' out on 't, no more 'n it out of you. Sometimes I used to think—

"Good Lord!" cried Jack. He laid down his oar again, and the dory wheeled to starboard sharply.

"Rowe Salt, you look there! You tell me if you see a woman yonder, on the water!"

"You've got the jim-jams, Jack. Women folks don't walk at Georges'. I can't see nothin' nowhere, but it's thick as"—

"It's thick as hell," interrupted Jack. "And there's a woman walkin' on the water,—Lord! Don't you see her? Lord! Her hair is yeller hair, and it's streamin' over her,—don't *you* see her? She's walkin' on this devilish fog to-wards the dory,—Teen? Teen! There! I'll swear off when I get home. I'll tell her so. I hate to see such things."

"You see, Rowe," Jack added presently,—for he had not spoken after that, but had fallen grimly to work. It was ten below, and the wind was taking the backward spring for a bitter blow; both men, tugging at their trawls through the high and icy sea, were suffering too much to talk,—"ye see we had some words before I come aboard, and she warn't right smart. The baby can't be very old. I don't know how old it is. I was oncommon drunk; I don't remember what I did to her. I'm afraid I hit her,—for I had some words with her. I wished I was at home. She won't tell nobody. She never does. But I'm set to be at home and tell her I've sworn off. I've got money for her this trip, too; I'm afraid she's in a hurry for it."

After this outburst of confidence, Jack seemed to cling to his dory-mate; he followed him about deck, and looked wistfully at him. Jack had begun to take on the haggard look of the abstainer once again. The crew thought he did not seem like himself. He had stopped drinking, abruptly, after that day in the fog, and suffered heavily from the weather and from exposure.

"I say, Rowe," he asked one day, "if anything was to happen, would you jest step in and tell my wife I didn't believe that yarn about her? She'll know."

Now it befell, that when they were rounding Eastern point, and not till then, they bespoke the *Destiny,* which was outward bound, and signaled them. She drew to speaking distance, and her skipper had a word with the master of the *Daredevil,* but he spoke none too loud, and made his errand quickly, and veered to his own course, and the two boats parted company, and the *Daredevil* came bustling in. They were almost home.

It was remembered afterward that Jack was badly frostbitten upon that voyage; he looked badly; he had strange ways; the men did not know exactly how to take him. He was overheard to say:

"*I* ain't goin' to go to Georges' again."

Rowe Salt overheard this, after the skipper of the *Destiny* had signaled and tacked. Jack was sitting aft alone, when he said it, looking seaward. He had paid little or no attention to the incident of the *Destiny,* but sat staring, plunged in some mood of his own which seemed as solitary, as removed from his kind and from their comprehension, as the moods of mental disorder are from the sane.

So then, with such dexterity as the ignorant man could muster, Salt got his friend down below, on some pretext, and stood looking at him helplessly.

"You don't look well, Rowe," Jack suggested pleasantly.

"Jack," said his dory-mate, turning white enough, "I'll make no bones of it, nor mince nothin', for somebody's got to tell ye, and they said it must be me. There's a warrant after ye. The sheriff's on the tug betwixt us and the wharf. She's layin' off of the island, him aboard of her."

"I never was in prison," faltered Jack. "The boys have always bailed me."

"T'ain't a bailin' matter, Jack, this time."

"What did you say?"

"I said it wasn't a bailin' business. Somebody's got to tell you."

Jack gazed confidingly up into his friend's face.

"What was it that I done, old boy? Can't ye tell me?"

"Let the sheriff tell you. Ask the sheriff. I'd rather it was the sheriff told you, Jack."

"Tell me what it is I done, Rowe Salt; I'd tell *you.*"

He looked puzzled.

"The sheriff knows more about it nor I do," begged the fisherman; "don't make an old messmate tell you."

"All right," said Jack, turning away. He had now grown very quiet. He pleaded no more, only to mutter once:

"I'd rather heard it from a messmate."

Rowe Salt took a step or two, turned, stopped, stirred, and turned again.

"You killed somebody, then, if you will know."

"*Killed* somebody?"

"Yes."

"I was drunk and killed somebody?"

"Lord help you, yes."

"I hope," hoarsely—"Look here, Salt. *I hope Teen won't know.*

"I say, Rowe," after a long pause, "who was it that I killed?"

"Ask the sheriff."

"Who was it that I killed?"

"The skipper'll tell you, mebby. I don't. No, I vow I won't. Let me go. I've done my share of this. Let me up on deck! I want the air!"

"I won't let you up on deck—so help me!—till you tell!"

"Let me off, Jack, let me off!"

"Tell me who it was, I say!"

"Lord in heaven, the poor devil don't *know,*—he really don't."

"I thought you would ha' told me, Rowe," said Jack with a smile,—his old winning smile, that had captivated his messmates all his life.

"I *will* tell you!" cried Rowe Salt with an oath of agony. "You killed your wife! You murdered her. She's dead. Teen ain't to home. She's dead."

VI

They made way for him at this side and at that, for he sprang up the gangway, and dashed among them. When he saw them all together, and how they looked at him, he stopped. A change seemed to strike his purpose, be it what it might.

"Boys," said Jack, looking all about, "ye won't have to go no bail for me. I'll bide my account this time."

He parted from them, for they let him do the thing he would, and got himself along into the bows, and there he sank down, crouching, and no one spoke to him.

The *Daredevil* rounded Eastern Point, and down the shining harbor, all sails set, came gayly in. They were almost home.

Straightway there started out upon the winter sea a strong, sweet tenor, like a cry. It was Jack's voice,—everybody knew it. He stood by himself in the bows, back to them, singing like an angel or a madman,—some said this; some said the other,—

"Rock of Ages, cleft for me!
Let me hide myself in thee; . . .

Thou must save, and thou alone . . .

When I soar to worlds unknown,
See thee on thy judgment throne."—

sang Jack.

With the ceasing of his voice, they divined how it was, by one instinct, and every man sprang to him. But he had leaped and gained on them.

The waters of Fairharbor seemed themselves to leap to greet him as he went down. These that had borne him and ruined him buried him as if they loved him. He had pushed up his sleeves for the spring, hard to the shoulder, like a man who would wrestle at odds.

As he sank, one bared arm, thrust above the crest of the long wave, lifted itself toward the sky. It was his right arm, on which the crucifix was stamped.

[Teen and Jack's baby is adopted by Mother Mary, and the fisher community of Fairharbor finds hope that the child will be reared in this new environment. *Ed.*]

MARY DWINELL CHELLIS
DATES UNKNOWN

Mary Dwinell Chellis, the most prolific of women temperance writers, provides a good example of the neglect with which scholars have approached women's temperance fiction. Chellis published at least forty-two novels and collections in addition to a large (but indeterminable) number of tracts and pamphlets between 1860 and 1891; her poetry is often included in collections for temperance speakers. Most of Chellis's works were published by the American Tract Society and the National Temperance Society and Publication House, although some were published by commercial houses and often printed later for Sunday school libraries. The National Temperance Society and Publication House registered a series of her works as "The Chellis Library," inscribing the honor on the covers of her books to make them easily recognizable by readers. Still, little information about Chellis remains, except for the cataloging of her works and occasional mentions of her writing in the *Union Signal,* the official newspaper of the Woman's Christian Temperance Union.

In *Our Homes* (New York: National Temperance Society and Publication House, 1881), Chellis tells the story of Madame Rénau, presumed wife of Alphonse Rénau, who has convinced her to marry him based on a false identity. Alphonse tells her he owns a large estate in France, but, once married, he uses his rights as her husband to demand the majority of money she earns in her lucrative dressmaking business. As the novel begins, the Rénaus have been married for ten years; their three children have all died in infancy.

85

Chellis addresses numerous issues of concern to women in *Our Homes*. Notions of a community among women is woven throughout the novel. When the distressed Madame Rénau seeks consolation from Mrs. Horton, telling her, "I have lived with him ten years, and he has spent thousands and thousands of dollars that I have earned. My customers complain of my prices, and I know I am hard with the poor girls who work for me, but my heart is turning to stone," the older woman counsels her to support other women: "Don't let it. Some of the women who work for you may be carrying a heavier burden than you carry. They may not be so well fed, or so comfortably clothed. It may be that their earnings are as ruthlessly taken as yours" (29). Madame Rénau resolves to pursue the notion of sisterhood, to "help some other woman to bear a burden, perhaps heavier than her own" (40).

Mrs. Horton also suggests women should not be too self-sacrificing. In trying to make sense of her situation, Madame Rénau believes she has been a good wife: "I certainly yielded to my husband in everything where yielding was possible. I lived and worked only for him." Mrs. Horton replies, "In that way you did more than your duty. You sacrificed yourself entirely to him, and I hardly think it is a woman's duty to quite forget herself" (97).

In the excerpt here, Madame Rénau and another woman, Madge Tubbs, discover both have been married to the same man. Alphonse Rénau is, in truth, Timothy Tubbs. Timothy had deserted Madge, their five children, and all accompanying responsibilities and convinced Augusta Blaine to become Madame Rénau. Augusta is relieved to know she can now be legally rid of a drunken brute who has claimed the money from her hard work, but she cannot understand why Mrs. Tubbs would seek out such an abusive husband, hoping for his return to his family. In her exploration of such reasoning, Chellis suggests that women's inability to escape such abusive situations is related to their lack of self-esteem.

from *Our Homes*

"What do you propose to do, now that you have found your husband?" asked Madame, after a somewhat prolonged silence, in which she had taken a hasty retrospect of the last ten years.

"I don't know ma'am. I didn't think I'd find Timothy as he is or I'd known he wouldn't go home with me. He was always grander than I was, but I was a good wife to him. I was a poor girl, and so was he poor, but I worked hard to make things comfortable for him, and when he'd let the liquor alone, he sometimes wa'n't so bad. It was when I wouldn't give him money I needed for the children, that he struck me, and I complained of him. That was what made him leave me. But I couldn't help it, with my children hungry, and I not able to do a stroke of work, for the blow he gave me."

"I should think you would have been glad never to see him again."

"Yes, ma'am, you'd think so, and I'd think so, but when I heard where he was, the longing in my heart wouldn't let me rest. I can't tell how it is, but women like me, who don't have anything to think of but their work and their families, don't give up a man they've loved once, as easy as women do that study books, or paint pictures, or dress so nice that folks praise them for their good looks. I don't know how it is, and I can't rightly say it, but such as I be, are always going back to the courting times. Timothy pretended to love me then, and seems as though, now, he couldn't undo it all. There wa'n't one of my mates had a beau as handsome as he was, and I was that proud of him, I didn't think about the liquor he drinked."

"That is something every woman *should* think of. The drinking habits of the men are the curse of the women."

"True for you, ma'am, and the men ai'n't alone in it. There's women that drink, and there's women, too, that eat opium to make them forget their troubles, but it only makes the bad worse."

"Mr. Rénau is coming up the stairs. Do you wish to see him?"

The question was asked too late. He hurried through the hall and rushed into their presence before reply could be made.

"You here, Madge!" he exclaimed with an oath, forgetting in his surprise, that he thus acknowledged his acquaintance with the woman he had denounced as an impostor and utter stranger.

"Yes, Timothy, I'm here. I wanted to see you. I thought it would be a comfort to me, but I'm sorry I come;" and there was a pathos in the speaker's voice, which would have touched any heart less hard than that of him she addressed.

"Get out of the house! I had enough of you, years ago," he retorted savagely.

"You will stay as long as you please," said her hostess, rising and going towards her. "If paying the rent of a house, furnishing it, and providing for it gives title to it, then this is my house; and you, Mr. Tubbs, have no right here."

The scene which followed can never be described. The man thus brought to bay was maddened with drink, and desperate with the taunts of the rabble and the importunities of his creditors. The day had been crowded with discomfiture and mortification. His old associates held themselves aloof from him, and strangers were wary of him. Mrs. Alden had passed him haughtily, and even the saloon keeper had refused to trust him for a single drink.

His pockets were empty, and his wife was indifferent. For ten years, he had lived a life of careless self-indulgence at the expense of others, and the possibility that this life was ended quite distracted him.

What he had intended to demand of her he called wife, he quite forgot, when he saw her companion. What he might have claimed from her, had he found her alone, he dared not claim in the presence of another.

But his rage found vent in terrible oaths and imprecations; in threats of violence, and curses upon both the dead and the living; while his distorted face and blood-shot eyes, gave him the appearance of a demon. It was evident, however, that he feared to match his physical strength against that of Madge, who wondered, as she looked at him, how she could have thought it worth her while to come in search of such a monster.

"I'm sorry I come," she more than once repeated.

"It is well that you came," at length said her hostess. "I am glad that you came. I am glad to know that this man is not my husband."

Every word augmented the frenzy which was fast exhausting its victim, until at last he sunk to the floor, paralyzed by the intensity of his emotions.

Then poor Madge sprang to him, pillowed his head in her lap, and smoothing back his hair, covered his brow with kisses. Wonder as she might, her love for him still survived; but, submitted even to this test, the younger and fairer woman felt no return of tenderness for him who had so embittered her life.

"He will die, and I have killed him!" said the faithful, long-suffering wife. "I didn't want to hurt him. I'm sorry I come;" and she burst into tears, which could not be repressed.

"He must be placed in bed and a physician called," said Madame. "He must not die for want of care."

"Let me stay and nurse him, lady," pleaded the weeping woman. "Let me stay. He belonged to me before he belonged to you, and if you'll let me nurse him, I'll go away and leave him to you when he's stronger."

"You are welcome to stay," was replied kindly. "You are more than welcome; and neither you nor your husband shall want for anything which money can buy."

"Thank you, dear lady. You deserved better than you've had, but I'd do for you always for your kindness," was responded to this assurance.

A physician was summoned, who said at once that the man was beyond reach of human skill. He might breathe a few hours, but he would never regain consciousness. Some general directions were given, and the women left to their task of watching and waiting for the departure of an immortal soul from its tenement of clay. The heavy breathing of the doomed man was the only sound which broke the stillness, until Madame said to her companion softly:

"Shall I leave you, or do you prefer to have me remain?"

"Would you mind going?" was asked in reply.

"I have no wish to remain unless I can help you in some way. This man is your husband, not mine, and I relinquish to you all claim I thought I had upon him. You love him. I wish to do my duty to him and you."

"Then leave me, lady. I'm used to watching, and I'd be thankful to have him all to myself for a little while. If he'd only speak and say he forgives me, I'd be able to bear the rest. Lady, can you pray? A prayer would help me so, and may be save him, now he can't pray for himself, dear man. I ain't used to praying, but I've wished many a time I was. My oldest boy can pray. I wish he was here to pray for his father. He didn't want me to come, but when he see how set I was, he didn't try to keep me. I'm sorry now that I come. I wish you could pray for him. Do, dear lady. You must have loved him once, and then there's the babies belonging to you both."

What could the woman, thus entreated, do but fall upon her knees and pour out her heart in supplication to God. Her babies were safe, but their father had need of mercy. She prayed for the forgiveness of his sins; prayed, too, for the wife who watched beside him; that she might be comforted, and strengthened to bear all that was in store for her. Rising, the suppliant touched her lips to the forehead of her suffering sister, who, with streaming eyes, uplifted, looked into her face.

"I will leave you now, but if you pull this bell-rope I shall hear you, and will come to you directly," she said softly, adding the benediction, "May God bless you."

When morning dawned the man was dead; and with her own hands, his wife, Madge, prepared his body for burial. She begged the privilege of doing this, and was not denied.

She remained to the funeral, which was conducted in the most quiet manner; tarried for one visit to the grave of her recreant husband, and then started homeward; a sad, yet wiser woman for the experience she had gained. She had won a friend, where she feared to meet an enemy; and sorrowed not only for herself, but for another, whose generous kindness was past her comprehension.

CAROLINE LEE WHITING HENTZ
1800–1856

Caroline Lee Hentz, a successful and popular writer during her lifetime, published tales, verse, drama, and novels. She also published a classroom elocution text, *The Flowers of Elocution* (1855). Unlike many such women, however, Hentz did not participate in other reform causes. In fact, her best-known novel, *The Planter's Northern Bride* (1854), is a pro-slavery response to Harriet Beecher Stowe's *Uncle Tom's Cabin*.

Hentz wrote for numerous periodicals, including the Philadelphia *Saturday Courier* and *Godey's Lady's Book*. She collected many of the stories previously published in periodicals in short story editions. The collections containing at least one temperance story include *The Mob Cap; and Other Tales* (1850); *Courtship and Marriage; or, The Joys and Sorrows of American Life* (1856); *Love After Marriage; and Other Stories of the Heart* (1857); and *The Victim of Excitement, The Bosom Serpent, etc., etc., etc.* (1853). In addition to *The Planter's Northern Bride*, Hentz's more popular novels include *Linda; or, The Young Pilot of Belle Creole* (1850) and its sequel, *Robert Graham* (1855).

"The Drunkard's Daughter," included here, appears in both *The Mob Cap* and *Courtship and Marriage* (Philadelphia: T. B. Peterson). In this story, Hentz describes the chagrin of a young woman, Kate Franklin, who faces the social prejudices heaped upon daughters of drunkards. In "The Drunkard's Daughter," Kate finally overcomes the bias that confronts her as the daughter of an alcoholic, but the price she pays is such a heavy one that "no one [can] say the horrors of intemperance are exaggerated." In Mr. Franklin's story of his own father's addiction to alcohol, Hentz attests to the belief of many nineteenth-century temperance advocates that heredity plays a role in the addiction to alcohol. In the distinguished member of Congress, she also suggests that addiction knows no socioeconomic or class boundaries.

"The Drunkard's Daughter" responds to nineteenth-century critics who argued for the perilous nature of distilled spirits but insisted that fermented beverages, such as wine and beer, presented no danger. Finally, Kate's understanding of the social biases toward those associated with the drunkard, especially toward women and children, suggests one basis for the conspiracy of silence in which those surrounding the alcoholic become complicit.

The Drunkard's Daughter

Kate Franklin sat at the window, watching the lightning that streamed through the sky, till her eyes were almost blinded by the glare. She was naturally timid, and had an unusual dread of a thunder-storm, yet though the lightning ran down in rills of fire, and the thunder rolled till the earth shook with its reverberations, she kept her post of danger, repeating, as she gazed abroad, "Oh! that I were a boy, that I might venture abroad in search of my father! It is almost midnight, yet he is not returned. He will perish in a storm like this. Oh! that I were a boy!" she again passionately exclaimed—while the rain began to drive against the casement, and the wind swept the branches of the trees roughly by the panes. She held a young baby in her arms, which she had just lulled to sleep, and her mother lay sleeping in a bed in the same apartment. All slumbered but Kate, who for hours had watched from the window for her father's return. At length her resolution was taken: she laid the babe by her mother's side, drew down the curtain to exclude the lightning's glare, and throwing a shawl around her, softly opened the door, and soon found herself in the street, in the midst of the thunder, the lightning, and the rain. How strong must have been the impulse, how intense the anxiety, which could have induced a timid young girl to come out at that lone, silent hour, on such a night, without a protector or a guide! She flew along at first, but the rain and the wind beat in her face, and the lightning bewildered her with its lurid corruscations. Then pausing for breath, she shaded her eyes, and looking fearfully around, gazed on every object, till her imagination clothed it with its own wild imagery.

At length her eye fell on a dark body extended beneath a tree by the way-side. She approached it, trembling, and kneeling down, bent over it, till she felt a hot breath pass burningly over her cheek, and just then a sheet of flame rolling round it, she recognized but too plainly her father's features. She took his hand, but it fell impassive from her hold. She called upon his name, she put her arms around his neck and tried to raise him from the earth, but his head fell back like lead, and a hoarse breathing sound alone indicated his existence.

"Father, dear father, wake and come home!" she cried, in a louder tone; but the thunder'd roar did not rouse him, how much less her soft, though earnest voice. Again she called, but she heard only the echoes of night repeating her own mournful adjuration— "Father, dear father, come home."

How long she thus remained, she knew not; but the wind and the rain subsided, the lightning flashed with a paler radiance, and at intervals the wan moon might be seen wading through the gray, watery clouds. She felt her strength exhausted, and clasping her hands together, lifted her eyes, streaming with tears, almost wishing a bolt would fall and strike them both simultaneously.

"My father is lost!" said she, "and why should I wish him to live? Why should I wish to survive him?"

The sound of horse's feet approaching startled her. The horseman checked his speed as he came opposite the tree, where Kate still knelt over her father, and as the lightning played over her white garments, which, being wet by the rain, clung closely around her, she might well be mistaken for an apparition. Her shawl had fallen on the ground, her hair streamed in dripping masses over her face, and her uplifted arms were defined on the dark background of an angry sky. The horse reared and plunged, and the rider dismounting, came as near to the spot as the impetuous animal would allow.

"Oh! Harry Blake, is it you?" exclaimed Kate. "Then my father will not be left here to die."

"Die!" repeated Harry; "what can have happened? Why are you both abroad such a night as this?"

"Alas!" said Kate, "I could not leave my father to perish. I sought him through the storm, and I find him thus."

While she was speaking, Harry had fastened the bridle of his horse to the tree, and stooped down on the other side of Mr. Franklin. Kate's first feeling on his approach was a transport of gratitude—now she was overwhelmed with shame; for she knew, as Harry inhaled the burning exhalation of his breath, his disgraceful secret would be revealed—that secret which her mother and herself had so long in anguish concealed.

"Poor Kate!" involuntarily burst from his lips, as he gazed on the prostrate and immoveable form of the man he had so much loved and respected. Had he seen him blasted by the lightning's stroke, he could not have felt more shocked or grieved. He comprehended in a moment the full extent of his degradation, and it seemed as if an awful chasm, yawning beneath his feet, now separated him, and would for ever separate him from his instructor and friend.

"Kate," said he, and his voice quivered from emotion, "this is no place for you. You are chilled by the rain—you will be chilled to death, if you remain in your wet garments. Let me see you safe at home, and I will return to your father, nor leave him till he is in a place of security."

"No, no!" cried Kate, "I think not of myself, only assist me to raise him, and lead him home, and I care not what happens to me. I knew it would come to this at last. Oh! my poor father!"

Harry felt that there was no consolation for such grief, and he attempted not to offer any. He put a strong arm round the unhappy man, and raised him from the ground still supporting the reeling body and calling his name in a loud, commanding tone. Mr. Franklin opened his eyes with a stupid stare, and uttered some indistinct, idiotic sounds, then letting his head fall on his bosom, he suffered himself to be led homeward, reeling, tottering, and stumbling at every step. And this man, so helpless and degraded, so imbruted and disgusting, that his very daughter, who had just periled her life in the night-storm to secure him from danger, and turned away from him, even while she supported him, with unconquerable loathing, was a member of Congress, a distinguished lawyer—eloquent at the bar, and sagacious in council—a citizen respected and beloved; a friend generous and sincere—a husband once idolized—a father once adored. The young man who had walked by his side, had been for more than a year, a student in his office, and sat under his instruction, as Paul sat at the feet of Gamaliel. Now, in the expressive language of Scripture, he could have exclaimed, "Oh,

Lucifer, thou son of the morning, how low art thou fallen!" but he moved on in silence, interrupted occasionally by the ill-repressed sobs of Kate. He had been that day to an adjoining town to transact some business for Mr. Franklin, and being detained to an unusually late hour, was overtaken by the storm, when the agonized voice of Kate met his ear.

Harry lingered a moment at Mr. Franklin's door before he departed. He wanted to say something expressive of comfort and sympathy to Kate, but he knew not what to say.

"You will never mention the circumstances of this night, Harry," said Kate, in a low, hesitating tone. "I cannot ask you to respect my father as you have done, but save him, if it may be, from the contempt of the world."

"If he were my own father, Kate," cried Harry, "I would not guard his reputation with more jealous care. Look upon me henceforth as a brother, and call upon me as such, when you want counsel, sympathy or aid. God bless you, Kate."

"Alas! there is no blessing for a drunkard's daughter," sighed Kate, as she turned from the door and listened to her father's deep, sonorous breathing, from the sofa on which he had staggered, and where he lay stretched at full length, till long after the dawning of morn, notwithstanding her efforts to induce him to change his drenched garments.

Mrs. Franklin was an invalid, and consequently a late riser. Kate usually presided at the breakfast table, and attended to her father's wants. This morning he took his accustomed seat, but his coffee and toast remained untasted. He sat with his head leaning upon his hand, his eyes fixed vacantly on the wall, and his hair matted and hanging in neglected masses over his temples. Kate looked upon his face and remembered when she thought her father one of the handsomest men she had ever seen—when dignity was enthroned upon his brow, and the purity as well as the majesty of genius beamed from his eyes. He lifted his head and encountered her fixed gaze—probably followed the current of her thoughts, for his countenance darkened, and pushing his cup far from him, he asked her, in a surly tone, why she stared so rudely upon him?

Kate tried to answer, but there was suffocation in her throat, and she could not speak.

Mr. Franklin looked upon her for a moment with a stern yet wavering glance, then rising and thrusting back his chair against the wall, he left the house, muttering as he went, "curses not loud, but deep."

Kate had become gradually accustomed to the lowering cloud of sullenness, which the lethargy of inebriation leaves behind it. She had heard by almost imperceptible degrees, the voice of manly tenderness assume the accents of querulousness and discontent; but she had never met such a glance of defiance, or witnessed such an ebullition of passion before. Her heart rose in rebellion against him, and she trembled at the thought that she might learn to hate him as he thus went on, plunging deeper and deeper in the gulf of sensuality.

"No, no, no!" repeated she to herself, "let me never be such a monster. Let me pity, pray for him, love him if I can—but let me never forget that he is my father still."

Young as Kate was, she had learned that endurance, not happiness, was her allotted portion. Naturally high spirited and impetuous, with impassioned feelings and headlong impulses, in prosperity she might have become haughty and ungovernable; but subjected in early youth to a discipline, of all others the most galling to her pride, her spirit became subdued, and her passions restrained by the same process by which her principles were strengthened, and the powers of her mind precociously developed. Her brothers and sisters had all died in infancy, except one, now an infant in the cradle, a feeble, delicate child, for whom every one prophesied an early grave was appointed.

Mrs. Franklin herself was constitutionally feeble, and yielding to the depression of spirits caused by her domestic misfortunes, indulged in constant and ineffectual complainings, which added to the gloom of the household, without producing amendment or reformation in its degraded master. She was very proud, and had been a very beautiful woman, who had felt for her husband an attachment romantically strong, for it was fed by the two strongest passions of her heart—pride, which exulted in the homage paid to his talents and his graces, and vanity, which delighted in the influence her beauty exercised over his commanding mind. Now, his talents and graces were obscured by the murky cloud of intemperance, and her languishing beauty no longer received its accustomed incense; the corrosions of mortification and peevish discontent became deeper and deeper, and life one scene of gloom and disquietude.

Kate grew up amidst these opposing influences like a beautiful plant in a barren, ungenial soil. To her father, she was the delicate but hardy saxifrage, blooming through the clefts of the cold, dry rock; to her mother, the sweet anemone, shedding its blossoms over the roots of the tree from which it sprung—fragrant, though un-nurtured, neglected and alone.

It would be too painful to follow, step by step, Mr. Franklin's downward course. Since the night of his public exposure he had gone down, down, with a fearfully accelerated motion, like the mountain stream, when it leaps over its rocky barrier. Public confidence was gradually withdrawn, clients and friends forsook him, and ruin trod rapidly on the steps of shame.

Harry Blake clung to him, till he saw his once powerful mind partaking so far of the degradation of his body, as to be incapable of imparting light to his. He now felt it due to himself to dissolve the connection subsisting between them—and he called, though reluctantly, to bid him farewell. Mr. Franklin seemed much agitated when Harry informed him of his intended departure. He knew the cause, and it seemed as if the last link was about to be severed that bound him to the good and honourable. Harry had been to him a delightful companion; and, in the days of his unsullied reputation, it had been one of his most interesting tasks to direct a mind so buoyant and aspiring, and which owned, with so much deference, the overmastering influence of his own.

"Do not go yet, Harry," said he; "I have much, much to say to you, and I may never have another opportunity. I have anticipated this moment. It is painful, but justice to yourself demanded it."

Harry seated himself, pale from suppressed emotion, while Mr. Franklin continued speaking, walking up and down the room, every feature expressive of violent agitation.

"I have never yet to a human being introduced the subject of which I am about to speak—not even to my wife and daughter. I have never rolled back the current of time, and revealed the spot where, standing on the quicksands of youth, the first wave of temptation washed over me. I could not bear to allude to the history of my degradation. But you, Harry, are going among strangers, amid untried scenes—and I would warn you now, with the solemnity of a man who knows he has sealed his own everlasting ruin, to beware of the first downward step. You do not know me, sir—no one knows me; they know not my parentage, or the accursed stream that runs in these veins.

"My father was called the King of the Drunkards! He drank till he was transformed, breath, bones, and sinew, into flame, and then he died—the most horrible of all deaths—of spontaneous combustion. Yes, he was the King of the Drunkards! I remember when a little boy, I saw him walking at the head of a long procession, with a banner flying, as if in triumph, and a barrel of whiskey rolling before, on which the drummer made music as they walked. And shouts went up in the air, and people applauded from the windows and the doors—and I thought the drunkard's was a merry life. But when I grew older, and saw my mother's cheek grow paler and paler, and that my father's curses and threats, and brutal treatment were the cause—when I saw her at length die of a broken heart, and heard the neighbours say that my father had killed her, and that he would have to answer for her death at the great bar of Heaven!—I began to feel an indescribable dread and horror, and looked upon my father with loathing and abhorrence! And when he died—when his body was consumed by flames, which seemed to me emblematical of the winding-sheet in which his soul was wrapped—I fled from my native town, my native State; I begged my bread from door to door. At length, a childless stranger took me in. He pitied my forlorn condition—clothed, fed, and educated me. Nature had given me talents, and now opportunity unfolded them. I became proud and ambitious, and I wanted to convince my benefactor that I was no vulgar boy. Conscious of the dregs from which I had been extracted I was resolved to make myself a name and fame—and I have done it. You know it, Harry—I have taken my station in the high places of the land; and the time has been, when but to announce yourself as my student, would have been your passport to distinction. Well, do you want to know what made me what I am?—what, when such a burning beacon was forever blazing before my memory, hurried me on to throw my own blasted frame into a drunkard's dishonoured grave? I will tell you, young man—it was the *wine* cup!—the glass offered by the hand of beauty, with smiles and adulation! I had made a vow over my mother's ashes that I would never drink. I prayed God to destroy me, body and soul, if I ever became a drunkard. But *wine,* they said, was one of God's best gifts, and it gladdened without inebriating—it was ingratitude to turn from its generous influence. I believed them, for it was alcohol that consumed my father. And I drank wine at the banquet and the board—and I drank porter and ale, and the rich scented cordial—and I believed myself to be a temperate man. I thought I grew more intellectual; I could plead more eloquently, and my tongue made more music at the convivial feast. But when the excitement of the scene was over, I felt languid and depressed. My head ached, and my nerves seemed unsheathed. A thirst was enkindled within me, that wine could no longer quench. A hereditary fire was burning in my veins. I had lighted up the smouldering spark, and it now blazed, and blazed. I knew I was destroying myself, but the power of resistance was gone. When I first tasted I was undone! Beware, Harry, beware! To save you from temptation, I have lifted the veil, and laid bare before you the hell of a drunkard's bosom. But no! that cannot be. The Invisible alone can witness the agonies of remorse, the corroding memories, the anticipated woes, the unutterable horrors that I endure and dread—and expect to endure as long as the Great God himself exists."

He paused, and sunk down exhausted into a chair. Large drops of sweat rolled down his livid brow—his knees knocked together, his lips writhed convulsively, every muscle seemed twisted, and every vein swollen and blackened. Harry was terrified at this paroxysm. He sprang toward him, and untying the handkerchief from his neck, handed him a glass of water with trembling hands. Mr. Franklin looked up, and meeting Harry's glance of deep commiseration, his features relaxed, and large tears, slowly gathering, rolled down his cheeks. He bent forward, and extending his arms across the table, laid his head on them; and deep, suffocating sobs burst forth, shaking his frame, as if with strong spasms. Harry was unutterably affected. He had never seen man weep thus before. He knew they were tears wrung by agony, the agony of remorse; and while he wept in sympathy, he gathered the hope of his regeneration from the intensity of his sufferings.

"I pity you, Mr. Franklin," said he, "from my soul I pity you—but you must not give yourself up as lost. God never yet tempted a man beyond his strength. You may, you can, you *must* resist. For your own sake, for your wife's—your daughter's sake, I conjure you."

"My daughter's!" interrupted Mr. Franklin, lifting his head. "Ah! that name touches the chord that still vibrates. Poor Kate! poor Kate! The hand that should have blessed has blighted her young hopes. My wife reproaches me, and gives me gall and vinegar, even when I would meet her with smiles. But Kate never gave me one reproach but her tears. I once thought you loved her, and that I should see the two objects I most loved, happy in each other's affections, and scattering roses over the pillow of my declining years. But that can never be now; your proud father will never permit you to marry a drunkard's daughter." He spoke this in a bitter tone, and a smile of derision for a moment curled his lips.

"You thought right," exclaimed Harry, passionately, "I have loved her, I do love her, as the best, the loveliest, the most exalted of human beings. I would not pain you, sir, but you constrain me to speak the truth: my father has forbidden me to think of such a union, and as I am now dependent on him, I could not brave his commands without seeking to plunge your daughter into poverty and sorrow. Yet I will not deceive you. I would have braved everything with her consent, but she refuses to listen to vows, unsanctioned by parental authority. The time, I trust, will come when, having secured an independence, by my energies, I may dare to speak and act as a man, and woo her to be my wife in the face of the world."

"Yes! yes!" repeated Mr. Franklin, "the time may come, but I shall not live to see it. There is at times such a deadly faintness, such a chilly weight here," laying his hand on his breast, "it seems as though I could feel the cold fingers of death clutching round my heart and freezing my life-blood. If I did not warm the current with fresh streams of alcohol, I should surely die. Then this aching brow, this throbbing brain, these quivering nerves, and shaking limbs, are they not all the heralds of coming dissolution?—Harry, I do not mean to distress you—I have but one thing more to say: if you resist temptation, and I pray God you may, dare not triumph over the fallen. Oh! you know not, you dream not, in the possession of unclouded reason and unblighted faculties, the proud master of yourself, what that wretch endures, who, beset by demons on every side, feels himself dragged down lower and lower, incapable of resistance, to the very verge of the bottomless pit."

He wrung Harry's hand in his, then turned and left the office. Harry followed, oppressed and awe-struck by the revelations he had heard. Temptation, sin, sorrow, disgrace, death, judgment, and eternity, swept like dark phantoms across his mind; chasing away hope, love, joy, and heaven; even the image of Kate Franklin flitted mournfully in the back-ground, fading and indistinct as a vanishing rainbow.

Kate grieved at Harry's departure, but it was a grief which vented itself in tears. She was affected by his disinterested attachment; she esteemed his virtues and admired his character, and in

sunnier hours she might have indulged in those sweet day dreams
of love, which throw over the realities of life the hues of heaven.
But she felt it was hers to endure and to struggle, not to enjoy—she
dared not fix her gaze on the single star that shone through the dark
clouds closing around her, lest it should charm her into a forget-
fulness of the perils and duties of her situation; so gathering all her
energies, as the traveller folds his mantle over his breast to shield
him from the tempest, the more fearful the storm, the more firm
and strong became her powers of resistance. It was summer when
Harry departed, and Kate, though she never mentioned his name,
found his remembrance associated with the flowers, the fragrance,
and the moonlight of that beautiful season; but when winter came
on, with its rough gales, and sleet and snow—for she lived on the
granite hills of New England, where the snow-spirit revels amid
frost-work and ice—she sat by a lonely fire, watching her father's
late return, or nursing the fretful and delicate babe in her mother's
chamber, all the anticipated ills of poverty hanging darkly over her,
Kate found her only comfort in communing with her God, to whom,
in the dearth of all earthly joy, she had turned for support and consolation, and as her religious faith increased, her fortitude strengthened, and her stern duties became easier of performance. One night
she sat alone by the fireside—and it was a most tempestuous night,
the wind howled and tossed the naked boughs of the trees against
the windows, which rattled as if they would shiver in the blast; and
the snow, drifted by its violence, blew in white wreaths on the glass
and hung its chill drapery on the walls. She sat on a low seat in the
corner, her Bible on her knees, a dim fire burning on the hearth, for
cold as it was, she would not suffer it to be replenished with fuel
which her mother might yet want for her own comfort. She was
gradually accustoming herself to personal privations, voluntarily ab-
staining from every luxury, not knowing how soon she might need
the necessaries of life. She was reading the sublime book of Job, and
when she came to the words, "Hast thou entered into the snow?
Hast thou seen the treasures of the hail?" she repeated them aloud,
struck with the force, mid the wintry scene around her. At this
moment her father entered. It was an unusually early hour for his
return, and as he walked forward she noticed with joy that his step
was less fluctuating than usual. He bent shivering over the fire,
which Kate immediately kindled afresh, and a bright blaze soon
diffused warmth and cheerfulness through the apartment.

"I heard your voice as I entered, Kate," said he; "where is your companion?"

"There," answered she, lifting the Bible from her knees—"here is the companion of my solitude, and a very pleasing one I find it."

Mr. Franklin fixed his eyes steadfastly on Kate for a few moments, throwing himself back in his chair, gazed upon the ceiling, and spoke as in a soliloquy—

"I remember when I was a little boy, reading that book at my mother's knee; and when she was dying she told me never to lay my head upon the pillow without reading a chapter and praying to the Great God for pardon and protection. But that was a long time ago. I would not open it now for the universe."

"Oh! father!" exclaimed Kate, "do not say so. Young as I am, I have lived too long if the promises written here be not true. They alone have saved me from despair."

"Despair!" repeated he, in a hollow tone—"yes, that is the fitting word, but it belongs to me alone. You are innocent and virtuous, and why should you talk of despair? You have no brand on your brow, no thunder-scar graven by the Almighty's hand, from which men turn away and women shrink with horror. I am an object of loathing and scorn to all. Even you, my own daughter, who once lived in my bosom, if I should open my arms to enfold you, as I was wont to do, would shrink from me, as from the leper's touch."

"Oh! no, no!" cried Kate, springing from her seat, and throwing her arms impulsively around his neck, while her tears literally rained on his shoulder.

It had been long months since she had heard such a gush of tenderness from his lips—since she had dared to proffer the caresses of affection. She thought all natural feeling was dried up in his heart—withered, scorched by the fiery breath of intemperance. She had locked her grief and humiliation in her own breast. She believed every appeal to her reason and sensibility would be as unavailing as if made to the granite of her native hills. She now reproached herself for her coldness and reserve. She accused herself of neglect and irreverence.

"Oh, my father!" she exclaimed, "if you still love me I will not despair. There is hope, there will be joy. You have but to make one great effort, and you will be free once more. Chains, strong as adamant, cannot bind the soul to sin, unless it is a willing captive. You are wretched now; we are all wretched. No smiles gladden our household. My mother lies on a bed of languishment, where a breaking heart has laid her. My little sister pines like a flower, which sunbeams never visited; and I—oh, father! words can never tell the wo, the anguish, the agony, which I have pent up in any bosom, till it threatened to destroy me. I would not reproach you—I would not add one drop to your cup of bitterness—but I must speak now, or I die."

Excited beyond her power of self-control, Kate slid from her father's relaxing arms, and taking the Bible, which lay upon her chair, in both hands, prostrated herself at his feet.

"By this blessed book," continued she, in an exalted voice, "this book which has poured oil and balsam in my bleeding heart, this book, so rich in promises, so fearful in threatenings—by the God who created you to glorify Him, the Saviour who died to redeem you—by your immortal and endangered soul—I pray thee to renounce the fatal habit, which has transformed our once blissful home into a prison-house of shame, sorrow, and despair."

She paused, breathless from intense emotion, but her uplifted hands still clasped the sacred volume; her cheek glistening with tears, was mantled with crimson; and her eyes, turned up to her father, beamed with the inspiration of the Christian's hope.

Mr. Franklin looked down upon his daughter, as she thus knelt before him, and it seemed as if a ray from the Divine intelligence darted like a glory from her eyes into the depths of his soul. Lost, ruined as he was, there was still hope of his redemption. He might be saved. She, like a guiding cherub, might still take him by the hand, and lead him back to the green paths of pellucid streams where he had once walked with undoubting footsteps. As these thoughts rolled through his mind, he bent forward, lower and lower, till his knees touched the floor. He wrapped his arms around Kate, and, leaning his head on her shoulder, sobbed aloud. The prayer of the publican trembled on his lips—"Oh, my God! have mercy upon me, a miserable sinner! Oh, Thou who was once tempted, yet never sinned, save me from temptation!"

It was long before other sounds interrupted the hallowed silence which succeeded. Kate hardly dared to breathe, lest she should disturb the communion her father's soul was holding with the being he invoked. Her heart ached with the fulness of hope that flowed into it from channels long sealed. Had he made promises of amendment in his own strength, she might have feared their stability, but now, when she saw him prostrate in the dust, in tears and humiliation, crying for mercy from the depths of a wounded and contrite spirit, she believed that He, "whose fan is in His hand," had come to winnow the chaff from the wheat, before the whole should be consumed with unquenchable fire.

It was midnight before she rose to retire to her chamber. She felt unwilling to leave her father. It seemed to her that this night was the crisis of her destiny—that angels and demons were wrestling for his soul—that the angels had prevailed; but might not the demons return? or the good angels, too sure of their victory, wing their way back to the skies? Long after she had retired to bed, she heard him walk backwards and forwards, and sometimes she heard his voice ascending as in prayer.

"Hear him, gracious Father!" cried she, from her moistened pillow, "hear him, answer and bless him!"

Then folding her arms closely round the infant, who slumbered by her side, she gradually fell asleep, and it will throw no shade over her filial piety to believe that no one thought of Henry Blake, associated with pure images of future felicity, gilded her dreams. How long she slept, she knew not; but she awoke with a strange feeling of suffocation, and, starting up in bed, looked wildly around her. She saw nothing, but the chamber seemed filled with smoke, and a hollow, crackling sound met her ear. The dread of fire for a moment paralyzed her limbs. It was but a moment—when springing from her bed, the infant still cradled on her arm, she opened the door, and found the terrible reality of her fears. Such a rush of hot air pressed upon her, she staggered back, panting and bewildered. The flames were rolling in volumes through the next apartment, and the wind, blowing in violence through the outer door, which was open, fearfully accelerated the work of destruction.

"My father!" shrieked Kate; "my father!—where is he?"

That fearful cry awoke the child, who screamed and clung in terror closer to her bosom; but her mother, who seldom slept except under the influence of powerful opiates, lay still unmoved, unconscious of the terrific element which was raging around her.

"Mother!" cried Kate, franticly, "wake or you die! The house is in flames!—they are rolling towards us!—they are coming! Oh! my God—mother, awake!"

She shook her arm with violence, and shrieked in her ear; but, though she moved and spoke, she seemed in a lethargy so deep, that nothing could rouse her to a sense of her danger.

The flames began to curl their forked tongues around the very door of the chamber, and the house shook and quivered as if with the throes of an earthquake. Kate knew she could make her own escape through a door, in an opposite direction; but she resolved, if she could not save her mother, to perish with her. She would have her lifted in her arms, were it not for the infant clinging to her bosom. Perchance that infant might be saved. She rushed through the door, made her way through the drifting snow to the street, laid the child down on the chill but soft bank by the wallside, silently commending it to the protection of God,—then winged her way back to the building, though the flames were now bursting from the roof, and reddening the snow with their lurid glare.

"Mother, dear mother, speak if you live," cried Kate, shuddering at the supernatural sounds of her own voice. A faint groan issued from the bed, round which the flames were rapidly gathering. It is astonishing what strength is given by desperation. Kate was a slender girl, of delicate frame, unused to physical exertion, but now she felt nerved with a giant's strength. She took up her mother in her arms, just as the fire caught the bed curtain, and communicated even to her night-dress. Smothering the blaze with the blanket she had dragged from the bed in rescuing her mother, she flew rather than walked, burdened as she was, the flames roaring and hissing behind her, gaining upon her at every step—the hot air almost stifling her breath, even while her naked feet were plunging through the snow drifts, and the frosts penetrating her thin night wrapper. It seemed as if ages of thought and feeling were compressed in that awful moment. Her father's dreaded fate—her little sister freezing on the snow—the servants probably perishing in the flames—her houseless mother fainting in her arms—her own desolate condition—all was as vividly impressed on her mind as the lurid blaze of the conflagration on the dark grey of the wintry night. She bent her steps to the nearest dwelling, which was the residence of Mr. Blake, the father of Harry. She reached the threshold, and fell with her now senseless burden, heavily against the door. She tried to call aloud for assistance, but no sound issued from her parched and burning lips. She endeavored to lift her right hand to the knocker, but it was numb and powerless, and in her left, which encircled her mother, she felt for the first time the most intense pain.

"Merciful Father!" thought she, "thou who has sustained us thus far, leave us not to perish!"

Even while this prayer burst from her soul, footsteps approached, the door opened, and Mr. Blake, accompanied by a servant, bearing a lamp, stood upon the threshold. He had been awakened a few minutes before by the reflection of the blaze in his chamber, and had just aroused his family, when the sudden jarring of the door excited his alarm. He recoiled at first with horror from the spectacle which he beheld. Mrs. Franklin, white, ghastly and still, lay to all appearance dead, in the nerveless arms of her daughter, who, pale, prostrate, and voiceless, could only lift her imploring eyes, and moan the supplication her lips vainly sought to express. Mr. Blake had forbidden his son to marry a *drunkard's daughter,* and he had looked coldly on Kate, secretly condemning her for the influence she unconsciously exercised over his destiny. But he was not a hard-hearted man, though very proud, and his wife was a repository of heaven's own influences. Under her anxious superintendence, the sufferers were soon placed in warm beds, and every means used for the resuscitation of the one, and the renovation of the other, while Mr. Blake, with the male part of the household, hastened to the scene of the conflagration. The main building was now enveloped in fire, but the kitchen was still standing, and he rejoiced to see the servants rushing to and fro, trying to save something, perhaps their own property, from the ruins. He looked around in search of the unhappy master, and trembled at the supposition that he might have found a funeral pyre. There was nothing to be done—the work of destruction was almost consummated, and he was turning away sick at heart, when he thought he saw a bundle lying near the wall where he stood. He stooped down, and beheld with astonishment a sleeping infant. At first he thought it dead, but when he raised it, and touched his cheek to its cold face, he felt its sweet breath stealing softly over his lips, and its little hand instinctively clasped his neck. He was inexpressibly affected, and gathering the folds of his cloak around it, he pressed it to his bosom with a father's tenderness. Never had he been so struck with the special providence of God, as in the preservation of this little outcast. Angels must have brooded over it, impressed their heavenly warmth upon its chilly bed. But who had laid it so tenderly in its snowy cradle, aloof from the smoke and the blaze? Who but she whose filial arms had borne her mother to his own door! As he answered this interrogation to himself, his heart smote him for his injustice to the heroic girl who had made such unparalleled exertions. He almost wished Harry was at home—but this was a moment of excitement; when he became calmer, he rejoiced at his absence.

Mr. Franklin had not perished in the ruins. After Kate had left him, his newly awakened feelings of remorse raged with frenzy in his bosom. No longer soothed by his daughter's caresses, and sustained by her prayers, the blackness of despair rolled over him. He could not compose himself to rest—the room seemed too small to contain the mighty conflict of his feelings. He could not bear to look upon the blazing hearth, and feel the fires raging within. He went to the door, and as the cold wind blew on his brow, he felt inexpressible relief, and leaving the door unlatched, he rushed abroad, reckless where he went, provided he could escape from himself. The farther he roamed from his own home, the more he seemed to lose the consciousness of his own identity, till exhausted in body and mind, he threw himself down on the floor of an uninhabited dwelling, which had often been the scene of his drunken orgies. There he lay, while the fire which he left blazing on the hearth, fanned by the blast howling through the open door, reveled uncontrolled and unconquerable. When at morning he sought his homestead, he found it a heap of smouldering ruins—and he knew the work of destruction was his. He remembered how the door creaked in the blast, and in his madness he would not return. While he stood gazing in speechless agony on the wreck, Mr. Blake approached, and taking him by the arm, drew him to his own dwelling. Like the friends of Job, he spoke not, for "he saw his grief was very great." His wife, whom he had once tenderly loved, and who, in his chastened mood, came back to his memory, clothed in all the sweetness of which his vices had robbed her, lay on her deathbed. Though rescued by filial devotion from a fiery grave, she had swallowed the breath of the flames, and her chafed and wounded spirit was passing into the presence of her Maker. She could not speak, but she knew him as he entered, and stretching out her feeble hand, her dying glance spoke only pity and forgiveness. The unhappy man knelt by her side, and burying his face in the bed-cover, gave way to a burst of anguish, that was like the rending asunder of body and soul. And Kate, too, lay there by the side of her dying mother, with frozen feet, blistered hands, and feverish brow—with her bright locks scorched and disheveled—her eyes bloodshot and dim. This, too, was *his* work. There are calamities which come immediately from the hand of God, and man bows in weakness before the majesty of the power that overwhelms him. The pestilence that walketh in darkness—the tempest that wasteth at noonday—the earthquake—the flood—are ministers of his vengeance, and come clothed with an authority so high and sacred, the boldest and strongest dare not rebel. But when the sufferer stands amid ruin his own hand has wrought—when conscience tells him he has arrogated to himself the fearful work of destruction, and stolen and winged the darts of death—there is an unfathomable wo, an immedicable wound, an undying remorse—an antepast on earth of the retributions of heaven. Let no one say the horrors of intemperance are exaggerated! Here fire and death had done their part, but murder had not yet reddened the black catalogue of sin. Happy, comparatively happy, the inebriate who is arrested in his headlong career, before the blood of innocence, mingling with the libations of Bacchus, brands him with the curse of Cain—the indelible stamp of infamy, which his own life, poured out on the scaffold, cannot efface, and which is handed down an inalienable heritage, to his children's children.

The day after the remains of the ill-fated Mrs. Franklin were consigned to the grave, the citizens of the place assembled in the town hall, to make arrangements for the relief of the suffering family. Their sympathies were strongly excited in behalf of the heroine, Kate—and in the hour of his calamity they remembered Mr. Franklin as he was in his high and palmy days, when his voice had so often filled the hall where they were met, with strains of the loftiest eloquence. They had seen him prostrated on the grave of his wife, in sorrow that refused consolation, and they felt towards him something of that tenderness which we feel for the dead—when vice is recollected with compassion rather than hatred, and scorn melts in forgiveness. Warmed by a common impulse, they contributed munificently, and made immediate preparations for the erection of a new building on the site of the old. Mr. Franklin, who was aware of their movements, entered the hall before they separated. It had been long since he had met his former friends, associated in such a respectable body, and a few days before he would have shrunk from their glances, conscious of his degraded condition. Now, strengthened by a solemn resolution, he came among them, and standing in their midst, he begged permission to address them a few moments. He began with the history of his boyhood, and told them his parentage, his flight, his temptation, his perjury, and guilt. His voice was at first faltering, but as he proceeded, it recovered much of its former richness of tone, and when he painted his remorse and despair, his solemn resolutions of amendment, and his trust in Almighty God for strength to fulfil them, his eloquence rose to the most thrilling sublimity.

"For myself," said he, in conclusion, "I would have asked nothing—hoped nothing. I would have buried in the deepest solitude the memory of my shame. But I have children—a daughter worthy of a better fate. For her sake I solicit the restoration of that confidence I have so justly forfeited—the birthright I have so shamefully sold. Low as I have sunk, I feel by the effort I have this moment made, that the indwelling Deity has not yet quite forsaken this polluted temple. I am still capable of being master of myself, and with God's help I will be so. I ask not for the hand of fellowship and friendship. I want it not till time shall have proved the sincerity of my reformation, and purified from defilement the drunkard's name."

Here every hand was simultaneously extended, in token of reviving confidence. Some grasped his in silence and tears—others fervently bid him Godspeed, and promised him encouragement, sympathy and patronage.

The introduction of a household scene—more than a twelvemonth after this—will close the history of The Drunkard's Daughter. Mr. Franklin was seated by his own fireside, reading; and when he raised his clear, dark eye from the book, and cast it on the domestic group at his side, you could read in his untroubled glance, quietude, self-respect, and confidence. The red signet of intemperance was swept from his noble brow; every look bore witness to his intellectual and moral regeneration. Kate sat near him—she, who, in the hands of God, had been made the instrument of his salvation—bearing on her youthful and lovely person a sad memento of her father's sin. Her left hand lay useless in her lap; its sinews had been contracted by the fires she smothered, when snatching her mother from the flames, and she was destined to carry through life a witness of filial heroism and devotion. But her right hand was clasped in that of Harry Blake, who, sanctioned by parental authority, had sought and received her wedded vows. Kate refused for a long time to assume the sacred duties of a wife, conscious of her impaired usefulness, but Harry pleaded most eloquently, and Harry's father declared that he considered the cause of her dependence as a mark of glory and honor. He had forbidden his son to claim alliance with a degraded name, but Kate had proved, during her sojourn in his dwelling, that a daughter's virtues could redeem a father's shame. Kate soon learned to be reconciled to a misfortune, which only endeared her the more to the hearts of her friends. She forgot to mourn over her physical dependence, in a father's and husband's devoted love. But, though dependent, she was not passive. She shared in all their intellectual pursuits, read for them, wrote for them, when weary from professional toils, and all that her right hand found to do, "she did diligently and in order." She was their inspiring companion, their modest counsellor, their spiritual friend.

There was one more figure added to this domestic scene. A fair-haired child sat on Mr. Franklin's knee, and twisted her chubby fingers in his still raven hair. It was the child once cradled on the snowy bed, whose blooming cheeks and bright lips corresponded more with the *rose-bud,* than the *snow-drop,* the pet name she bore.

"Let no man say, when he is tempted, I am tempted of God," or having once yielded to the power of the tempter, that, like the giant slumbering in the lap of Delilah, he cannot break the green withs with which his passions have bound him, and find in after years the shorn locks of his glory clustering once more around his brow.

JULIA PERKINS (PRATT) BALLARD [KRUNA]
1828–1894

Although most information about her life has been lost, Julia Perkins Ballard published widely, under various names. She penned much of her temperance fiction under the pseudonym Kruna, although she also used a variety of other forms, usually incorporating the name Ballard. Her most popular book, *Among the Moths and Butterflies,* was a "revised and enlarged edition" of a previously published work primarily for children, *Insect Lives, or Born in Prison,* initially published in 1879. The revised edition found a popular audience with at least ten printings between 1890 and 1908 and enjoyed continued publication for years after Ballard's death.

Ballard is representative of many women temperance writers in that she wrote in a variety of genres: poetry (*The Scarlet Oak, and Other Poems* [1878], with Annie Lenthal Smith); short tracts (*Up or Down* [n.d.]); short stories (*The Hole in the Bag, and Other Stories* [1872], *The Lost Estate, and Other Stories* [1882], and *The Jonas Fund, and Other Stories* [1889]); and novels (*The Broken Rock* [1868] and *Jem and Velvet* [ca. 1870]).

The following short story from *The Hole in the Bag* (New York: National Temperance Society and Publication House) typifies many temperance stories intended to diminish prejudicial treatment that wives and children of drunkards endured. The story, like Hentz's "The Drunkard's Daughter," exposes the unjust treatment toward the children of alcoholics and models a kinder approach. Perkins presents the "sorrow of a drunkard's family—the bitter hopelessness of their lot." Ballard's protagonist, Barbary Carwell, models appropriate behavior for others treated badly because of their association with drunkards.

Only a Drunkard's Daughter

Barbary Carwell sat in her room very busy with a pile of butternuts in a broken basket at her side. She was not eating nuts. Oh! no, she had hardly time or wish for that. The little saw she had borrowed of Will Floy, who had always been Barbary's friend and helper, was heated from hurrying its way through the hard nut; and layer after layer of the curious open-work segments was laid on the table beside her. Then the little red tin cup, in which she had melted her pennyworth of glue, was taken from the mantel, and the parts of shells neatly fastened on a plain pine frame. A coat of varnish finished her afternoon's work, and Barbary was delighted with her success. "How glad I should be to keep it, and put in that sweet picture of 'Jessie and her Fawns!'" she thought; "but as long as I can get my geography in no other way, Jessie must wait awhile."

Barbary took the frame, almost before it was dry, to a little drygoods and fancy store on the corner near her home; and the money she got in return made her heart very light. She had an arithmetic and a slate before; and now she would have a new geography, and she could go to the free-school, and be as happy as anybody. Besides, now that she had learned to make frames, and had secured some pretty patterns for brackets, and had plenty of basket patterns running through her little head, and a whole large basketful of butternuts, and cones, and acorns, and beechnuts in the attic, she was sure she should hardly need for anything for a good while to come.

"Here is my new book," she said, running in breathlessly to her mother the next morning. "Now, if my dress is ready, I can start this very day."

Mrs. Carwell went to a closet, and, taking down a checked black and white frock, over which she had spent one day's close work altering it for Barbary, handed it to her, together with a clean barred white apron. There was scarcely a smile on the mother's face, as the eager child took them gladly, and was soon dressed and on her way to school.

"Dear child!" thought Mrs. Carwell, as Barbary closed the door,

"I am glad she is so easily pleased. I fear I have thought of my own troubles too much, and neglected to make her happy."

A little past twelve Mrs. Carwell was glad to hear Barbary's step at the door. But instead of coming in, as she had expected, full of pleasant news about the school, Barbary went straight through the little kitchen and hall up to her own room. Not so fast, however, as to conceal from her mother's notice swollen eyes and tear-stained cheeks. She said nothing, however, until after dinner, when the school-hour came, and Barbary made no sign of going.

"It is nearly two; are you ready for school?" asked Mrs. Carwell in a quiet voice.

The tone and manner brought fresh tears to Barbary's eyes, as she replied:

"I would rather study at home, and then I can help you more."

Mrs. Carwell looked up in surprise. After all Barbary's eagerness to have her books and clothing ready that she might attend the school, was this to be the result?

"What has happened, Barbary? Some one has said something to hurt your feelings—either about your clothes, or home, or something else."

Barbary knew very well what the "something else" meant. This "something else" was the great grave where lay buried half Barbary's, and well-nigh all her mother's, hopes and joys.

"Yes, mother. I don't suppose it was my clothes; for although many of the girls were very nicely dressed, yet I was whole and neat, and looked as well as many who are much better able to dress than I am. The teacher gave me a pleasant seat at a double desk. Mary Cranston sat at the desk. She was once in a Sabbath-school class with me. She did not speak to me, but I did not expect that in school-hours. At recess, however, she asked the teacher if Barbary Carwell was to share her desk, and I saw her countenance fall when Miss Harte said 'Yes.' Then the girls all drew off in knots by themselves, and there wasn't any one I could talk with, or that seemed to want me near them, so I went to my seat, and tried to read through the recess. But I could not help hearing what Mary Cranston said when Nettie Reyle asked her how she should like her new seat-mate."

"What was it, Barbary?"

"I didn't hear every word, but I know she said something like this—that I might be good enough, but was, after all, only 'a drunkard's daughter.'"

Mrs. Carwell's face burned with indignation, none the less real that the remark was true.

"Did Mary know you heard her?"

"Yes; as she said it, she looked towards me, and our eyes met. She came to the desk a little before the bell rang, and I said to her: 'Mary, I am sorry Miss Harte gave me this seat. I will ask her for another, if I come any more. If what you said is true, it is not my fault.'"

"I am glad you had the firmness to speak so to Mary, Barbary; and I hope the same feeling will lead you now to go to school, and try to do right. Do not lose this opportunity to improve yourself. You can tell your teacher you would like a seat by yourself, if you choose. I have seldom spoken to you of this great burden I bear about daily, Barbary; but, if we cannot help your father's habits—and I do not see as we can—let us try not to lose our self-respect—let us be more to each other, Barbary."

There was a feeling of womanly strength in Barbary's heart as she went up to her teacher and asked her for a seat by herself, at the close of the afternoon school. Mary Cranston heard the request, and a feeling of shame sent a flush over her face, as she lingered behind her old mates until Barbary came out. Then she said: "I am sorry I spoke as I did, Barbary. Do not leave my seat—I will be a friend to you." Tears came into Barbary's eyes, but from a very different source from those she had shed at noon.

"I like the stuff she is made of," said Mary to one of her friends that night, "and I shall be kind to her, if she *is* a drunkard's daughter."

Who is there that realizes the sorrow of a drunkard's family—the bitter hopelessness of their lot? Surely not those who can wilfully add scorn to their cup of woe. Are there not some very near you, perhaps within a stone's throw of your dwelling, of whom you have never thought save as "only a drunkard's child"? Hasten, then, by word or act of sympathy, to show them that some, at least, can feel kindly toward, and bear some regard for, those who already have more than they know how to bear of bitter sorrow. Never *think,* much less *say,* "It is only a drunkard's daughter."

CORRA LYNN
DATES UNKNOWN

Details of Corra Lynn's life have been lost. *Durham Village; A Temperance Tale* (Boston: John P. Jewett & Company, 1854), excerpted here, was also published as *Fast Life; or, The City and the Farm* by the Scottish Temperance League.

While most women's temperance fiction exposing the fallacy of men's protection for and care of women specifically addresses the need for legal reform, some simply unmasks the hypocrisy underlying assumptions of male protection. The greatest number of women's temperance works portray the misconception attending notions of spousal protection; next most abundant in debunking these ideas are stories about fathers, both illustrated in this anthology. But brothers, also assumed to be protectors of mothers and sisters, provide another avenue for writers to reveal the error of arguments claiming men provide the only protection women need. An excerpt of one such example is available to today's readers in Lucy Freibert and Barbara White's *Hidden Hands* (1985). Metta Fuller Victor's *The Senator's Son* (1853) depicts a brother, Parke Madison, whose drinking problem so engulfs him that he becomes liable to prosecution for forgery. His sister Alice marries the holder of the forged documents, a despicable man, after Parke begs her to thus save him from imprisonment.

In *Durham Village*, Lynn demonstrates the failure of William Lundley to protect his younger sister, Edith, who has been entrusted to his care. Not only does William fail to protect Edith, his irresponsible behavior places both Edith and their sister, Julia, in jeopardy. Lynn demonstrates that women provide their own best protection. Their quick thinking and self-composure save Edith from rape and Julia from harassment and blackmail. While *Durham Village* does not address specifically legal inequities for women, it belies notions that women do not need legal protections because men better serve that function. The author makes clear, in fact, that men create dangers for women.

In the first excerpt provided, Edith Lundley, at age eighteen, has come to live with her brother, William, a successful lawyer. Their other sister, Julia, chooses to remain with their parents in the quiet village she calls home.

When William becomes increasingly addicted to drink, Edith cares for him and protects her family from discovering the truth. She finally must disclose details to Julia, but she remains in the city to care for William. Rather than serve as her protector, William places Edith in danger by getting drunk and allowing Fitzgerald Dunlap access to his keys.

Dunlap, unbeknownst to those in the city where he now lives, has abandoned a wife and child. He, nonetheless, courts young women and is considered one of the city's most eligible bachelors. In the second excerpt, Dunlap has discovered that Edith knows his true background and leaves the city, along with his friend, Diamond, in search of Julia in an effort to assure the secrecy of his history.

The sisters demonstrate extraordinary composure under distressing circumstances. Their safety comes not from male protectors. Instead, they become the protectors for men in their lives. Edith cares for William until his total insanity. When catastrophic events take place, it is Edith's composure that commands—"she whom God had made the weaker must become, and was, the stronger" (122). Likewise, Julia's strength and composure continue after she refuses to serve Dunlap's purposes and Dunlap writes her father with the truth about William—"as she took the letter to read, she heard the heart beat violently and convulsively in her father's breast, and felt the necessity of being calm" (167). Julia is calm, and her grieving mother also becomes a paragon of strength and composure. It is her father who must be comforted and cared for.

In this excerpt, Mrs. Corneille, the widow of a drunkard, has come to live with the Lundley family after the death of her husband.

from *Durham Village; A Temperance Tale*

Edith watched for Mr. Henley all that evening. She had expected he would return there, but as eleven o'clock struck from the "old city bell" she gave up her hopes of his visit, took her light, and went up to her room.

Her efforts had all been ineffectual to keep William from his wine. She could hear him in his room now, mixing his evening beverage, and determined once more to argue with him. Knocking at the closet-door, he bade her come in, and she entered.

"What's wanted, Dithie—here? It is high time such as you were sleeping. Why, half the night is gone at the farm!"

"William," she said, "I have come in to ask you if I might give a sick lady room here for a while; she is needy."

He set down the glass which he held in his hand, with its contents untasted, and heard Edith's simple narrative of the facts.

"And that is Dunlap's history, wretched man!" he exclaimed. "I will help her. Come here? That she may; and I'll have nothing more to do with him. These are his doings are they?"

"Not his alone, but *wine's*," replied Edith. "O, brother, do not take this, to-night. Think of Dunlap, and think of home."

"No danger of me, Dithie; I'm a strong man, heart and head."

"Many have fallen, as good as you," she added, as she laid her hand on his shoulder. "Do not *take* it."

He moved slowly to the window, opened it, and threw the brandy out. Edith retired to her room in fine spirits. Hope, angel hope, for a moment hovered with his shining wing over her, but hastened away,—for the lifting of the wine-cup was heard from the adjoining room, and sorrow came with it.

Edith could not sleep, and lay restless upon her bed. She thought she heard a noise below; she listened. The noise continued. It seemed like some one stealing up the stairs. She sprang to her door, and, as she did so, she distinctly heard the handle turn. She fled through the closet, to see if William were sleeping, and if his door were fastened. It was not, and she had just time to turn the key, when that door was tried, also. William was sleeping, a hard, beast-like sleep, and she knew there was no safety in waking him; he could be no protection, and she would let him sleep on. It so happened that the doors were supplied with a bolt, as well as a lock and key, and she fastened both. Soon she heard a rattling as of a bunch of keys; then she heard her own lock spring back, and the latch raised. Fast and firm, it did not yield to the pressure without. William's door was tried in the same manner. She then heard the footsteps descend the stairs, and the front-door open. She looked out of the window, and could distinguish the figure of a man walking up the street. He did not hurry at all, but walked leisurely along. At this moment the watchman came under the window, and Edith raised it. He stopped, and looked up.

"Yonder," said she, in a low voice, "goes a housebreaker. He has been in here; but that is he."

The watchman quickened his pace, but the man walked on just as slowly.

"Stop!" demanded the watchman.

The man obeyed without hesitation, turned, and asked what he wanted.

"Excuse me," Edith heard the watchman say, "I mistook you. Yonder must be the man," and he started in pursuit of another figure, which seemed to be hurrying on. Presently two others joined him; the watchman sprang his rattle, and gave chase, while Dunlap (for it was he) turned the corner of the street and went up into his rooms.

Since Julia had received the sad news of her brother's downfall, she felt a constant fear lest it might become known to her mother. It weighted upon her, day after day, like a leaden weight. She started at every knock at the door, and felt relieved when each visitor left the house. This state of suspense was leaving its impress upon her. Ever delicate, she grew still more so, and the sunken cheeks and pale lips alarmed her friends.

She felt conscious that the change must be apparent to them, and rallied each day every energy to the conflict of concealment. She often spent much of the night weeping.

It was on one evening, when sitting alone by the fire-light, she heard a gentle tap at the door, and, opening it, found Mr. Dunlap standing upon the steps. Surprised at the call, she civilly asked him in. He entered and sat down.

"I called rather late, Miss Lundley, hoping to find you alone. It is a little matter of business; in fact, it is that that brought me down here. You see, I thought I would like to see you first, because Mr. Downer says your parents don't know of your brother's condition, and perhaps you can do the thing for me."

"If it is an honorable thing to do, perhaps I can."

"No dishonor about it. You see, your sister, down there in the city, is engaged to a Mr. Henley,—a man whom I hate, there's no mincing that. Well, he has papers of mine which he has no right to. I know he has handed them over to Edith; she has had them for some time. I have tried every way to obtain them,—every lawful way. Have them I will. Now, if you can obtain them for me, I will keep still about your brother; but, if you will not, I will blazon it around the town, and tell your parents, too."

"If you suppose you can intimidate me in that way, you are mistaken, sir," replied Julia, with a calmness which surprised him, for he had understood that she was a timid creature.

"I mean what I say, Miss Lundley; I want those papers, and, really, you can obtain them easily. Just write for them,—she will trust them with you, I know,—then hand them to me. They are of no importance to any one but myself."

"I shall do no such thing. I never play a double part."

"But you must, or I will tell everything I know. And that is a disgrace you cannot well endure."

It would seem that Mr. Dunlap was forgetting his courteous manners, for his tone now was rude and insolent. Nevertheless, Julia did not appear disconcerted, but replied,

"I think it must come from a more reliable source, before it will be believed."

"Few believe it! I can bring facts,—facts that I know of. Did not I see him once beat his head against the door, and howl? Have not I heard him use oaths that made *me* tremble, though I am used to oaths? Have not I seen him under the table in my own room, and had him carried out by servants, dead drunk? Have not I seen him—"

"Stop, sir!" exclaimed Julia, rising from her seat. "I bid you stop, or go."

"Ha! well, that looks rather keen; I like it."

"You see," he said, softening his tone a little, "I do not mean to tell all this but to you, unless you will not write for my papers. If you will write for them, I will publish another story around. I will tell them how kind he is, how devoted,—worthy the care of such a sister!" he added, in a satirical tone.

"If you suppose, sir, that by any means you can drive me to do that which I will not consent to, you do not understand my character, or my *will*."

"You *will* not, then?" and he drew his chair nearer her side. She neither moved hers, nor spoke.

"You *will* not, then? Well, just listen," and he dropped his voice into a thrilling whisper. "Listen; I will—"

"Stop, sir!—I command you; or I will call my father."

"O, no, that you will not," he said, putting his arm about her, and holding her firmly in the chair. "I mean no violence; I simply want you to hear what I have to say. Well, then, I will—"

"Let me go, or I will call for help!"

"No use, for I can help that,—stop it easily. Just listen. Your brother signed a paper,—I made him sign it, when he was drunk,— a paper that would carry him to prison. Do you hear? But that is not all; O, no!—"

But, ere he had finished the sentence, a blow fell upon his head, and he dropped to the floor.

So intense had been his excitement that he had not heard the soft, sylph-like tread of Mr. Diamond, who had followed him thither and listened unseen to the whole of the conversation, and ended it in this manner,—the first spirited act he was ever guilty of performing.

Dunlap almost instantly arose, it being the suddenness, rather than the violence of the blow, which had levelled him.

By this time Mrs. Corneille was aroused. The heavy fall of the man had jarred her room to such a degree as to awaken her, and, springing up, she hastened down stairs just as Dunlap had arisen, and seated himself in the chair.

"O, Mrs. Corneille!" exclaimed Julia. "Hist! be silent; but come, send these men away."

"And ken ya na better than to be here such an hour o' the night? Out with ye, each one, or I'll drive ye out! It's no good ye are here for."

"Not so fast, my good woman," replied Mr. Diamond; "this friend of mine is pale, and I think needs care."

"Take him home and care for him, then. I dinna like the looks of either of you, and, if ye winna go soon, I will see that ye are sent. Come here!" and she opened the door wide upon its hinges, and stood for a moment irresolute.

"Come, I say,—out with ye; na's the good ye are after. But Miss Julia is not a bird of your kind. Come, go!"

She was fairly aroused, and, before Mr. Diamond could make his exit, she seized him, unresisting, by the arm, and led him to the outer door, where she gave him one good hard push, and returned after Mr. Dunlap. He had just time to whisper something to Julia, and clench his fist, ere she returned.

"Now," said she, "out! An ye have na manners, I will teach you some. It's na the thing for ye to be here; no, come."

Had Mr. Dunlap not seen fit to go, she never could have led him, as she did the yielding Diamond; but the truth was, he felt strangely, and thought it best to reach home as speedily as possible,—therefore he went. Mrs. Corneille doubly barred the door, and listened long to be sure they were nowhere about the farm.

It was not the fall which had aroused these strange feelings in Mr. Dunlap's heart; but, he was thwarted in the plans where his only resource lay. He had unintentionally, exposed his own baseness, and was now adrift.

Early the next morning, the sudden departure of the city gentlemen filled the country folks with surprise, and brought, for a few days, peace to Julia's agitated heart.

Part 2

LEGAL INEQUITIES

MARIETTA HOLLEY
1836–1926

While not actively involved in reform causes, humorist Marietta Holley wrote primarily about woman's rights issues, often incorporating them into the popular travel motif of her time. She corresponded with reform leader Frances E. Willard, and this correspondence apparently influenced her writing of *Sweet Cicely or Josiah Allen as a Politician* (New York: Funk & Wagnalls, 1885), a portion of which is included here. Holley published more than twenty-five novels, including her most popular work, *Samantha at Saratoga; or, Racin' after Fashion* (1887).

Holley's narrator, Samantha Allen, Josiah Allen's wife, demonstrates the ridiculous nature of arguments against woman's rights and stresses the hypocrisy of sentiments extolling men's protection of women. In *Sweet Cicely,* published in at least thirteen editions between 1885 and 1895, Samantha highlights the ills of intemperance, telling of her niece Cicely's marriage to Paul Slide, whose intemperance leads to heartbreak for Cicely and those who love her. The frame permits Holley to address the many inequities that Cicely then experiences under the law.

In one subplot, Samantha's husband, Josiah, decides to become a politician, and Samantha and Cicely travel—take a "tower" (tour)—to Washington to determine the feasibility of Josiah's moving there. Samantha's travels permit Holley to expose more unjust and unequal laws. The second excerpt included here features Samantha's discussion with Dorlesky Burpy, one of the string of neighbors who approaches Samantha requesting a favor while she is in Washington. Concerned with "the lawful sufferin's of . . . wimmen," Dorlesky asks Samantha to lobby for temperance and more equitable rights for women while she is in Washington.

from *Sweet Cicely or Josiah Allen as a Politician*

Chapter I

It was something about the middle of winter, along in the forenoon, that Josiah Allen was telegrafted to, unexpected. His niece Cicely and her little boy was goin' to pass through Jonesville the next day on her way to visit her aunt Mary (aunt on her mother's side), and she would stop off, and make us a short visit if convenient.

We wuz both tickled, highly tickled; and Josiah, before he had read the telegraf ten minutes, was out killin' a hen. The plumpest one in the flock was the order I give; and I was beginnin' to make a fuss, and cook up for her.

We loved her jest about as well as we did Tirzah Ann. Sweet Cicely was what we used to call her when she was a girl. Sweet Cicely is a plant that has a pretty white posy. And our niece Cicely was prettier and purer and sweeter than any posy that ever grew: so we thought then, and so we think still.

Her mother was my companion's sister,—one of a pair of twins, Mary and Maria, that thought the world of each other, as twins will. Their mother died when they wus both of 'em babies; and they wus adopted by a rich aunt, who brought 'em up elegant, and likely too: that I will say for her, if she was a 'Piscopal, and I a Methodist. I am both liberal and truthful—very.

Maria was Cicely's ma, and she was left a widow when she wus a young woman; and Cicely wus her child. And the two wus bound up in each other as I never see a mother and daughter in my life before or sense.

The third year after Josiah and me wus married, Maria wusn't well, and the doctor ordered her out into the country for her health; and she and little Cicely spent the hull of that summer with us. Cicely wus about ten; and how we did love that girl! Her mother couldn't bear to have her out of her sight; and I declare, we all of us wus jest about as bad. And from that time they used to spend most all of their summers in Jonesville. The air agreed with 'em, and so did I: we never had a word of trouble. And we used to visit them quite a good deal in the winter season: they lived in the city.

Wall, as Cicely got to be a young girl, I used often to set and look at her, and wonder if the Lord could have made a prettier, sweeter girl if he had tried to. She looked to me jest perfect, and so she did to Josiah.

And she knew so much, too, and wus so womanly and quiet and deep. I s'pose it wus bein' always with her mother that made her seem older and more thoughtful than girls usially are. It seemed as if her great dark eyes wus full of wisdom beyond—fur beyond—her years, and sweetness too. Never wus there any sweeter eyes under the heavens than those of our niece Cicely.

She wus very fair and pale, you would think at first; but, when you would come to look closer, you would see there was nothing sickly in her complexion, only it was very white and smooth,—a good deal like the pure white leaves of the posy Sweet Cicely. She had a gentle, tender mouth, rose-pink; and her cheeks wuz, when she would get rousted up and excited about any thing; and then it would all sort o' die out again into that pure white. And over all her face, as sweet and womanly as it was, there was a look of power, somehow a look of strength, as if she would venture much, dare much, for them she loved. She had the gift, not always a happy one, of loving,—a strength of devotion that always has for its companion-trait a gift of endurance, of martyrdom if necessary.

She would give all, dare all, endure all, for them she loved. You could see that in her face before you had been with her long enough to see it in her life.

Her hair wus a soft, pretty brown, about the color of her eyes. And she was a little body, slender, and sort o' plump too; and her arms and hands and neck wus soft and white as snow almost.

Yes, we loved Cicely: and no one could blame us, or wonder at us for callin' her after the posy Sweet Cicely; for she was prettier than any posy that ever blew, enough sight.

Wall, she had always said she couldn't live if her mother died.

But she did, poor little creeter! She did.

Maria died when Cicely was about eighteen. She had always been delicate, and couldn't live no longer: so she died. And Josiah and me went right after the poor child, and brought her home with us.

She lived, Cicely did, because she was young, and couldn't die. And Josiah and me was dretful good to her; and many's the nights that I have gone into her room when I'd hear her cryin' way along in the night; many's the times I have gone in, and took her in my

Paul Slide. From Marietta Holley, *Sweet Cicely or Josiah Allen as a Politician.*
New York: Funk & Wagnalls, 1885, p. 7.

arms, and held her there, and cried with her, and soothed her, and got her to sleep, and held her in my arms like a baby till mornin'.

Wall, she lived with us most a year that time; and it wus about two years after, while she wus to some of her father's folks'es (they wus very rich), that she met the young man she married,—Paul Slide.

He was a handsome young man, well-behaved, only he would drink a little once in a while: he'd got into the habit at college, where his mate was wild, and had his turns. But he wus very pretty in his manners, Paul was,—polite, good-natured, generous-disposi- tioned,—and very rich.

And as to his looks, there wusn't no earthly fault to find with him, only jest his chin. And I told Josiah, that how Cicely could marry a man with such a chin was a mystery to me.

And Josiah said, "What is the matter with his chin?"

And I says, "Why, it jest sets right back from his mouth: he hain't got no chin at all hardly," says I. "The place where his chin ort to be is nothin' but a holler place all filled up with irresolution and weakness. And I believe Cicely will see trouble with that chin."

And then—I well remember it, for it was the very first time af- ter marriage, and so, of course, the very first time in our two lives— Josiah called me a fool, a "dumb fool," or jest the same as called me so. He says, "I wouldn't be a dumb fool if I was in your place."

I felt worked up. But, like warriors on a battle-field, I grew stronger for the fray; and the fray didn't scare me none.

But I says, "You'll see if you live, Josiah Allen"; and he did.

But, as I said, I didn't see how Cicely ever fell in love with a man with such a chin. But, as I learned afterwards, she fell in love with him under a fur collar. It was on a slay-ride. And he wuz very hand- some from his mouth up, very: his mouth wuz ruther weak. It wus a case of love at first sight, which I believe in considerable; and she couldn't help lovin' him, women are so queer.

I had always said that when Cicely did love, it would go hard with her. Many's the offers she'd had, but didn't care for 'em. But I knew, with her temperament and nater, that love, if it did come to her, would come to stay, and it would come hard and voyalent. And so it did.

She worshipped him, as I said at first, under a fur collar. And then, when a woman once gets to lovin' a man as she did, why, she can't help herself, chin or no chin. When a woman has once throwed herself in front of her idol, it hain't so much matter whether it is stuffed full of gold, or holler: it hain't so much matter *what* they be, I think. Curius, hain't it?

It hain't the easiest thing in the world for such a woman as Cicely to love, but it is a good deal easier for her than to unlove, as she found out afterwards. For twice before her marriage she saw him out of his head with liquor; and it wus my advice to her to give him up.

And she tried to unlove him, tried to give him up.

But, good land! She might jest as well have took a piece of her own heart out, as to take out of it her love for him: it had become a part of her. And he told her she could save him, her influence could redeem him, and it wus the only thing that could save him.

And Cicely couldn't stand such talk, of course; and she believed him—believed that she could love him so well, throw her influence so around him, as to hold him back from any evil course.

It is a beautiful hope, the very beautifulest and divinist piece of folly a woman can commit. Beautiful enough in the sublime martyrdom of the idee, to make angels smile; and vain enough, and foolish enough in its utter uselessness, to make sinners weep. It can't be done—not in 98 cases out of a 100 at least.

Why, if a man hain't got love enough for a woman when he is tryin' to win her affection—when he is on probation, as you may say,—to stop and turn round in his downward course, how can she expect he will after he has got her, and has let down his watch, so to speak?

But she loved him. And when I warned her with tears in my eyes, warned her that mebby it wus more than her own safety and happiness that wus imperilled, I could see by the look in her eyes, though she didn't say much, that it wusn't no use for me to talk; for she wus one of the constant natures that can't wobble round. And though I don't like wobblin', still I do honestly believe that the wobblers are happier than them that can't wobble.

I could see jest how it wuz, and I couldn't bear to have her blamed. And I would tell folks,—some of the relations on her mother's side,—when they would say, "What a fool she wus to have him!"—I'd say to 'em, "Wall, when a woman sees the man she loves goin' down to ruination, and tries to unlove him, she'll find out jest how much harder it is to unlove him than to love him in the first place: they'll find out it is a tough job to tackle."

I said this to blamers of Cicely (relatives, the best blamers you can find anywhere). But, at the same time, it would have been my way, when he had come a courtin' me so far gone with liquor that he could hardly stand up—to set myself up as a rival to alcohol, and he might pay to that his attentions exclusively hereafter.

But she didn't. And he promised sacred to abstain, and could, and did, for most a year; and she married him.

But, jest before the marriage, I got so rousted up a thinkin' about what I had heard of him at college,—and I studied on his picture, which she had sent me, took sideways too, and I could see plain (why, he hadn't no chin at all, as you may say; and his lips was weak and waverin' as ever lips was, though sort o' amiable and fascinating),—and I got to forebodin' so about that chin, that I went to see her on a short tower, to beset her on the subject. But, good land! I might have saved my breath, I might have saved my tower.

I cried, and she cried too. And I says to her before I thought,— "He'll be the ruin of you, Cicely."

And she says, "I would rather be beaten by his hand, than to be crowned by another. Why, I love him, aunt Samantha."

You see, that meant a awful sight to her. And as she looked at me so earnest and solemn, with tears in them pretty brown eyes, there wus in her look all that that word could possibly mean to any soul.

But I cried into my white linen handkerchief, and couldn't help it, and couldn't help sayin', as I see that look,—

"Cicely, I am afraid he will break your heart—kill you"—

"Why, I am not afraid to die when I am with him. I am afraid of nothing—of life, or death, or eternity."

Well, I see my talk was no use. I see she'd have him, chin or no chin. If I could have taken her up in my arms, and run away with her then and there, how much misery I could have saved her from! But I couldn't: I had the rheumatiz. And I had to give up, and go home disapp'inted, but carryin' this thought home with me on my tower,—that I had done my duty by our sweet Cicely, and could do no more.

As I said, he promised firm to give up drinking. But, good land! What could you expect from that chin? That chin couldn't stand temptation if it came in his way. At the same time, his love for Cicely was such, and his good heart and his natural gentlemanly intuitions was such, that, if he could have been kep' out of the way of temptation, he would have been all right.

If there hadn't been drinking-saloons right in front of that chin, if it could have walked along the road without runnin' right into 'em, it would have got along. That chin, and them waverin'-lookin', amiable lips, wouldn't have stirred a step out of their ways to get ruined and disgraced: they wouldn't have took the trouble to.

And for a year or so he and the chin kep' out of the way of temptation, or ruther temptation kep' out of their way; and Cicely was happy,—radiantly happy, as only such a nature as hern can be. Her face looked like a mornin' in June, it wus so bright, and glowing with joy and happy love.

I visited her, stayed 3 days and 2 nights with her; and I almost forgot to forebode about the lower part of his face, I found 'em so happy and prosperous and likely.

Paul was very rich. He was the only child: and his pa left 2 thirds of his property to him, and the other third to his ma, which was more than she could ever use while she was alive; and at her death it wus to go to Paul and his heirs.

They owned most all of the village they lived in. His pa had owned the township the village was built on, and had built most all the village himself, and rented the buildings. He owned a big manufactory there, and the buildings rented high.

Wall, it wus in the second year of their marriage that that old college chumb—(and I wish he had been chumbed by a pole, before he had ever gone there). He had lost his property, and come down in the world, and had to work for a livin'; moved into that village, and opened a drinking-saloon and billiard-room.

He had been Paul's most intimate friend at college, and his evil genius, so his mother said. But he was bright, witty, generous in a way, unprincipled, dissipated. And he wanted Paul's company, and he wanted Paul's money; and he had a chin himself, and knew how to manage them that hadn't any.

Wall, Cicely and his mother tried to keep Paul from that bad influence. But he said it would look shabby to not take any notice of a man because he wus down in the world. He wouldn't have much to do with him, but it wouldn't do to not notice him at all. How curius, that out of good comes bad, and out of bad, good. That was a good-natured idee of Paul's if he had had a chin that could have held up his principle; but he didn't.

So he gradually fell under the old influence again. He didn't mean to. He hadn't no idee of doin' so when he begun. It was the chin.

He begun to drink hard, spent his nights in the saloon, gambled,—slipped right down the old, smooth track worn by millions of jest such weak feet, towards ruin. And Cicely couldn't hold him back after he had got to slippin': her arms wuzn't strong enough.

She went to the saloon-keeper, and cried, and begged of him not to sell her husband any more liquor. He was very polite to her, very courteous: everybody was to Cicely. But in a polite way he told her that Paul wus his best customer, and he shouldn't offend him by refusing to sell him liquor. She knelt at his feet, I hearn,—her little, tender limbs on that rough floor before that evil man,—and wept, and said,—

"For the sake of her boy, wouldn't he have mercy on the boy's father."

But in a gentle way he gave her to understand that he shouldn't make no change.

And he told her, speakin' in a dretful courteous way, "that he had the law on his side: he had a license, and he should keep right on as he was doing."

And so what could Cicely do? And time went on, carryin' Paul further and further down the road that has but one ending. Lower and lower he sunk, carryin' her heart, her happiness, her life, down with him.

And they said one cold night Paul didn't come home at all, and Cicely and his mother wus half crazy; and they wus too proud, to the last, to tell the servants more than they could help: so, when it got to be most mornin', them two delicate women started out through the deep snow, to try to find him, tremblin' at every little heap of snow that wus tumbled up in the path in front of 'em; tremblin' and sick at heart with the agony and dread that was rackin' their souls, as they would look over the cold fields of snow stretching on each side of the road, and thinkin' how that face would look if it was lying there staring with lifeless eyes up towards the cold moonlight,— the face they had kissed, the face they had loved,—and thinkin', too, that the change that had come to it—was comin' to it all the time— was more cruel and hopeless than the change of death.

So they went on, clear to the saloon; and there they found him,— there he lay, perfectly stupid, and dead with liquor.

And they both, the broken-hearted mother and the broken-hearted wife, with the tears running down their white cheeks, besought the saloon-keeper to let him alone from that night.

The mother says, "Paul is so good, that if you did not tempt him, entice him here, he would, out of pity to us, stop his evil ways."

Cicely in the saloon. From Marietta Holley, *Sweet Cicely or Josiah Allen as a Politician*. New York: Funk & Wagnalls, 1885, p. 15.

And the saloon-keeper was jest as polite as any man wus ever seen to be,—took his hat off while he told 'em, so I hearn, "that he couldn't go against his own interests: if Paul chose to spend his money there, he should take it."

"Will you break our hearts?" cried the mother.

"Will you ruin my husband, the father of my boy?" sobbed out Cicely, her big, sorrowful eyes lookin' right through his soul—if he *had* a soul.

And then the man, in a pleasant tone, reminded 'em,—

"That it wuzn't him that wus a doin' this. It was the law: if they wanted things changed, they must look further than him. He had a license. The great Government of the United States had sold him, for a few dollars, the right to do just what he was doing. The law, and all the respectability that the laws of our great and glorious Republic can give, bore him out in all his acts. The law was responsible for all the consequenses of his acts: the men were responsible who voted for license—it was not him."

"But you *can* do what we ask if you will, out of pity to Paul, pity to us who love him so, and who are forced to stand by powerless, and see him going to ruin—we who would die for him willingly if it would do any good. You *can* do this."

He was a little bit intoxicated, or he wouldn't have gin 'em the cruel sneer he did at the last,—though he sneered polite,—a holdin' his hat in his hand.

"As I said, my dear madam, it is not I, it is the law; and I see no other way for you ladies who feel so about it, only to vote, and change the laws."

"Would to God I *could!*" said the old white-haired mother, with her solemn eyes lifted to the heavens, in which was her only hope.

"Would to God I could!" repeated my sweet Cicely, with her eyes fastened on the face of him who had promised to cherish her, and comfort her, and protect her, layin' there at her feet, a mark for jeers and sneers, unable to speak a word, or lift his hand, if his wife and mother had been killed before him.

But they couldn't do any thing. They would have lain their lives down for him at any time, but that wouldn't do any good. The lowest, most ignorant laborer in their employ had power in this matter, but they had none. They had intellectual power enough, which, added to their utter helplessness, only made their burden more unendurable; for they comprehended to the full the knowledge of what was past, and what must come in the future unless help came quickly. They had the strength of devotion, the strength of unselfish love.

They had the will, but they hadn't nothin' to tackle it onto him with, to draw him back. For their prayers, their midnight watches, their tears, did not avail, as I said: they went jest so far; they touched him, but they lacked the tacklin'-power that was wanted to grip holt of him, and draw him back. What they needed was the justice of the law to tackle the injustice; and they hadn't got it, and couldn't get holt of it; so they had to set with hands folded, or lifted to the heavens in wild appeal,—either way didn't help Paul any,—and see him a sinkin' and a sinkin', slippin' further and further down; and they had to let him go.

He drunk harder and harder, neglected his business, got quarrelsome. And one night, when the heavens was curtained with blackness, like a pall let down to cover the accursed scene, he left Cicely with her pretty baby asleep on her bosom, went down to the saloon, got into a quarrel with that very friend of hisen, the saloonkeeper, over a game of billiards,—they was both intoxicated,—and then and there Paul committed *murder,* and would have been hung for it if he hadn't died in State's prison the night before he got his sentence.

Awful deed! Dreadful fate! But no worse, as I told Josiah when he was a groanin' over it; no worse, I told the children when they was a cryin' over it; no worse, I told my own heart when the tears wus a runnin' down my face like rain-water,—no worse because Cicely happened to be our relation, and we loved her as we did our own eyes.

And our broad land is *full* of jest such sufferin's, jest such crimes, jest such disgrace, caused by the same cause;—as I told Josiah, suffering, disgrace, and crime made legal and protected by the law.

And Josiah squirmed as I said it; and I see him squirm, for he believed in it: he believed in licensing this shame and disgrace and woe; he believed in makin' it respectable, and wrappin' round it the mantilly of the law, to keep it in a warm, healthy, flourishin' condition. Why, he had helped do it himself; he had helped the United States lift up the mantilly; he had voted for it.

He squirmed, but turned it off by usin' his bandana hard, and sayin', in a voice all choked down with grief,—

"Oh, poor Cicely! Poor girl!"

"Yes," says I, "'poor girl!' and the law you uphold has made her 'poor girl'—has killed her; for she won't live through it, and you and the United States will see that she won't."

He squirmed hard; and my feelin's for him are such that I can't bear to see him squirm voyalently, as much as I blamed him and the United States, and as mad a I was at both of 'em.

So I went to cryin' again silently under my linen handkerchief, and he cried into his bandana. It was a awful blow to both on us.

Wall, she lived, Cicely did, which was more than we any of us thought she could do. I went right there, and stayed six weeks with her, hangin' right over her bed, night and day; and so did his mother,—she was a broken-hearted woman too. Her heart broke, too, by the United States; and so I told Josiah, that little villain that got killed was only one of his agents. Yes, her heart was broke; but she bore up for Cicely's sake and the boy's. For it seemed as if she felt remorsful, and as if it was for them that belonged to him who had ruined her life, to help her all they could.

Wall, after about three weeks Cicely begun to live. And so I wrote to Josiah that I guessed she would keep on a livin' now, for the sake of the boy.

And so she did. And she got up from that bed a shadow,—a faint, pale shadow of the girl that used to brighten up our home for us. She was our sweet Cicely still. But she looked like that posy after the frost has withered it, and with the cold moonlight layin' on it.

Good and patient she wuz, and easy to get along with; for she seemed to hold earthly things with a dretful loose grip, easy to leggo of 'em. And it didn't seem as if she had any interest at all in life, or care for any thing that was a goin' on in the world, till the boy was about four years old; and then she begun to get all rousted up about him and his future. "She *must* live," she said; "she had got to live, to do something to help him in the future."

"She couldn't die," she told me, "and leave him in a world that was so hard for boys, where temptations and danger stood all round her boy's pathway. Not only hidden perils, concealed from sight, so he might possibly escape them, but open temptations, open dangers, made as alluring as private avarice could make them, and made as respectable as dignified legal enactments could make them,—all to draw her boy down the pathway his poor father descended." For one of the curius things about Cicely wuz, she didn't seem to blame Paul hardly a mite, nor not so very much the one that enticed him to drink. She went back further than them: she laid the blame onto our laws; she laid the responsibility onto the ones that made 'em, directly and indirectly, the legislators and the voters.

Curius that Cicely should feel so, when most everybody said that he could have stopped drinking if he had wanted to. But then, I don't know as I could blame her for feelin' so when I thought of Paul's chin and lips. Why, anybody that had them on 'em, and was made up inside and outside accordin', as folks be that have them looks; why, unless they was specially guarded by good influences, and fenced off from bad ones,—why, they *could not* exert any self-denial and control and firmness.

Why, I jest followed that chin and that mouth right back through seven generations of the Slide family. Paul's father was a good man, had a good face; took it from his mother: but his father, Paul's grandfather, died a drunkard. They have got a oil-portrait of him at Paul's old home: I stopped there on my way home from Cicely's one time. And for all the world he looked most exactly like Paul,—the same sort of a irresolute, handsome, weak, fascinating look to him. And all through them portraits I could trace that chin and them lips. They would disappear in some of 'em, but crop out agin further back. And I asked the housekeeper, who had always lived in the family, and was proud of it, but honest; and she knew the story of the hull Slide race.

And she said that everyone of 'em that had that face had traits accordin'; and 'most every one of 'em got into trouble of some kind.

One or two of 'em, especially guarded, I s'pose by good influences, got along with no further trouble than the loss of the chin, and the feelin' they must have had inside of 'em, that they wuz liable to crumple right down any minute.

And as they wus made with jest them looks, and jest them traits, born so, entirely unbeknown to them, I don't know as I can blame Cicely for feelin' as she did. If temptation hadn't stood right in the road in front of him, why, he'd have got along, and lived happy. That's Cicely's idee. And I don't know but she's in the right ont.

But as I said, when her child wus bout four years old, Cicely took a turn, and begun to get all worked up and excited by turns a worryin' about the boy. She'd talk about it a sight to me, and I hearn it from others.

She rousted up out of her deathly weakness and heart-broken, stunted calm,—for such it seemed to be for the first two or three years after her husband's death. She seemed to make an effort almost like that of a dead man throwin' off the icy stupor of death, and risin' up with numbed limbs, and shakin' off the death-robes, and livin' again. She roused up with jest such a effort, so it seemed, for the boy's sake.

She must live for the boy; she must work for the boy; she must try to throw some safeguards around his future. What *could* she do to help him? That wus the question that was a hantin' her soul.

It wus jest like death for her to face the curius gaze of the world again; for, like a wounded animal, she had wanted to crawl away, and hide her cruel woe and disgrace in some sheltered spot, away from the sharp-sot eyes of the babblin' world.

But she endured it. She came out of her quiet home, where her heart had bled in secret; she came out into society again; and she did every thing she could, in her gentle, quiet way. She joined temperance societies,—helped push 'em forward with her money and her influence. With other white-souled wimmen, gentle and refined as she was, she went into rough bar-rooms, and knelt on their floors, and prayed what her sad heart was full of,—for pity and mercy for her boy, and other mothers' boys,—prayed with that fellowship of suffering that made her sweet voice as pathetic as tears, and patheticker, so I have been told.

But one thing hurt her influence dretfully, and almost broke her own heart. Paul had left a very large property, but it wus all in the hands of an executor until the boy wus of age. He wus to give Cicely a liberal, a very liberal, sum every year, but wus to manage the property jest as he thought best.

He was a good business man, and one that meant to do middlin' near right, but wus close for a bargain, and sot, awful sot. And though he was dretful polite, and made a stiddy practice right along of callin' wimmen "angels," still he would not brook a woman's interference.

Wall, he could get such big rents for drinkin'-saloons, that four of Cicely's buildings wus rented for that purpose; and there wus one billiard-room. And what made it worse for Cicely seemin'ly, it wus her own property, that she brought to Paul when she wus married, that was invested in these buildings. At that time they was rented for dry-goods stores, and groceries. But the business of the manufactories had increased greatly; and there wus three times the population now there wus when she went there to live, and more saloons was needed; and these buildings wus handy; and the executer had big prices offered to him, and he would rent 'em as he wanted to. And then, he was something of a statesman; and he felt, as many business men did, that they wus fairly sufferin' for more saloons to enrich the government.

Why, out of every hundred dollars that them poor laboring-men had earned so hardly, and paid into the saloons for that which, of course, wus ruinous to themselves and families, and, of course, rendered them incapable of all labor for a great deal of the time,— why, out of that hundred dollars, as many as 2 cents would go to the government to enrich it.

Of course, the government had to use them 2 cents right off towards buyin' tight-jackets to confine the madmen the whisky had made, and poorhouse-doors for the idiots it had breeded, to lean up aginst, and buryin' the paupers, and buyin' ropes to hang the murderers it had created.

But still, in some strange way, too deep, fur too deep, for a woman's mind to comprehend, it wus dretful profitable to the government.

Now, if them poor laborin'-men had paid that 2 cents of thiern to the government themselves, in the first place, in direct taxation, why, that wouldn't have been statesmanship. That is a deep study, and has a great many curius performances, and it has to perform.

Cicely tried her very best to get the executor to change in this one matter; but she couldn't move him the width of a horse-hair, and he a smilin' all the time at her, and polite. He liked Cicely: nobody could help likin' the gentle, saintly-souled little woman. But he wus sot: he wus makin' money fast by it, and she had to give up.

And rough men and women would somtimes twit her of it,— of her property bein' used to advance the liquor-traffic, and ruin men and wimmen; and she a feelin' like death about it, and her hands tied up, and powerless. No wonder that her face got white and whiter, and her eyes bigger and mournfuller-lookin'.

Wall, she kep' on, tryin' to do all she could: she joined the Woman's Temperance Union; she spent her money free as water, where she thought it would do any good, and brought up the boy jest as near right as she could possibly bring him up; and she prayed, and wept right when she wus a bringin' of him, a thinkin' that *her* property wus a bein' used every day and every hour in ruinin' other mothers' boys. And the boy's face almost breakin' her heart every time she looked at it; for, though he wus jest as pretty as a child could be, the pretty rosy lips had the same good-tempered, irresolute curve to 'em that the boy inherited honestly. And he had the same weak, waverin' chin. It was white and rosy now, with a dimple right in the centre, sweet enough to kiss. But the chin wus there, right under the rosy snow and the dimple; and I foreboded, too, and couldn't blame Cicely a mite for her forebodin', and her agony of sole.

Chapter V

Wall, it wuzn't more'n 2 or 3 days after I begun my preprations, that Dorlesky Burpy, a vegetable widow, come to see me; and the errents she sent by me wuz fur more hefty and momentous than all the rest put together, calves, hen-coop, and all.

And when she told 'em over to me, and I meditated on her reasons for sendin' 'em, and her need of havin' 'em done, I felt that I would do the errents for her if a breath was left in my body. I felt that I would bear them 2 errents of hern on my tower side by side with my own private, hefty mission for Josiah.

She come for a all day's visit; and though she is a vegetable widow, and very humbly, I wuz middlin' glad to see her. But thinks'es I to myself as I carried away her things into the bedroom, "She'll want to send some errent by me;" and I wondered what it wouldn't be.

And so it didn't surprise me any when she asked me the first thing when I got back "if I would lobby a little for her in Washington."

And I looked agreeable to the idee; for I s'posed it wuz some kind of tattin', mebby, or fancy work. And I told her "I shouldn't have much time, but I would try to buy her some if I could."

And she said "she wanted me to lobby, myself."

And then I thought mebby it wus some new kind of waltz; and I told her "I was too old to lobby, I hadn't lobbied a step since I was married."

And then she said "she wanted me to canvass some of the senators."

And I hung back, and asked her in a cautius tone "how many she wanted canvassed, and how much canvass it would take?"

I knew I had a good many things to buy for my tower; and, though I wanted to obleege Dorlesky, I didn't feel like runnin' into any great expense for canvass.

And then she broke off from that subject, and said "she wanted her rights, and wanted the Whiskey Ring broke up."

And then she says, going back to the old subject agin, "I hear that Josiah Allen has political hopes: can I canvass him?"

And I says, "Yes, you can for all me." But I mentioned cautiously, for I believe in bein' straightforward, and not holdin' out no false hopes,—I said "she must furnish her own canvass, for I hadn't a mite in the house."

But Josiah didn't get home till after her folks come after her. So he wuzn't canvassed.

But she talked a sight about her children, and how bad she felt to be parted from 'em, and how much she used to think of her husband, and how her hull life was ruined, and how the Whiskey Ring had done it,—that, and wimmen's helpless condition under the law. And she cried, and wept, and cried about her children, and her sufferin's she had suffered; and I did. I cried onto my apron, and couldn't help it. A new apron too. And right while I wus cryin' onto that gingham apron, she made me promise to carry them two errents of hern to the President, and to get 'em done for her if I possibly could.

"She wanted the Whiskey Ring destroyed, and she wanted her rights; and she wanted 'em both in less than 2 weeks."

I wiped my eyes off, and told her I didn't believe she could get 'em done in that length of time, but I would tell the President about it, and "I thought more'n as likely as not he would want to do right by her." And says I, "If he sets out to, he can haul them babys of yourn out of that Ring pretty sudden."

And then, to kinder get her mind off of her sufferin's, I asked her how her sister Susan wus a gettin' along. I hadn't heard from her for years—she married Philemon Clapsaddle; and Dorlesky spoke out as bitter as a bitter walnut—a green one. And says she,

"She is in the poorhouse."

"Why, Dorlesky Burpy!" says I. "What do you mean?"

"I mean what I say. My sister, Susan Clapsaddle, is in the poorhouse."

"Why, where is their property all gone?" says I. "They was well off—Susan had five thousand dollars of her own when she married him."

"I know it," says she. "And I can tell you, Josiah Allen's wife, where their property is gone. It has gone down Philemon Clapsaddle's throat. Look down that man's throat, and you will see 150 acres of land, a good house and barns, 20 sheep, and 40 head of cattle."

"Why—ee!" says I.

"Yes, you will see 'em all down that man's throat." And says she, in still more bitter axents, "You will see four mules, and a span of horses, two buggies, a double sleigh, and three buffalo-robes. He has drinked 'em all up—and 2 horse-rakes, a cultivator, and a thrashin'-machine.

"Why! Why-ee!" says I agin. "And where are the children?"

"The boys have inherited their father's evil habits, and drink as bad as he duz; and the oldest girl has gone to the bad."

"Oh, dear! oh, dear me!" says I. And we both sot silent for a spell. And then, thinkin' I must say sunthin', and wantin' to strike a safe subject, and a good-lookin' one, I says,—

"Where is your aunt Eunice'es girl? that pretty girl I see to your house once."

"That girl is in the lunatick asylum."

"Dorlesky Burpy!" says I. "Be you a tellin' the truth?"

"Yes, I be, the livin' truth. She went to New York to buy millinary goods for her mother's store. It wus quite cool when she left home, and she hadn't took off her winter clothes: and it come on brilin' hot in the city; and in goin' about from store to store, the heat and the hard work overcome her, and she fell down in the street in a sort of a faintin'-fit, and was called drunk, and dragged off to a police court by a man who wus a animal in human shape. And he misused her in such a way, that she never got over the horror of what befell her—when she come to, to find herself at the mercy of a brute in a man's shape. She went into a melancholy madness, and wus sent to the asylum. Of course, they couldn't have wimmen in such places to take care of wimmen," says she bitterly.

I sithed a long and mournful sithe, and sot silent agin for quite a spell. But thinkin' I *must* be sociable, I says,—

"Your aunt Eunice is well, I s'pose?"

"She is a moulderin' in jail," says she.

"In jail? Eunice Keeler in jail?"

"Yes, in jail." And Dorlesky's tone wus now like wormwood, wormwood and gall.

"You know, she owns a big property in tenement-houses, and other buildings, where she lives. Of course, her taxes wus awful high; and she didn't expect to have any voice in tellin' how that money, a part of her own property, that she earned herself in a store, should be used.

"But she had jest been taxed high for new sidewalks in front of some of her buildin's.

"And then another man come into power in that ward, and he natrully wanted to make some money out of her; and he had a spite against her, too, so he ordered her to build new sidewalks. And she wouldn't tear up a good sidewalk to please him or anybody else, so she was put to jail for refusin' to comply with the law."

Think'es I to myself, I don't believe the law would have been so hard on her if she hadn't been so humbly. The Burpys are a humbly lot. But I didn't think it out loud. And I didn't uphold the law for feelin' so, if it did. No: I says in pityin' tones,—for I was truly sorry for Eunice Keeler,—

"How did it end?"

"It hain't ended," says she. "It only took place a month ago; and she has got her grit up, and won't pay: and no knowin' how it will end. She lays there a moulderin'."

I myself don't believe Eunice wus "mouldy;" but that is Dorlesky's way of talkin',—very flowery.

"Wall," says I, "do you think the weather is goin' to moderate?"

I truly felt that I dassent speak to her about any human bein' under the sun, not knowin' what turn she would give to the conversation, bein' so embittered. But I felt the weather was safe, and cotton stockin's, and factory-cloth; and I kep' her down onto them subjects for more'n two hours.

But, good land! I can't blame her for bein' embittered against men and the laws they have made; for, if ever a woman has been tormented, she has.

It honestly seems to me as if I never see a human creeter so afflicted as Dorlesky Burpy has been, all her life.

Why, her sufferin's date back before she wus born; and that is goin' pretty fur back. You see, her father and mother had had some difficulty: and he wus took down with billious colic voyolent four weeks before Dorlesky wus born; and some think it wus the hardness between 'em, and some think it wus the gripin' of the colic at the time he made his will; anyway, he willed Dorlesky away, boy or girl, whichever it wuz, to his brother up on the Canada line.

So, when Dorlesky wus born (and born a girl, entirely onbeknown to her), she was took right away from her mother, and gin to his brother. Her mother couldn't help herself: he had the law on his side. But it jest killed her. She drooped right away and died, before the baby wus a year old. She was a affectionate, tender-hearted woman; and her husband wus kinder overbearin', and stern always.

But it was this last move of hisen that killed her; for I tell you, it is pretty tough on a mother to have her baby, a part of her own life, took right out of her arms, and gin to a stranger.

For this uncle of hern wus a entire stranger to Dorlesky when the will wus made. And almost like a stranger to her father, for he hadn't seen him sence he wus a boy; but he knew he hadn't any children, and s'posed he wus rich and respectable. But the truth wuz, he had been a runnin' down every way,—had lost his property and his character, wus dissipated and mean (onbeknown, it was s'posed, to Dorlesky's father). But the will was made, and the law stood. Men are ashamed now, to think the law wus ever in voge; but it wuz, and is now in some of the States. The law wus in voge, and the poor young mother couldn't help herself. It has always been the boast of our American law, that it takes care of wimmen. It took care of her. It held her in its strong, protectin' grasp, and held her so tight, that the only way she could slip out of it wus to drop into the grave, which she did in a few months. Then it leggo.

But it kep' holt of Dorlesky: it bound her tight to her uncle, while he run through with what little property she had; while he sunk lower and lower, until at last he needed the very necessaries of life; and then he bound her out to work, to a woman who kep' a drinkin'-den, and the lowest, most degraded hant of vice.

Twice Dorlesky run away, bein' virtuous but humbly; but them strong, protectin' arms of the law that had held her mother so tight, jest reached out, and dragged her back agin. Upheld by them, her uncle could compel her to give her service wherever he wanted her to work; and he wus owin' this woman, and she wanted Dorlesky's work, so she had to submit.

But the 3d time, she made a effort so voyalent that she got away. A good woman, who, bein' nothin' but a woman, couldn't do any thing towards onclinchin' them powerful arms that wuz protectin' her, helped her to slip through 'em. And Dorlesky come to Jonesville to live with a sister of that good woman; changed her name, so's it wouldn't be so easy to find her; grew up to be a nice, industrious girl. And when the woman she was took by, died, she left Dorlesky quite a handsome property.

And finally she married Lank Rumsey, and did considerable well, it was s'posed. Her property, put with what little he had, made 'em a comfortable home; and they had two pretty little children,—a boy and a girl. But when the little girl was a baby, he took to drinkin', neglected his business, got mixed up with a whisky-ring, whipped Dorlesky—not so very hard. He went accordin' to law; and the law of the United States don't approve of a man whippin' his wife enough to endanger her life—it says it don't. He made every move of hisen lawful, and felt that Dorlesky hadn't ort to complain and feel hurt. But a good whippin' will make anybody feel hurt, law or no law. And then he parted with her, and got her property and her two little children. Why, it seemed as if every thing under the sun and moon, that *could* happen to a woman, had happened to Dorlesky, painful things, and gaulin'.

Jest before Lank parted with her, she fell on a broken sidewalk: some think he tripped her up, but it never was proved. But, anyway, Dorlesky fell, and broke her hip-bone; and her husband sued the corporation, and got ten thousand dollars for it. Of course, the law give the money to him, and she never got a cent of it. But she wouldn't never have made any fuss over that, knowin' that the law of the United States was such. But what made it gaulin' to her wuz, that, while she was layin' there achin' in splints, he took that very money and used it to court up another woman with. Gin her presents, jewellry, bunnets, head-dresses, artificial flowers, and etcetery, out of Dorlesky's own hip-money.

And I don't know as any thing could be much more gaulin' to a woman than that wuz,—while she lay there, groanin' in splints, to have her husband take the money for her own broken bones, and dress up another woman like a doll with it.

But the law gin it to him; and he was only availin' himself of the glorious liberty of our free republic, and doin' as he was a mind to.

And it was s'posed that that very hip-money was what made the match. For, before she wus fairly out of splints, he got a divorce from her. And by the help of that money, and the Whisky Ring, he got her two little children away from her.

And I wonder if there is a mother in the land, that can blame Dorlesky for gettin' mad, and wantin' her rights, and wantin' the Whisky Ring broke up, when they think it over,—how she has been fooled round with by men, willed away, and whipped and parted with and stole from. Why, they can't blame her for feelin' fairly savage about 'em—and she duz. For as she says to me once when we wus a talkin' it over, how every thing had happened to her that could happen to a woman, and how curious it wus,—

"Yes," says she, with a axent like boneset and vinegar,—"and what few things there are that hain't happened to me, has happened to my folks."

And, sure enough, I couldn't dispute her. Trouble and wrongs and sufferin's seemed to be epidemic in the race of Burpy wimmen. Why, one of her aunts on her father's side, Patty Burpy, married for her first husband Eliphalet Perkins. He was a minister, rode on a circuit. And he took Patty on it too; and she rode round with him on it, a good deal of the time. But she never loved to: she wus a woman who loved to be still, and be kinder settled down at home.

But she loved Eliphalet so well, she would do any thing to please him: so she rode round with him on that circuit, till she was perfectly fagged out.

He was a dretful good man to her; but he wus kinder poor, and they had hard times to get along. But what property they had wuzn't taxed, so that helped some; and Patty would make one doller go a good ways.

Dorlesky's trials. From Marietta Holley, *Sweet Cicely or Josiah Allen as a Politician.* New York: Funk & Wagnalls, 1885, p. 153.

No, their property wasn't taxed till Eliphalet died. Then the supervisor taxed it the very minute the breath left his body; run his horse, so it was said, so's to be sure to get it onto the tax-list, and comply with the law.

You see, Eliphalet's salary stopped when his breath did. And I s'pose mebby the law thought, seein' she was a havin' trouble, she might jest as well have a little more; so it taxed all the property it never had taxed a cent for before.

But she had this to console her anyway,—that the law didn't forget her in her widowhood. No: the law is quite thoughtful of wimmen, by spells. It says, the law duz, that it protects wimmen. And I s'pose in some mysterious way, too deep for wimmen to understand, it was protectin' her now.

Wall, she suffered along, and finally married again. I wondered why she did. But she was such a quiet, home-lovin' woman, that it was s'posed she wanted to settle down, and be kinder still and sot. But of all the bad luck she had! She married on short acquaintance, and he proved to be a perfect wanderer. Why, he couldn't keep still. It was s'posed to be a mark.

He moved Patty thirteen times in two years; and at last he took her into a cart,—a sort of a covered wagon,—and travelled right through the Eastern states with her. He wanted to see the country, and loved to live in the wagon: it was his make. And, of course, the law give him the control of her body; and she had to go where he moved it, or else part with him. And I s'pose the law thought it was guardin' and nourishin' her when it was a joltin' her over them praries and mountains and abysses. But it jest kep' her shook up the hull of the time.

It wus the regular Burpy luck.

And then, another one of her aunts, Drusilla Burpy, she married a industrius, hard-workin' man,—one that never drinked a drop, and was sound on the doctrines, and give good measure to his customers: he was a grocer-man. And a master hand for wantin' to foller the laws of his country, as tight as laws could be follered. And so, knowin' that the law approved of "moderate correction" for wimmen, and that "a man might whip his wife, but not enough to endanger her life," he bein' such a master hand for wantin' to do every thing faithful, and do his very best for his customers, it was s'posed that he wanted to do his best for the law; and so, when he got to whippin' Drusilla, he would whip her *too* severe—he would be *too* faithful to it.

You see, the way ont was, what made him whip her at all wuz, she was cross to him. They had nine little children. She always thought that two or three children would be about all one woman could bring up well "by hand," when that one hand wuz so awful full of work, as will be told more ensuin'ly. But he felt that big families wuz a protection to the Government; and "he wanted fourteen boys," he said, so they could all foller their father's footsteps, and be noble, law-making, law-abiding citizens, jest as he was.

But she had to do every mite of the housework, and milk cows, and make butter and cheese, and cook and wash and scour, and take all the care of the children, day and night, in sickness and in health, and spin and weave the cloth for their clothes (as wimmen did in them days), and then make 'em, and keep 'em clean. And when there wuz so many of 'em, and only about a year's difference in their ages, some of 'em—why, I s'pose she sometimes thought more of her own achin' back than she did of the good of the Government; and she would get kinder discouraged sometimes, and be cross to him.

And knowin' his own motives was so high and loyal, he felt that he ought to whip her. So he did.

And what shows that Drusilla wuzn't so bad as he s'posed she wuz, what shows that she did have her good streaks, and a deep reverence for the law, is, that she stood his whippin's first-rate, and never whipped him.

Now, she wuz fur bigger than he wuz, weighed 80 pounds the most, and might have whipped him if the law had been such.

But they was both law-abidin', and wanted to keep every preamble; so she stood it to be whipped, and never once whipped him in all the seventeen years they lived together.

She died when her twelfth child was born: there wus jest 13 months difference in the age of that and the one next older. And they said she often spoke out in her last sickness, and said,—

"Thank fortune, I have always kept the law."

And they said the same thought wus a great comfort to him in his last moments.

He died about a year after she did, leaving his 2nd wife with twins and a good property.

Then, there was Abagail Burpy. She married a sort of high-headed man, though one that paid his debts, and was truthful, and considerable good-lookin', and played well on the fiddle. Why, it seemed as if he had almost every qualification for makin' a woman happy, only he had jest this one little excentricity,—that man would lock up Abagail Burpy's clothes every time he got mad at her.

Of course the law give her clothes to him; and knowin' it was one of the laws of the United States, she wouldn't have complained only when she had company. But it was mortifyin', and nobody could dispute it, to have company come, and nothin' to put on.

Several times she had to withdraw into the wood-house, and

Beating his wife. From Marietta Holley, *Sweet Cicely or Josiah Allen as a Politician*. New York: Funk & Wagnalls, 1885, p. 158.

stay most of the day, shiverin', and under the cellar-stairs, and round in clothes-presses.

But he boasted in prayer-meetin's, and on boxes before grocery-stores, that he wus a law-abidin' citizen; and he wuz. Eben Flanders wouldn't lie for anybody.

But I'll bet that Abagail Flanders beat our old Revolutionary 4 mothers [foremothers] in thinkin' out new laws, when she lay round under stairs, and behind barrells, in her nightdress.

You see, when a man hides his wive's corset and petticoat, it is governin' without the "consent of the governed." And if you don't believe it, you ort to have peeked round them barrells, and seen Abagail's eyes. Why, they had hull reams of by-laws in 'em, and preambles, and "declarations of independence." So I have been told.

Why, it beat every thing I ever heard on, the lawful sufferin's of them wimmen. For there wuzn't nothin' illegal about one single trouble of theirn. They suffered accordin' to law, every one of 'em. But it wus tuff for 'em—very tuff.

And their all bein' so dretful humbly wuz and is another drawback to 'em; though that, too, is perfectly lawful, as everybody knows.

And Dorlesky looks as bad agin as she would otherways, on account of her teeth.

It wuz after Lank had begun to kinder get after this other woman, and wus indifferent to his wive's looks, that Dorlesky had a new set of teeth on her upper jaw. And they sort o' sot out, and made her look so bad that it fairly made her ache to look at herself in the glass. And they hurt her gooms too. And she carried 'em back to the dentist, and wanted him to make her another set.

But the dentist acted mean, and wouldn't take 'em back, and sued Lank for the pay. And they had a lawsuit. And the law bein' such that a woman can't testify in court in any matter that is of mutual interest to husband and wife—and Lank wantin' to act mean, too, testified that "they wus good sound teeth."

And there Dorlesky sot right in front of 'em with her gooms achin', and her face all pokin' out, and lookin' like furyation, and couldn't say a word. But she had to give in to the law.

And ruther than go toothless, she wears 'em to this day. And I do believe it is the raspin' of them teeth aginst her gooms, and her discouraged and mad feelin's every time she looks in a glass, that helps to embitter her towards men, and the laws men have made, so's a woman can't have the control over her own teeth and her own bones.

Wall, Dorlesky went home about 4 P.M., I a promisin' at the last minute as sacred as I could, without usin' a book, to do her errents for her.

ELIZABETH CADY STANTON
1815–1902

Elizabeth Cady Stanton, best known today for her leadership in the woman's suffrage movement, was a principal organizer of the Seneca Falls Convention, the first woman's rights convention. Along with Susan B. Anthony and Matilda Joslyn Gage, she edited the first three volumes of the *History of Woman Suffrage*. Stanton was active in other reform causes early in her career. Her husband, Henry Stanton, was a leader in the abolition movement, and while accompanying him to the world's anti-slavery convention, she met Lucretia Mott; the two began making plans to call a woman's rights convention, which resulted in the Seneca Falls Convention. Stanton also participated in early women's temperance activities. She wrote numerous addresses on marriage and divorce, often connecting her call for women's right to divorce with intemperance. She often wrote stories and articles for Amelia Bloomer's temperance and woman's rights newspaper, *The Lily*.

Stanton severed her ties with temperance reform after the June 1853 New York state women's temperance convention. She had been president of the organization during the previous year; however, disagreements among members as to whether or not to admit men as voting members led to dissension, and Mary C. Vaughan was elected president in place of Stanton. Stanton left the temperance cause permanently and for the remainder of her life gave her attention only to woman's rights and suffrage reform.

Stanton wrote "Henry Neil and His Mother" as a monthly series of conversations for *The Lily* from November 1849 through March 1850 under the name of Sun Flower, a name she often used when writing for *The Lily*. The conversations both respond to arguments against Prohibition legislation and provide a sample text for other women in defending the need for improved laws. Stanton's conversations make use of many contemporaneous arguments in opposition to the legalization of the manufacture and marketing of liquor. She models an approach to educating children about temperance but also suggests to women further means of involvement in rectifying laws that affect them.

Henry Neil and His Mother

Conversation No. I

Henry: Now mother, said Henry taking a seat by her side, my vacation has come and you must redeem your promise to discuss with me some interesting question every day, and as I hope at some future day to identify myself with the glorious temperance cause as one of its advocates, I should like with you to review the whole subject in its various branches.

Mother: I am glad my son, you have chosen for our first conversation a subject of such interest and importance. Would that I were sufficiently informed to do it full justice; however I feel that I shall be able to point out to you the right in all moral questions. To begin then with the monster intemperance, as he has many horns, let me take hold of him by one at a time, give it a powerful shake and pull, and thus find out his weakest and his strongest points. First, let us consider him civilly, (tho' a most uncivil beast he is) or as a creature of law.

Henry: Oh! mother, I am sorry you have begun with that horn, for the whole problem of government and law is beyond my comprehension, and so much has been said upon both sides of the "no license" question, that I am completely *mystified.*

Mother: Then I have hit the very point on which you need light. The "no license" question is a simple one as are all questions of right and wrong. Men are seldom if ever troubled to know what is right, but when they come down one step to decide on what is politic or expedient then opens a wide field for debate, on which, the love of pure justice should not appear. The object of all just government is to protect the weak against the strong, and to make laws by which the greatest amount of happiness can be secured to the greatest number.

Henry: Well, mother, this government certainly has no such object in view, it is from what you have mentioned quite the opposite. The helpless wife and children of the poor drunkard are not protected against the grasping rumseller but on the contrary, the law allows him to strip our fields of their luxuriant crops, and torture what is intended for man's sustenance into a horrible poison, which if he will give the government a certain sum of money, he may sell to any one who sees fit to buy. How comes it with such an army of temperance men, with crowds of christians at our polls, that a distillery is allowed to stand, or a rumseller hold up an unblushing face in our midst?

Mother: The fact is, my son, that government thus far is a failure. Our leading men have invariably sacrificed what they know to be right to their own personal popularity. They fully believe that there should be laws to prevent the distilling and vending of alcohol, but how many of them would sustain their lawmakers in the passing of such laws, or their officers in seeing them enforced? Public sentiment is higher than law—laws in advance of the people are mere chaff.

Henry: Then it seems that the first step to be taken in all reforms is to teach the people what is right, and is it not clearly right that no man should be allowed to poison his neighbor, either at once or by degrees? But in the meantime, while we are getting public sentiment right, what would you do with your vote?

Mother: To vote right is one way to right public sentiment. Let every man who is not a tetotaler, understand that he cannot be supported for any office, and his conversion might be considered hopeful, though there is one difficulty in this class of converts, they do not stay converted.

Henry: I should think a majority in all our towns were temperance men, and public sentiment seems to be right, for the clergy generally have come into the ranks, and we hear no more of Christ's drinking wine, or the Bible allowing the moderate use of it, and now where are the laws? It seems to me we are in advance of them.

Mother: I have my fears from the slow movement of the political engine in this matter, that very many of the temperance host are like some christians in our churches, mere nominal members, who seize on certain empty forms and let go the essential substance, but I do not know the statistics on this point of numbers. I must ask some of the Lily ladies, and if it be true that the tetotalers do outnumber the wine bibbers, we shall have a right to demand that the drunkard be restored to his manhood, that the rumseller and distiller be at once educated at the expense of the State, for some higher employment, and that the rich harvests of grain that have hitherto been doomed to the horrid den and smoke of the infernal distillery, be sent across the mighty ocean, on missions of love, to the starving children of the Emerald Isle.

Conversation No. II

Henry: Since our last conversation I have still been thinking of the license law; now tell me mother what you think the duty of government is on this question.

Mother: There is a great difference of opinion among even great men on this point. Some say there should be no law about it, that every one should be free to sell as much alcohol as he pleases. They see no reason why it should have more attention, or peculiar legislation, than arsenic, nux vomica, or many other poisons. They say there is as much alcohol sold under the present laws as before. It is now done covertly, yet the laws are continually violated, but by trickery and false swearing the offenders avoid detection. Some say that those who sell should pay government something for the injury they do others, as well as for the great *respect* and *honor* they secure for themselves!!

Henry: Why pay government anything?

Mother: Because government must take care of all the paupers made by the rumseller, and whatever poor goose he takes in hand is generally picked pretty clean.

Henry: But by receiving pay does not government sanction the traffic?

Mother: Certainly, the partaker is as bad as the thief.

Henry: But you have not told me what you think the duty of government to be in this matter.

Mother: I think instead of playing bo-peep any longer with the rumseller, government should pass some stringent laws, forbidding altogether the distilling and importing of intoxicating drinks.

Henry: But if this could be done where wo'd we get what we need for medicinal purposes?

Mother: Prestnitz tells us that cold water is the best medicine, both for the inner and the outer man and I incline to agree with him. I should feel much safer, to have you pledge me, now that you are starting in life, never "to touch, taste, or handle" the unclean thing under any circumstances than if you made an exception in case of sickness,—for I should have my fears that you would be like poor Pat who signed the pledge and never kept it. On being asked, how it was that he a temperance man got drunk every day, ah! said he, "I take it as a medicine, and faith I have never seen a well day since I took the pledge."

Henry: But could government put down the distilleries?

Mother: Certainly, she could do it absolutely, as Gen. Jackson put down the United States Bank, and turn the distillers out to graze, or she could buy him out, compensate him, as Great Britain did her West Indian planters when she emancipated their slaves, and save money in the operation.

Henry: How could she save money?

Mother: She could put the grain which makes the alcohol to a better purpose, also the man who makes the pauper. Political economists will all agree that grain and sober men are far better property to a state than distilleries, alcohol and rumsellers. But as the majority rules in this country, the laws will come from the people and can be no better than they are and if by some accidental advantage a virtuous minority succeed in passing a wise law, it is of no value unless the mass so regard it, and this brings us to the consideration of the superiority of moral power, over all other kinds.

Henry: Well; how would you use moral power effectually? We have talked our political power into a thin mist, so that there seems to be no such thing unless backed up by something else; now I hope this other power has a spine of its own.

Mother: It has. How straight it can stand, and how much it can do, shall be the subject of our next conversation.

Conversation No. III

Mother: Having found in our former discussions that political power had no solid foundations of its own, but relied on some unseen power, let us now see what this is, and in what its strength consists.

Henry: I suppose you mean moral power.

Mother: Yes, an appeal to man's highest sentiments rather than to his pecuniary interests: to vote a man down does not put him down, to vote him good does not make him so. We have decided by law that there shall be no rumselling, yet the rumseller lives, and grows rich. Depend on it that kindness and truth will do for the rumseller what it has done for the drunkard.

Henry: Do you think the rumseller is governed by the same laws of mind that we are?

Mother: Certainly. Moral beings can only judge rightly of others by themselves; the moment they give a different nature to any of their own kind, they utterly fail. The drunkard was considered hopeless until it was discovered that he was governed by the same laws of mind as the sober man, then with what magic power by kindness and love, was he raised from the slough of despond, and placed rejoicing upon high land. Thus will it be with the rumseller. He too is a man,—formed in the image of God, and though by a false life that image may be dimmed, yet brush aside the dust of a perverted education, and the likeness will appear though ever so faintly seen. Law and denunciation have failed to do the work, let us try the power of sympathy.

Henry: Why, Mother, how could you feel any sympathy for the rumseller, whose heart seems so hardened against the poor perishing drunkard?

Mother: The golden rule tells us to feel for others as we would have others feel for us. Now suppose, my son, that you were so benighted as not to see the sin of rumselling, or if you saw it, so wicked as to sacrifice your sense of right to your love of gain,—how would you like me to treat you—with detestation and abhorrence, denouncing you at the corners of the street, and in all the public assemblies of the people, or with kindness and consideration?

Henry: I should rather have you sit down with me as now, and calmly reason the subject together; abuse might make me angry and array all my bad passions against you,—that whatever truths you might utter would all be colored by my hate. But if you made a kind appeal to me, I would listen, and no doubt think of what you said.

Mother: Just so, that is the whole secret of moral power. Let us look a little into the philosophy of it. I will still suppose you the ignorant, degraded, wicked rumseller. Now to take a phreno-logical view of you, certain organs in your brain are too active, others not enough so; all that is necessary to make you a good man is to restore the balance of power, rouse up your benevo-lence and conscientiousness, and enlighten your reason, that great helmsman of the brain.

Henry: But how is this to be done!

Mother: By constant appeals to these higher organs. A man is never radically better through fear or force, but each time you rouse into action one of the moral sentiments, you strengthen it and it will the more readily act again.

Henry: What organ makes a man sell rum?

Mother: Too much acquisitiveness, and too little conscientiousness, the same that makes a man sell tough chickens, rancid butter, wet sugar, milk well-watered, damaged muslin, calicoes that fade, measly pork and asthmatic horses. The same that induces the dentist to dig holes in good teeth, the doctor to bleed, blis-ter and dose his patient for every trifling ailment, the lawyer to council his client to go to law when he knows he has no case, and the minister to pervert the truth to please his people.

Henry: Alas! "for poor humanity." I shall begin to think, in spite of all your teachings to the contrary, that man is totally depraved. But do you think all these men equally guilty with the rumseller?

Mother: Infinitely more so. The intelligent, the thinking men of our land are they who have public sentiment in their keeping. Who seems to you the most in fault, the poor, ignorant rumseller, or our distinguished politicians, who on the eve of an election place hundreds of dollars in the hands of their emissaries through all our cities and towns, to be spent in rum,—that unwary and simple souls may be made to vote the *right way?*

Henry: The latter class clearly. The rumseller is such a contempt-ible little devil that he had no influence aside from his rum,—but who can estimate the evil done our cause, by the intelligent, respectable gentlemen, who spout *temperance* most eloquently in the forum but live it not in their lives?

Mother: I am glad you agree with me.

Henry: Yes, you are right, and now instead of firing that moral gun of yours at the rumsellers alone,—that dismal bird, more "grim, ungainly, ghastly, gaunt and ominous" than ever was the raven sung by Edgar Poe, you must have one of those six-barrelled California revolvers, that you may bring down at the same time from their airy heights more than one strong bird of prey.

Mother: Be sure that you understand me.—I do not excuse the rumseller. He is deeply guilty,—the blood of many a soul lies at his door,—neither do I object to political action on this question; if it be possible, the traffic in intoxicating drinks should be stopped at once, and by law; all that I say is, public sentiment is higher than law and to have this right you must enlarge the heads and hearts of the people.

Conversation No. IV

Mother: I heard a sermon a few days since that pleased me very much. It was on Temperance, and the comparative guilt of the rum-seller, distiller, and the law-maker, who encourages the traffic.

Henry: Did the preacher agree with you in thinking them all equally guilty?

Mother: Yes, and he illustrated his position in this way. Suppose a peaceable traveller is waylaid—one man compels him to stop, a second robs him of all he has, and a third blows out his brains; now which of these men does the law hold most guilty? Does it take no notice of the first two, but visit the penalty of the crime on him alone who finished the work? By no means.—In the eye of the law they are all equally guilty, and would receive the same sentence at a bar of justice.

Henry: Was anything said of the license laws?

Mother: He said our legislators might with the same propriety, license a certain number of men to go about setting fire to their own and their neighbors' houses, according as their pleasure or interest might dictate. If any one complained, they might argue that this was a natural taste that must be gratified; men as well as children love to see fire. If in the exercise of this taste, any injury were done, the State would pay damages. If any were stripped of home and all its comforts, the State had prepared Poor Houses where they could be sheltered, fed, and clothed. If any lives were lost, the State would supply them with a fine coffin and decent burial. Surely such magnanimity on the part of the State—such even handed justice places it above all blame.

Henry: And this I suppose is the true state of the case. A number of *wise men* get together and create a kind of rumselling aristocracy. They give a certain number of men the right to destroy with their liquid fire, both the lives and property of their neighbors. Then, when the rumseller has finished his work—clothed the drunkard in rags, turned his wife and children into the street, these *wise* ones make another law, by which the drunkard and his family shall be re-housed and supported at the public crib.

Mother: Burning up houses and getting men drunk are very expensive amusements, and fall most heavily on those who are the least amused. For instance, all the drunkards' widows who, by diligence and industry, may have provided homes for themselves, are taxed from their small earnings to build and keep up these Poor Houses. Such a woman is doubly wronged. First, the rumseller sanctioned by the State, robs her of husband and all she has of this world's goods. Then if she have the native energy, by hard labor to get for herself a new home, and gather round her something she can call her own, the State comes to collect its annual poor tax, and she must pay her proportion.

Henry: I think the law-maker and rumseller should pay the poor tax. It seems to be grossly unjust, that woman should be taxed when she has no voice in making the laws. I begin to view all the reforms of our day in a new light. It is now plain to me that to make our race better we must begin much deeper than at first I had supposed.

Mother: Reformers err in trying to make the surface of things smooth, whilst the waters of pollution run deep and fierce below. This brings us to the third part of our subject, a social power. We have seen that political power is a mere name and can do nothing of itself. We have seen that no good work can be done but by moral fervor; let us now see the value of social power in the temperance cause.

Henry: I thought we had already done what we could socially. We have banished wine from most of our churches, our homes, and places of employment and a young man can now be considered quite respectable, without ever being drunk, or even drinking a glass of champaigne.

Mother: Here is the field where we feel the weight of woman's influence. I blush for my sex that woman is not always found on the side of those who love truth, justice, and mercy. Much has been done socially, but more remains to be done. Wine is still used in our fashionable hotels, at many public places of amusement, at private parties, and alas! for the ignorance of woman, even in the nursery.

Henry: Are there any mothers in our days so wicked as to give their young children alcohol?

Mother: Theirs is the sin of ignorance; they know not what they do. There are kind, generous, respectable women in our day, who drink wine and beer, and give it to their friends, their husbands, brothers, and children. No true mother would deliberately injure her own child, therefore when I hear of one who takes stimulating drinks during the period of lactation, and uses brandy as the panacea for all her children's ills, I set her down as ignorant of great physiological laws, for the violation of which she and her offspring must certainly suffer.

Henry: Do you think the use of intoxicating drinks injures the mind as well as the body?

Mother: Yes. No man, woman, or child, can take alcohol in any form, with impunity.—Though the light of the mind may not be wholly put out, yet its brightness will be somewhat dimmed. All physiologists agree that the intellect of a young child is permanently injured by the frequent use of cordials, paragoric or brandy. To say nothing then of the long train of bodily diseases that follow this treatment in infancy—there is the mind, a wreck to folly and ignorance. O! ye drunken fathers, and thoughtless mothers, how great is your responsibility. Be not surprised that your sons and daughters are fools or idiots. Wonder not at the *inscrutable ways of Providence,* but begin now to learn and obey the immutable laws which govern all mind and matter. Thus you see the children suffer in being weak in body and mind, and the parents in seeing them so. Verily, "a foolish son is heaviness to his mother."

Henry: Do you think temperance people ought to attend parties at houses where a room is set aside for drinking brandy and wines?

Mother: No parents should trust their sons and daughters in such houses, unattended by a wise Mentor.

Henry: But may not parents too be tempted? It seems to me that the same principle that would keep us from the rum hotel in our travels, would also keep us from the rum parties. I would not for the world go where I might chance to see one of Eve's fair daughters with the wine cup in her hand. I have learned to look up to woman with a kind of veneration, as the repository of all that is left us of truth and goodness on the earth, and I would not see her stoop to minister to man's baser appetites, nor to degrade herself to his level.

Mother: In regard to these parties, now that the mass of the people are professedly tetotalers, it is in bad taste to have wine at all. If the lady or gentleman who give the party, chance that day to *need a little as medicine,* why let them take it secretly. There is no use in dosing all their guests, or in disgusting them with the sight of that compound of log wood, sugar, water, and alcohol, called wine. I have often thought on seeing a group of these wine bibbing lords and ladies standing round, sipping their nectar, descanting on its peculiar merits, its delicious flavour, rich color and delicate perfume, how the manufacturer would laugh in his sleeve, could he but be for a while an invisible listener. Alas! for these epicures, these connoiseurs, they do not in fact know the difference between the pure juice of the grape, and the chemical compound now extant, called wine.

Henry: What do you think of using wine at the communion?

Mother: I think in so doing, christians are more governed by custom than principle. Cold water might as well be substituted for the pure juice of the grape, as the so called wine of our times.

Henry: I wish, mother, you would mention some of the things to be done in our social relations.

Mother: All reform must begin here, and with the women first. It is the mother who stamps her sons. Make the women of a nation wise and virtuous, and the men will be so too. In this case each one has a special duty on his own.

The Pastor—he can teach and preach temperance wherever he goes, and he ought to go into a great many places where he does not,—he can banish wine from the communion, and the rumseller with it.

The Doctor—should not prescribe wine and beer for the weak and dyspectic. Many a man and woman owe their ruin to an M.D.'s proscription. They might better far have died of dyspepsia or enervation, than to sleep in a drunkard's grave.

The Lawyer—he should not so demean himself as ever to be

found on the rum side of any case in court. Let him see that the rumseller has justice at all times, when his rum is not in question, but there let him take care of himself.

The Farmer—shame on the honest farmer,—who claims to be a temperance man, and then sells his grain to the distiller. His hard labor thus applied is worse than lost to the world.

The Rumseller's Wife—she holds a most responsible position. There is, alas! a kind of tradition among women, that they must defend their husbands' actions and opinions, whatever they may be. Now this is all wrong. A wife who sustains her husband in sin, is not a true friend to him. I have often thought what I would do were I a rumseller's wife. Well, I should take the most pungent temperance papers I could find, and give them to the bar-room loafers to read. I should have as much temperance literature as possible all over the house, and discourse on the subject whenever I could get an audience in the bar-room, *his honour, the master,* being out. I should often propose moral problems to his *honour,* such as the justice of taking all the drunkard's earnings from his wife and children. I should make the children sing temperance songs, and ask questions on the medicinal properties of alcohol. I should water the whiskey barrels, jugs, and bottles freely, and give every drunkard I caught on the premises a cold shower. I should have a large watering-pot painted on the sign that all drunkards might know what they had to expect at that house—and fifty other things I could do to make my husband uncomfortable in his business, and thin out his daily visitors. I know I could end one rum establishment, unaided and alone.

Henry: I fear the rumseller would cut short your glorious campaign by proposing to you to find some other field for your operations, or in other words, turn you out of doors.

Mother: Not if he knew there was such a public sentiment among women, that he could get no other wife to play second fiddle to him in such a business. I have no doubt if we could call a convention of all our countrywomen, and after due counsel and consideration, commence an united and systematic mode of attack, we could torment every rumseller in the land, out of his business in one year, and utterly ruin the logwood *speculators* for all coming time.

Conversation No. V

Henry: What is the reason that Temperance is not a party question?

Mother: Because it is generally considered *unwise* to carry one's principles into his politics or religion.

Henry: I am sure they are making slavery a test question, both in church and state.

Mother: Not in those states where the evil exists. Here in New York our politicians can afford to discourse on slavery, picture forth all its evils, and denounce those who abet and support it; because there are no slaveholders to vote here. But think you we could get any of these *humane politicians* on the eve of an election to deliver a course of lectures on temperance; condemning the liquor traffic—urging the people to demand stringent laws against the rumseller, distiller, and the farmer who helps to support the traffic? Verily, no!! There are rumsellers to *vote* in New York!

Henry: Instead of granting licenses as is now done for a stipulated sum of money, would it not be well to set the price a little higher, and forbid the exercise of the right to the elective franchise during the continuance in the traffic? The rumseller cannot pay too dear for all the evil he does. In this way he would be stripped of all political influence, and the state might still reap her unjust gains.

Mother: The state gains nothing by the liquor traffic. Let me give you some statistics that you may judge how great her taxes must be. "There are 1,700 criminals in the New York state prisons, of whom 1,300 are indebted to the rumseller's merchandize for their crimes. The Empire state has to make provision for 880 insane persons. Of these 400 owe their loss of reason to rum and rumsellers. Of the 1,900 paupers in the poorhouses of this state, 1,700 owe their pauperism to strong drink." The city of New York alone supports 8,000 houses for the worship of Bachus. Now can the small sum of money which each rumseller pays yearly for his license be any compensation for the evil he does in a pecuniary point of view? Your idea of taking from the rumseller all voice in the government, would undoubtedly end the traffic.

Henry: I would not *take* it from him; that would be a violation of right. It would be a fair exchange, voluntary on his part. For I suppose these rumsellers are so wedded to their business, that like Esau of old, they would sell their birthright for a mess of potage.

Mother: Could we induce the rumseller to give up his vote, we should no doubt soon see a new state of things. Our candidates for office would then find temperance a grand theme for eloquence, and a subject very dear to their hearts; and our legislators would be full of sympathy for the poor drunkard, and propose many plans to relieve the state of the unnecessary expenditures caused by the rum traffic.

FRANCES ELLEN WATKINS HARPER
1825–1911

Frances Ellen Watkins Harper, an African American poet and novelist, was a tireless worker for reform. Watkins Harper actively supported abolition, temperance, and woman's rights. After emancipation, she worked persistently to improve circumstances for blacks.

Watkins Harper became an officer of the Philadelphia WCTU in 1875 and, later, of the Pennsylvania state WCTU; in 1876, Frances E. Willard introduced her formally to the WCTU national convention in Newark. By 1883, Harper had become National Superintendent of Work among Colored People for the national WCTU. She was the first black woman to serve on the executive committee and the board of superintendents for the national union.

Although Harper challenged some members and local unions for their racist treatment of African American members, especially in the South, she acknowledged the "Christian affiliation" she found among others. Believing that the WCTU "has in its hands one of the grandest opportunities that God ever pressed into the hands of womanhood of any country" (Boyd 206), she continued her association with the union as both organizer and lecturer throughout the century. In her capacity as leader, "she tried to help those who wished to join the white group to do so and those who preferred to organize themselves separately to do that" (Hine 535). (For further information on Harper's association with the WCTU, see Mattingly.)

Harper is best known for her novel *Iola Leroy; or Shadows Uplifted* (1892), a story set in the reconstruction South that deals primarily with matters of racial politics; for her temperance short story, "The Two Offers" (1859); and for her poetry. *Sowing and Reaping,* excerpted here, was serialized in the *Christian Recorder* (1876–1877). Protagonist Belle Gordon breaks her engagement to Charles Romaine because of his drinking. Her cousin, Jeanette Roland, chides her for tossing aside such a likely prospect—a handsome, wealthy young man. According to Jeanette, "young men will sow their wild oats," but Belle insists that "a young man has no more right to sow his wild oats than a young woman" and fears to join her future with someone of intemperate character. Jeanette eventually marries Charles Romaine, and Belle marries an admirable and temperate friend, Paul Clifford, whom she has come to know while ministering to the poor and sick. In chapter 17, below, Paul first seeks Belle's assent to marriage, and concerned friends react to developments in Jeanette's marriage. The discussion permits Harper to provide arguments, not only against association with intemperate men, but also in favor of greater rights for women, especially the right to vote.

from *Sowing and Reaping*

"I am sorry, very sorry," said Belle Gordon, as a shadow of deep distress flitted over her pale sad face. She was usually cheerful and serene in her manner; but now it seemed as if the very depths of her soul had been stirred by some mournful and bitter memory. "Your question was so unexpected and—"

"And what!" said Paul in a tone of sad expectancy, "so unwelcome?"

"It was so sudden, I was not prepared for it."

"I do not," said Paul, "ask an immediate reply. Give yourself ample time for consideration."

"Mr. Clifford," said Belle, her voice gathering firmness as she proceeded, "while all the relations of life demand that there should be entire truthfulness between us and our fellow creatures, I think we should be especially sincere and candid in our dealings with each other on this question of marriage, a question not only as affecting our own welfare but that of others, a relation which may throw its sunshine or shadow over the track of unborn ages. Permit me now to say to you, that there is no gentleman of my acquaintance whom

I esteem more highly than yourself; but when you ask me for my heart and hand, I almost feel as if I had no heart to give; and you know it would be wrong to give my hand where I could not place my heart."

"But would it be impossible for you to return my affection?"

"I don't know, but I am only living out my [vow] of truthfulness when I say to you, I feel as if I had been undone for love. You tell that in offering your hand that you bring me a heart unhackneyed in the arts of love, that my heart is the first and only shrine on which you have ever laid the wealth of your affections. I cannot say the same in reply. I have had my bright and beautiful day dream, but it has faded, and I have learned what is the hardest of all lessons for a woman to learn. I have learned to live without love."

"Oh no," said Paul, "not to live without love. In darkened homes how many grateful hearts rejoice to hear your footsteps on the threshold. I have seen the eyes of young Arabs in the street grow brighter as you approached and say, 'That's my lady, she comes to see my mam when she's sick.' and I have seen little girls in the street quicken their face to catch a loving smile from their dear Sunday school teacher. Oh Miss Belle instead of living without love, I think you are surrounded with a cordon of loving hearts."

"Yes, and I appreciate them—but this is not the love to which I refer. I mean a love which is mine, as anything else on earth is mine, a love precious, enduring and strong, which brings hope and joy and sunshine over one's path in life. A love which commands my allegiance and demands my respect. This is the love I have learned to do without, and perhaps the poor and needy had learned to love me less, had this love surrounded me more."

"Miss Belle, perhaps I was presumptuous, to have asked a return of the earnest affection I have for you; but I had hoped that you would give the question some consideration; and may I not hope that you will think kindly of my proposal? Oh Miss Gordon, ever since the death of my sainted mother, I have had in my mind's eye the ideal of a woman nobly planned, beautiful, intellectual, true and affectionate, and you have filled out that ideal in all its loveliest proportions, and I hope that my desire will not be like reaching out to some bright particular star and wishing to win it. It seems to me," he said with increasing earnestness, "whatever obstacle may be in the way, I would go through fire and water to remove it."

"I am sorry," said Belle as if speaking to herself, and her face had an absent look about it, as if instead of being interested in the living present she was groping amid the ashes of the dead past. At length she said, "Mr. Clifford, permit me to say in the first place, let there be truth between us. If my heart seems callous and indifferent to your love, believe me it is warm to esteem and value you as a friend, I might almost say as a brother, for in sympathy of feeling and congeniality of disposition you are nearer to me than my own brother; but I do not think were I so inclined that it would be advisable for me to accept your hand without letting you know something of my past history. I told you a few moments since that I had my day dream. Permit me to tell you, for I think you are entitled to my confidence. The object of that day dream was Charles Romaine."

"Charles Romaine!" and there was a tone of wonder in the voice, and a puzzled look on the face of Paul Clifford.

"Yes! Charles Romaine, not as you know him now, with the marks of dissipation on his once handsome face, but Charles Romaine, as I knew him when he stood upon the threshold of early manhood, the very incarnation of beauty, strength and grace. Not Charles Romaine with the blurred and bloated countenance, the staggering gait, the confused and vacant eye; but Charles Romaine as a young, handsome and talented lawyer, the pride of our village, the hope of his father and the joy of his mother; before whom the future was opening full of rich and rare promises. Need I tell you that when he sought my hand in preference to all the other girls in our village, that I gave him what I never can give to another, the first, deep love of my girlish heart. For nearly a whole year I wore his betrothal ring upon my finger, when I saw to my utter anguish and dismay that he was fast becoming a drunkard. Oh! Mr. Clifford if I could have saved him I would have taken blood from every vein and strength from every nerve. We met frequently at entertainments. I noticed time after time, the effects of the wine he had imbibed, upon his manner and conversation. At first I shrank from remonstrating with him, until the burden lay so heavy on my heart that I felt I must speak out, let the consequences be what they might. And so one evening I told him plainly and seriously my fears about his future. He laughed lightly and said my fears were unfounded; that I was nervous and giving way to idle fancies; that his father always had wine at the table, and that he had never seen him under the influence of liquor. Silenced, but not convinced, I watched his course with painful solicitude. All remonstrances on my part seemed thrown away; he always had the precedent of his father to plead in reply to my earnest entreaties. At last when remonstrances and entreaties seemed to be all in vain, I resolved to break the engagement. It may have been a harsh and hard alternative, but I would not give my hand where my respect could not follow. It may be that I thought too much of my own happiness, but I felt that marriage must be for me positive misery or positive happiness, and I feared that if I married a man so lacking in self-control as to become a common drunkard, that when I ceased to love and respect him, I should be constantly tempted to hate and despise him. I think one of the saddest fates that can befall a woman is to be tied for life to a miserable bloated wreck of humanity. There may be some women with broad generous hearts, and great charity, strong enough to lift such men out of the depths, but I had no such faith in my strength and so I gave him back his ring. He accepted it, but we parted as friends. For awhile after our engagement was broken, we occasionally met at the houses of our mutual friends in social gatherings and I noticed with intense satisfaction that whenever wine was offered he scrupulously abstained from ever tasting a drop, though I think at times his self-control was severely tested. Oh! what hope revived in my heart. Here I said to myself is compensation for all I have suffered, if by it he shall be restored to manhood usefulness and society, and learn to make his life not a thing of careless ease and sensuous indulgence, but of noble struggle and high and holy endeavor. But while I was picturing out for him a magnificent future, imagining the lofty triumphs of his intellect—an intellect grand in its achievements and glorious in its possibilities, my beautiful daydream was rudely broken up, and vanished away like the rays of sunset mingling with the shadows of night. My Aunt Mrs. Roland, celebrated her silver-wedding and my cousin's birth-day by giving a large entertainment; and among other things she had a plentiful supply of wine. Mr. Romaine had lately made the acquaintance of my cousin Jeanette Roland. She was both beautiful in person and fascinating in her manners, and thoughtlessly she held a glass of wine in her hand and asked Mr. Romaine if he would not honor the occasion, by drinking her mother's health. For a moment he hesitated, his cheek paled and flushed alternately, he looked irresolute. While I watched him in silent anguish it seemed as if the agony of years was compressed in a few moments. I tried to catch his eye but failed, and with a slight tremor in his hand he lifted the glass to his lips and drank. I do not think I would have felt greater anguish had I seen him suddenly drowned in sight of land. Oh! Mr. Clifford that night comes before me so vividly, it seems as if I am living it all over again. I do not think Mr. Romaine has ever recovered from the reawakening of his appetite. He has since married Jeanette. I meet her occasionally. She has a beautiful home, dresses magnificently, and has a retinue of servants; and yet I fancy she is not happy. That somewhere hidden out of sight there is a worm eating at the core of her life. She has a way of dropping her eyes and an absent look about her that I do not fully understand, but it seems to me that I miss the old elasticity of her spirits, the merry ring of her voice, the pleasant thrills of girlish laughter, and though she never confesses it to me I doubt that Jeanette is happy. And with this sad experience in the past can you blame me if I am slow, very slow to let the broken tendrils of my heart entwine again?"

"Miss Belle," said Paul Clifford catching eagerly at the smallest straw of hope, "if you can not give me the first love of a fresh young life, I am content with the rich [aftermath?] of your maturer years, and ask from life no higher prize; may I not hope for that?"

"I will think on it but for the present let us change the subject."

"Do you think Jeanette is happy? She seems so different from what she used to be," said Miss Tabitha Jones to several friends who were spending the evening with her.

"Happy!" replied Mary Gladstone, "don't see what's to hinder her from being happy. She has everything that heart can wish. I was down to her house yesterday, and she has just moved in her new home. It has all the modern improvements, and everything is in excellent taste. Her furniture is of the latest style, and I think it is really superb."

"Yes," said her sister, "and she dresses magnificently. Last week she showed me a most beautiful set of jewelry, and a camel's hair shawl, and I believe it is real camel's hair. I think you could almost run it through a ring. If I had all she has, I think I should be as happy as the days are long. I don't believe I would let a wave of trouble roll across my peaceful breast."

"Oh, Annette," said Mrs. Gladstone, "don't speak so extravagantly, and I don't like to hear you quote those lines for such an occasion."

"Why not mother? Where's the harm?"

"That hymn has been associated in my mind with my earliest

religious impressions and experience, and I don't like to see you lift it out of its sacred associations, for such a trifling occasion."

"Oh mother you are so strict. I shall never be able to keep time with you, but I do think, if I was well off as Jeanette, that I would be blithe and happy as a lark, and instead of that she seems to be constantly drooping and fading."

"Annette," said Mrs. Gladstone, "I knew a woman who possesses more than Jeanette does, and yet she died of starvation."

"Died of starvation! Why, when, and where did that happen? and what became of her husband?"

"He is in society, caressed and [petted?] on by the young girls of his set and I have seen a number of managing mammas to whom I have imagined he would not be an objectionable son-in-law."

"Do I know him mother?"

"No! and I hope you never will."

"Well mother I would like to know how he starved his wife to death and yet escaped the law."

"The law helped him."

"Oh mother!" said both girls opening their eyes in genuine astonishment.

"I thought," said Mary Gladstone, "it was the province of the law to protect women, I was just telling Miss Basanquet yesterday, when she was talking about woman's suffrage that I had as many rights as I wanted and that I was willing to let my father and brothers do all the voting for me."

"Forgetting my dear, that there are millions of women who haven't such fathers and brothers as you have. No my dear, when you examine the matter, a little more closely, you will find there are some painful inequalities in the law for women."

"But mother, I do think it would be a dreadful thing for women to vote Oh! just think of women being hustled and crowded at the polls by rude men, their breaths reeking with whiskey and tobacco, the very air heavy with their oaths. And then they have the polls at public houses. Oh mother, I never want to see the day when women vote."

"Well I do, because we have one of the kindest and best fathers and husbands and good brothers, who would not permit the winds of heaven to visit us too roughly, there is no reason we should throw ourselves between the sunshine and our less fortunate sisters who shiver in the blast."

"But mother, I don't see how voting would help us, I am sure we have influence. I have often heard papa say that you were the first to awaken him to a sense of the enormity of slavery. Now mother if we women would use our influence with our fathers, brothers, husbands, and sons, could we not have everything we want."

"No, my dear we could not, with all our influence we never could have the same sense of responsibility which flows from the possession of power. I want women to possess power as well as influence, I want every Christian woman as she passes by a grog-shop or liquor saloon, to feel that she has on her heart a burden of responsibility for its existence, I hold my dear that a nation as well as an individual should have a conscience, and on this liquor question there is room for woman's conscience not merely as a persuasive influence but as enlightened and aggressive power."

"Well Ma I think you would make a first class stump speaker. I expect when women vote we shall be constantly having calls, for the gifted and talented Mrs. Gladstone to speak on the duties and perils of the hour."

"And I would do it, I would go among my sister women and try to persuade them to use their vote as a moral lever, not to make home less happy, but society more holy. I would have good and sensible women, grave in manner, and cultured in intellect, attend the primary meetings and bring their moral influence and political power to frown down corruption, chicanery, and low cunning."

"But mother just think if women went to the polls how many vicious ones would go?"

"I hope and believe for the honor of our sex that the vicious women of the community are never in the majority, that for one woman whose feet turn aside from the paths of rectitude that there are thousands of feet that never stray into forbidden paths, and today I believe there is virtue enough in society to confront its vice, and intelligence enough to grapple with its ignorance."

MARY DWINELL CHELLIS
DATES UNKNOWN

In her prolific writing about intemperance, Mary Dwinell Chellis addresses most of the issues typical of women's temperance fiction. In *Wealth and Wine* (New York: National Temperance Society and Publication House, 1874), for example, she acknowledges the widespread nature of hardships intemperance brings on women, confirming the hypocrisy of conventional wisdom that women are protected by men:

> It is not necessary that I trace the gradual descent of this family from poverty to abject want. Theirs was no peculiar experience of wretchedness. All over our land there are wives and children, who have once known the comforts of luxurious homes, now working in close rooms to earn a meagre supply of the coarsest food; while husbands and fathers, false to every sacred pledge, and every obligation or duty, spend their time in drunken revelry and debauch. (60)

Chellis attempts to gain acceptance for the necessity of divorce for some women by characterizing Jane Warland as someone who had never considered the possibility for herself. Out of desperation, Jane asks her friend Dr. Saunders for help in obtaining a divorce. Never having expected to be concerned with such a rupture, she knows nothing about correct legal procedure:

> Please tell the doctor for me, that whatever it is, I will pay it so soon as I can earn the money. I have never before wished to know how divorces are obtained. I consider them dreadful, and dis-

graceful; but there are alternatives more dreadful, and more disgraceful. The time has been when I thought otherwise; and there are those who believe that a woman should endure all wrong and outrage, rather than claim a release from her marriage vows. If they are right, then God forgive me, for I must claim this release. (68–69)

Chellis establishes women's right to divorce by supporting Jane with two sources, the authority figure Dr. Saunders, as illustrated in the chapter below, and her son, John. Dr. Saunders tells Jane, "There's no law of God or man that makes it [your] duty to live with him" (96). And John's pleading with his mother demonstrates the imperative for legal changes in custody laws:

I am growing older every day, and I ought to get started in the business I am to follow. You must get the lawyers, or the judges, or somebody else—I don't exactly know who—to give me all to you, so no one else will have any claims upon me. You'll do that, won't you, mother? . . . [Y]ou must get a divorce from your husband. Mother! mother! (64–65)

Chellis also affirms Jane's wish to be independent. When she leaves her husband, Hastings, Jane returns to her father's farm: "The cottage was repaired, and furnished comfortably. She could be happier there than in her brother's family, and she had already made plans for her own support" (61). Jane insists on working and taking care of her son and herself financially rather than depending upon her father or brother.

In addition, Chellis illustrates the double standard for women and men. In the chapter provided below, Jane tells her son and nephew of her own association with alcohol. Prior to this chapter, Chellis has told her reader of Jane's one-time overindulgence, explaining Hastings's reaction to Jane's indiscretion:

Often had her husband returned to her in a like state, and as often had she received him without reproaches. In the first years of their marriage, she had reason to feel herself injured by his conduct.

But now *his honor* was sullied. His feelings were outraged. No man could forgive such conduct in a wife. He waited only until she could appreciate her condition, when, gazing at the beautiful woman he had lured from the simple habits of her childhood, he exhausted his rage in words which would pollute the ears of the vilest outcast. (89)

The chapter provided below demonstrates Chellis's support of divorce for women married to alcoholic or abusive husbands. Jane Bedlow has married Hastings Warland, a young lawyer and son of wealthy parents. But Hastings is not interested in practicing law; instead, he participates in continuous rounds of festivity and general dissipation. The family's living standard declines as Hastings wastes their resources, and eventually he becomes physically abusive to Jane and to their son, John. Hungry and desperate, Jane returns to live in a cottage on her father's property, but Hastings follows and demands to live with her.

Hastings becomes drunk and attacks John, now fifteen, so severely that John's life is threatened. Dr. Saunders takes this opportunity to provide travel money for Hastings with the agreement that Hastings leave and remain out of town, threatening that if John dies, Hastings will be liable to legal action. Thus, Chellis underscores the fact that the law sanctions abuse of women and children; only when physical assault becomes life-threatening might the law take action. Dr. Saunders not only encourages Jane in her pursuit of divorce but also suggests that she refuse to let her marital mistake darken her future.

Other characters are Mabel Pease, orphaned at birth and heir to a fortune (another example of Chellis's independent women, Mabel takes an interest in business and decides she will manage her own money when she comes of age), and Raleigh Bedlow, John's seventeen-year-old cousin; all live on the family property.

(See additional biographical information on Mary Dwinell Chellis in part 1.)

from *Wealth and Wine*

One dreary winter evening, Mr. Bedlow, anxious for his daughter's comfort, sent Raleigh to visit her, and, if necessary, to remain through the night. Her husband had been away since early in the morning, and could not be expected to return for many hours.

"I am so glad you have come," exclaimed John, as his cousin entered, bringing a well-filled basket. "Mother and I have been lonely. Hickory-nuts too. That was a kind thought in you."

"That was grandfather's thought. He said it was a good evening to crack nuts, roast apples, and drink cider; only your mother don't quite approve of cider."

"But *I* do," replied John. "I wholly approve of it. I have drunk it when it was sparkling as champagne."

"That is why I disapprove of it," said Mrs. Warland with a sigh. "O boys! I wish I could make you feel about such things as I do."

"Why, Aunt Jane, do you think there is any danger of our becoming drunkards, because we drink some cider once in a while!"

"I don't think there is any danger of your becoming a drunkard, Raleigh. Your father was a consistent temperance man. But it is different with John. He must fight an inherited appetite. No one is really safe who drinks moderately."

"But there are a great many people who drink moderately all their lives. You know that, Aunt Jane."

"Yes, I do know it. But there are not so many moderate drinkers as are counted such. You don't know their private life. You don't live with them day after day, and see them when they are free from all restraint, except such as they impose upon themselves."

"You are right, Aunt Jane. You know a great deal more about it than I do, and I don't know what made me provoke you to an argument. I hate liquor-drinking as bad as you do, and moderate or not, there is no need of it."

"So do I hate it," added John. "I should think I had reason to. But I don't see why mother need be so particular about cider. Grandfather always drinks it, and I don't a bit doubt that what mother used to drink it herself."

"I did, and there was a time in my life when I drank wine and champagne."

"And you didn't get drunk either," was urged in reply.

"Yes, I did," she answered, the words dying out in a wailing sob. "Sit down here, and let me tell you all about it," she added with great effort. "I shall never have courage to tell you, unless I do so to-night. Don't hate me, boys. It was a terrible thing, but I believe God has forgiven me."

"Hate you!" murmured her son, throwing his arms around her. "I couldn't do that. But it don't seem possible that my mother—"

Here the boy laid his head upon his mother's shoulder, and wept bitterly; while Raleigh turned away to wipe the tears from his eyes.

"I must do myself justice," at length said Mrs. Warland. "I cannot have you think worse of me than I deserve. It may not seem generous, but I am unwilling to bear more of blame than belongs to me."

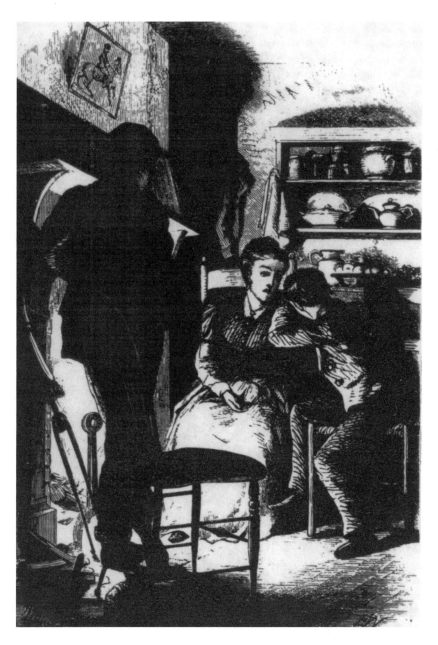

The sad story told. From Mary Dwinell Chellis, *Wealth and Wine,* frontispiece.
New York: National Temperance Society and Publication House, 1874.

"Don't mother. Tell us all about it, and put the blame just where it belongs. I don't doubt but what father was at the bottom of it."

"He was," she replied softly. "Yet I ought to have had more principle. I began by yielding a little, and drinking because it was fashionable. Raleigh, shall you despise me after this?"

"No, indeed, Aunt Jane. Why should I?" answered her nephew.

Nuts were forgotten, and the rosy apples stood untasted, while this woman described with startling minuteness her gradual enslavement by the siren of the wine-cup. There were frequent pauses in the narrative; but at length it was all told. The wind howled, the storm raged, and the fire burned low on the hearth; yet this group within the cottage heeded neither wind, nor storm, nor increasing cold.

Thus did Jane Warland make her first confession. To the second, only Mabel Pease listened; and with rare delicacy, the young lady offered neither question nor comment. She did not count her friend one whit the less worthy of esteem; and the evening had not passed, before she found opportunity to say this without referring to what had transpired.

Her own previous resolves were strengthened. Now that she had been made to realize the terrible effects of fashionable dram-drinking, she wondered that she had not discovered them for herself.

John Warland, too, had ample time to form his plans anew, and fortify himself against temptation. His mother would be free, and with her freedom, his own would be secured. Good Dr. Saunders would permit no unnecessary delay in the business entrusted to him.

When the showers of April had swept away the last vestiges of winter's snow, the cottage, which had been closed since the first of March, was reopened; and it was known somewhat generally that Jane Warland would be glad of employment as dressmaker or plain seamstress.

Her relatives had objected to this; her father assuring her that the resources of the old farm were sufficient for all; yet she was not deterred from her purpose.

"I have had my full share from the old farm," she answered cheerfully. "I thank you all the same. But I have earned my own support under greater difficulties than I shall meet with here, and I cannot be dependent. I shall be almost happy, when I am fairly established in my business. There is work enough here to be done, and I think I am the one to do it."

Dr. Saunders commended her, adding, "I know in one way it

seems hard. But that is more than counterbalanced by what you will gain. I want to see the color come back to your cheeks, and the old light shine in your eyes. John is going to be strong enough to help Raleigh this summer, and everything promises well for you all. You must let an old man say his say, and I tell you you are better off today, than you have been any time before, since you went to Mr. Beman's to spend a year and learn city ways. That's what I think."

"I think the same," she answered. "My friends have done more for me than I had a right to expect; and now I hope to do for myself."

"Your father's house was always open to you. You should have come home sooner than you did."

"Situated as I was, I never felt at liberty to do so. I was very proud, too, and I could bear some things among strangers better than I could bear them here. Knowing that I *could* come whenever I thought best gave me strength to struggle on. I have much to be thankful for; and not the least of my blessings are the two friends who always speak to me encouragingly. You and Mabel Pease would have me believe that there is something left for me in life, after all I have suffered."

"There is," replied the doctor with emphasis. "If I remember right—and I guess I do—you are hardly thirty-eight years old. There may be forty, fifty years of life before you; and if you are as sensible a woman as you ought to be, you won't feel it to be your duty to wear sack-cloth and ashes all that time, because you made a mistake when you were twenty. I'm not making light of your troubles, child; and I'm not making light of marriage-vows, either. But what our Savior allowed must be right; and when a woman has borne enough, and made up her mind that it's not her duty to bear any more, there's no reason why her conscience should accuse her of doing wrong, when she appeals to the law for the right to live in comfort and safety. I don't know what would happen if all the incorrigible drunkards in the country were deserted by their wives and children; but I've thought sometimes I should like to see the experiment tried. If the tables were turned, and the majority of drunkards were *women,* instead of *men,* there wouldn't be so much forbearance. I know that, and I wish there was less now."

"But, Dr. Saunders, if one of these drunkards was a member of your own family, I think you would feel that every possible means should be used to reclaim him; even though this involved a great sacrifice on the part of others. It has been proved that the lowest and most degraded may rise to a respectable position."

"I know it," said the old man with a shake of his head. "But I was speaking of *incorrigible* drunkards, and then there is one consideration, which with me outweighs all others. The children of drunkards are born under the worst conditions; and the sin of transmitting to another generation the tendency to drunkenness is a fearful one. Forgive me, Jane," added the speaker, interrupting himself. "In my earnestness, I forgot some things I ought to remember."

"There is no need to ask my forgiveness," she replied. "I think I know all you would say; and I know, too, that the curse which rests upon her children is the hardest of all for a drunkard's wife to bear. The mother of a drunkard's children is, of all women, the most to be pitied. I have but one, and it will break my heart if he goes wrong."

"I believe he will do right, and be a blessing to you," quickly responded the doctor. "This last trial has impressed him, as perhaps nothing else could. Then, too, Raleigh's companionship will do a great deal for him. That nephew of yours is a remarkable boy. He was always above the average of boys; but since Mabel Pease came here, he has developed wonderfully."

All this was but preliminary to a conversation from which both Mrs. Warland and Dr. Saunders would gladly have been excused. It was necessary to speak of the divorce then pending; and many of the visitor's remarks had been made for the purpose of reassuring his friend, who even now sometimes reproaches herself for the decision she had made.

"I don't think it will be necessary for me to trouble you again in this matter," he said as he was about to leave. "I would have spared you this if I could. My wife is coming over to-morrow to see about some sewing she wants done. I told her she had better speak in season."

SOPHIA LOUISA ROBBINS LITTLE
1799–?

Details of Little's life are sketchy. She evidently supported at least two major reform efforts: abolition and temperance. Two of her publications, *The Branded Hand* (1845) and *Thrice through the Furnace* (1852), support abolition; *The Reveille: or, Our Music at Dawn* (Providence: Benjamin T. Albro, 1854), excerpted here, promotes temperance and women's involvement in destroying saloons. In addition to her full-length works, Little published in popular nineteenth-century periodicals and in the gift book *The Token.* Her earliest works were written under the pseudonym Rowena.

The Reveille employs a framing device in which two women in an apartment overlooking the street of a small town converse about the goings-on below. They relate the story of Mary Grove, who had her choice of many lovers but married Jerry Woodliffe. The narrative follows Jerry's introduction to alcohol, his decline, and his efforts at reform; the rum club, a group supported by local profiteers in the alcohol industry, continually undermines his and others' efforts to remain sober. The women in the novel take rational, commonsense approaches to combat the influences of alcohol and its promoters; antagonism builds as the women battle the forces of intemperance and the "rum club" grows violently resentful of such interference by women.

Typically, Little incorporates many messages favorable to women. She takes Shakespeare to task for his presentation of women in *The Taming of the Shrew;* she presents admirable single women; and she illustrates women speaking in meetings where only men usually participate. Mary capably supports the family through the periods of Jerry's drunkenness. After his reformation, Jerry takes turns staying home with their children so that both may get out and attend services; he tells Mary, "You have been father and mother a long time, and it is but just that I should take my turn and do some of your work till I find employment" (8).

Mary consistently outsmarts the rum club. In fact, men serve as foils for women's intelligence and common sense throughout the narrative. Finally, Jerry, tricked by members of the rum club, falls again, and Mary beseeches tavern owners not to sell him more alcohol. All agree except Hal Wood. In this excerpt from the final chapter, Little celebrates the many women in the 1850s who, impatient with men's laws, took matters into their own hands, destroying saloons and their wares.

from *The Reveille: or, Our Music at Dawn*

"I will tell you what to do next," said Rockheart. "Bring round his dray, lay him on it, and have him driven home, so that his wife may see how pretty he looks! I guess it will make Mary Woodliffe look blue."

"Good," said Stronghead, "I should like to mortify her."

So round they brought poor Jerry's dray. On that dray they placed poor Jerry, dead drunk; and followed by a mob of boys and low people, hooting and hallowing, he was driven towards his house. Like all good housekeepers, when they return home, after absence, Mary Woodliffe had spent a busy day in getting her little domain, in yankee phrase, "to rights"—But every thing was now in ample order; all clean and right. And Mary, having last of all, made her own person clean and neat, sat down at her open window, to enjoy the evening breeze, little dreaming of the killing spectacle, soon to be presented to her. Imagine her, reader, now at the window, (and this is no fiction,) the cheerful, innocent, happy wife and mother. She hears a noise, and looking out, perceives a dray coming towards the house, followed by the rabble. As it draws near, she sees a seemingly lifeless form extended on the dray.

"Mercy!" she exclaims, "it is my husband; he is dead, and they are bringing him home on his dray!"

Down stairs she rushed, and out of the door, up to the dray. What words can describe her feelings on discovering the truth. She shrieked aloud. The bitter, bitter cries of her anguish went up to heaven, even after they had carried in her husband; but at last she was persuaded to go in. The rum fiends went home, rejoicing in this day of her calamity; but it was a dear bought exultation,—a costly victory, for the "army of the aliens." God is repaying them even now.—Their hour of triumph was their hour of doom.

As soon as Mary grew calmer, she caused her children to retire to rest and seated herself by the bed where they had laid her husband. She watched over that loved, though fallen husband, all night. O, what a night for that faithful, devoted heart. But though her sensibility was strong, so was her energy. The wrestling she had that night with the God of Miriam, of Deborah, of Judith, strengthened her "with strength in her soul." When Jerry began to rouse from his drunkenness, in the morning, and had come to sufficient consciousness, he looked up to his wife, and said, "Oh, Mary! can you ever forgive me?"

"Yes, I can forgive you," said she, but added in a calm, decisive tone, "Jerry Woodliffe, where did you get the liquor you got drunk with?"

"Oh, wife," said he, "don't ask me now; I don't want to tell you now; I am very hungry."

"Jerry," she repeated, "tell me where you got the liquor you got drunk with. I must know this moment."

"No! I never will tell you," said he, "so you need not ask."

Mary then rose and deliberately locked the door; then opening the window, she called her son William. He came, as usual, at her first call. She threw the key out of the window. "William," said she, "take that key and don't unlock the door, till I bid you."

Then she sat down again beside her husband.

"Mary," said he, "what do you mean? Do you mean to make me a prisoner, and keep me here to starve? Come, I am hungry, and I want something to eat."

"Jerry," said she firmly, "I am not going out of this chamber, nor shall you, till you tell me where you got the liquor to get drunk with. Depend upon it, I shall sit here, if it is forever, till you tell me."

Jerry knew that his wife's word meant something. He turned about uneasily on the bed.

"If you are bent to have your way, and I know you will, I got the liquor at Hal Wood's."

Mary at once rose from her seat, threw up the window, and

called her son. "William," said she, "come now, and unlock the door."

She then put on her shawl and bonnet. "Where are you going now?" asked Jerry.

"Down to Harry Wood's," she replied.

"Don't do that, Mary; his shop is full just now. That's the reason I was loth to tell you where I got the liquor; I knew that you would go there, straight as a gun."

William now unlocked the door. "You are at liberty now," said she, "and I am going to Harry Wood's." She passed down the street with a rapid step, and a flushed cheek. At last, she drew near the shop. Hal Wood's morning customers were gathering; among them were some very genteel ones, and one whom Mary Woodliffe well knew. Mary composedly entered the shop, and advancing to Mr. Wood, who was behind his counter, asked to him,—

"Mr. Wood, I have called to ask you to promise me not to sell my husband any more liquor."

"I shall not promise any such thing," said he.

She again earnestly repeated her request.

"I shall not," said he, "you are an impudent woman, and I order you to quit my shop."

Very much moved, but not to be thus driven away, she knelt before him weeping, and besought him to have mercy on her and her children; but at sight of her tears and her perseverance, he only grew harder, and in order to compel her to leave the shop, began to wound her delicacy by improper language. This stung her to the quick, and rousing all her womanly pride, gave a turn to her feelings. When he began his gross attack, she was kneeling at his feet in tears; but now, the fire in her kindling eye quietly drying up her tears, and, in the very rage of her chaste womanhood, she struck the offender several severe blows, in the presence of a dozen spectators. Young Charles Bigland, the person whom Mary recognized on entering the store, was one of them. He had never, until lately, been a frequenter there. He stood just on the verge of the precipice.—He knew Mary Woodliffe,—knew her respectability and worth. He came forward and said,—

"Wood, are you not ashamed to insult that respectable woman in that style? If you are not, I am ashamed for you, and she has given you just what you deserve."

"I thank you, Mr. Bigland," said Mary, "and as a proof of my gratitude, I beseech you to come no more to this dangerous place."

That was a timely warning to Charles Bigland, and saved one of the finest young men in the city, despite his parentage.

After this faithful warning to him, she turned again to the rum-seller.—"For you, sir," she said, "if you dare to sell my husband another glass of liquor, I will punish you more severely than I have done." So saying, she left the shop, and returned home.

She found her husband out; when he did return home, he was drunk, and continued from day to day, to keep up his debauchery. But one morning, a lawyer, a temperance man, and a friend of Mrs. Woodliffe's, came in, and said to her, "Mrs. Woodliffe, the temperance friends feel very badly about your husband's fall, and the dreadful excess he is now plunging into."

"They cannot feel so badly as I do," said the wife, with a deep sigh.

"We think," said the gentleman, "there is but one thing we can do, and that is, to take him up and put him in jail."

"Put him in jail?" exclaimed Mary, "put my husband in Jail? No, never! Put the rumseller in jail, not his victim!!"

"We by no means wish to injure your feelings, Mrs. Woodliffe," said the lawyer, "but we feel that extreme measures, only, will reclaim him, such is his condition. At this moment, that I am talking with you, he is in Harry Wood's shop in a state of intoxication."

"In Hal Wood's shop, drunk?" said Mary, her eyes flashing lightning through her tears.

"Yes, Madam!" said the lawyer, "it is indeed the fact."

She said no more, but rose and hastily put on her bonnet and shawl.—"Pray excuse me, sir," said she to her visitor, and instantly left.

How little may we realize it, at the moment when we are fulfilling some great destiny. As Mary Woodliffe passed down street, she little thought she had entered upon an act, which was to consummate her destiny; as the mover, the originator, of the great movement which is to complete a most important moral revolution. But though unconscious of this, there was a sort of prophecy of it in her noble appearance as she passed along embodying all that is strong in affection, or firm in purpose. Her beautiful hair waved back from her glowing cheek, in the rapidity of her motion; her high soul sat enthroned in her eye. Her mien and appearance drew attention as she went on, and this more especially, as her encounter with Hal Wood on the day it came off, had been the theme of every tea-table and news-corner in the city. There was whispering as she went, "there goes Mrs. Woodliffe to Hal Wood's to give him another dressing down." She stopped at several rum-shops as she passed, all assenting to her wish.

There was an auction in progress at an auction store, opposite Hal Wood's shop, and the attention of the crowd there was attracted as Mary Woodliffe entered the shop. Beside the counter stood her drunken husband, and Wood was in the very act of filling up his glass.

"How can you do that, Mr. Wood?" said she.

At the first sound of her voice, her husband, drunk though he was, left the shop.

"Oh! Mr. Wood," said she, "every other liquor seller to whom I have been, has promised me not to sell liquor to my husband; you alone have refused me."

She then added every moving entreaty, her aching heart could suggest, but all in vain; he was insensible, and rudely ordered her to leave his shop. But she only fell at his feet and the more earnestly besought him. By this time a crowd were attracted from the opposite side of the street, and Wood determined to drive her out by fair means or foul, used foul means indeed, and again insulted her by language more obscene than before. One could have thought the first lesson would have taught him that he could not with impunity offend Mary Woodliffe's keen sense of honor, and delicacy. But he was also, a destined instrument.

As from his lips impure words fell, her spirit rose, and rising from the posture of entreaty, she came upon him. The counter this time was no protection. She flew behind it, and dragging out Wood, inflicted on him a severe chastisement. She dealt her blows upon him well, and after she had finished, she thrust him out of the back door of his own shop.—He was given into her hands, and the heroine now stood on the field she had conquered. Her powers had driven out the enemy, now the weapons of his warfare were to be destroyed. Now the crowd without, soon heard in the clashing of the vessels as she dashed them together, the music of our *reveille* awaking to sterner warfare the soldiers who serve under the Temperance Banner. And every crash was music, our Music at the Dawn of a Day, which shall yet subdue rum oppression, and break the yoke from the drunkard's neck.

Standing behind the counter, in full view of the increasing throng at the door, at one sweep of her arm, the fine glittering vessels that contained the liquor, gave up, not the ghost, but the fiery spirit within them, and it ran in streams on the floor. Next, those costly mirrors, bought at no less a price than the drunkard's soul, were dashed in pieces, and their glittering fragments strewed the floor. Then, as Hawkins phrased it, "she turned the bungs of the little painted barrels, the right way to let their contents out, and thus turned the current of public opinion." Demijohns, bottles, all were broken and overturned. The next thing that met her eye was some superb glass vases, full of tempting confectionery and other dainties. "See, gentlemen," said she to the crowd, "these are baits to draw on our children to the drunkard's bowl.["] Soon the vases were destroyed, and their contents mingled with the melange upon the floor. The crowd stood at the door gazing on in fixed astonishment. No one offered to stay her hand as she stood, like an avenging angel, among the ruins she had made. For, strange to tell, there was no appearance of headlong passion or rashness, in all this, but a bold, deliberate purpose, if there was no legal redress for her wrongs, that she would be her own avenger.

But just then, Rockheart came pushing through the crowds. "Now this is a shame!" said he; "will none of you prevent this woman from destroying Mr. Wood's property?" Rockheart, you know, was a man six feet in height, and a foe not to be despised. But Mary Woodliffe was now above all fear. She looked upon him with contempt, and proceeded to roll back her little sleeves from her firm and rounded arm, as if to prepare for action. But Rockheart caught the glance of her eye, and slunk out of the shop without daring to speak to her.

Her work being now done, Mary Woodliffe passed out of the shop and through the crowd, which opened to give her way. The Mayor was just coming up with his posse, to quell the mob. But Mary Woodliffe stood upon the pavement of the sidewalk; she turned round, and thus spoke,—"Gentlemen if you will not give us protection, we will protect ourselves!" Then that vast multitude shouted, as with one voice,—"Protection!—Protection!"

Many years have passed away since this achievement, but our heroine still lives with her reclaimed husband, a happy wife, reposing on the laurels of her conjugal fidelity.

MRS. E. N. GLADDING
DATES UNKNOWN

L ittle information remains about Mrs. E. N. Gladding. She published her 285-page collection, *Leaves from an Invalid's Journal,
and Poems* in 1858 (Providence: George H. Whitney). "Minnie—
A Temperance Tale" is taken from that collection.

In "Minnie," Gladding depicts her protagonist's destruction of
portions of the liquor industry. Mid-century frustration with alcoholic excesses led many women to attack and destroy places that
sold and manufactured alcohol. Although they were often arrested,
as is Minnie, they seldom were convicted. Judges generally sympa-
thized with women who had suffered gravely from alcoholic husbands. Newspaper accounts also championed these women as desperate and with no other alternative.

"Minnie" offers a terrorist manual of sorts for anyone wishing
to destroy liquor wares. Minnie stakes out her sites well beforehand,
making sure they are isolated, where "no one can be injured by the
flames." She attacks in the dead of night, scattering shavings she
has brought to the scene, and rushes home immediately, only turning to look at the result when she is safely removed from the scene.
She then offers a calm response when informed of the fire.

Gladding provides several sentences noting Minnie's "great mistake" in not seeking advice from her mother; however, she actually
rewards Minnie munificently: the isolated family gains many sympathetic friends; her parents are cared for; she acquires, through
adoption, a wealthy father; she becomes a celebrity; and she mar-

ries a promising young lawyer. None of these advantages would have been available to Minnie prior to her taking unlawful action. Perhaps most important, appeals to her God not to forsake her are answered, suggesting the truth in her belief that God has spoken to her in a dream. The glowing defense of Minnie's counsel, Arthur P., erases any lingering doubts about the correctness of her actions. Gladding validates and encourages women in such tactics. Her nod to Minnie's "error" is typical of many stories by nineteenth-century women that provide the token nod to men's laws and customs but deliberately subvert them.

Gladding supports the view of temperance as a woman's issue not only in her strong protagonist but also in her dedication to "suffering mothers and broken-hearted wives . . . desponding sisters and despised children."

Minnie—A Temperance Tale

"Dear mother, why do you look so sad every day, and night too; and why do you keep looking out of the window? And when I ask you questions, you do not hear me, but sometimes say, 'yes darling;' and then you say, 'mother did not understand you;' and often I see tears on your cheek—but you try to hide them from me. You did not use to cry; and when dear father came home, we used to be *so* happy!—Now, he does not laugh and talk, and take me on his knee, and let me lay my head upon his shoulder. Once, when I looked up in his face and kissed him, and said, 'dear father,' he would kiss me, and always call me his precious little Minnie. And little Charlie does not now creep up to him and say, 'Papa,' as he used to. Why is all this, dear mother? I cannot go to sleep after you have kissed me and bid me good night; what is it dear mother? do tell your little Minnie." The mother clasped her child to her bosom, with a convulsive grasp, and the tears would force their way through the closed fingers, as she said, "My precious, precious child! have I indeed betrayed the bitter anguish of this tortured heart? I had hoped that thy childhood would be as sunny as was thy mother's; so that, in after life, it should be to thee ever as a beautiful dream of sunshine and of flowers. I have no right to drop pebbles into the pure and guileless fountain of thy innocent heart, and I have struggled hard not to do so; but thou art like that delicate plant that shrinks and trembles at the slightest approach, and closes its little petals even before the rude hand is laid upon it. I cannot deceive *thee*, my little cherished flower." Then, the mother put back the soft curls from her child's forehead, and gazed into those mild, thoughtful eyes,— thoughtful beyond their years,—and said, "what if thy fate should be like thy mother's!" And she clasped her close to her heart, and shuddered. She held her there, for a few moments, in silence, and then said "Minnie, my first-born darling—my precious one, I cannot tell thee what makes thy mother sad, and why a change has come over our once happy home, but thou wilt know it soon enough, for it comes on apace. I would not have a shadow darken thy pathway; but stern duties are before us both, and instead of being refreshed with the flowers, thou wilt feel nothing but the thorns. Tis hard for me to think this, much more to speak it; but thou art old beyond thy years, and you and little Charlie are all I have in the world,—now, *now* that I cannot."—She paused, for she could not speak against the father of that trusting, loving little being. Ella Howard was an only child; the idol of her parents, the bright cherished flower that for seventeen summers, bloomed in their elegant and tasteful mansion. But, although it was adorned with rare paintings and statuary; to their fond hearts, and to the hearts of their visitors, Ella seemed the most worthy of admiration. Simple in manners, and affectionate in heart; without one particle of coquetry, or affectation; she grew up beloved by all who knew her. Ella was a christian—thus following the example of her good and excellent parents. It seemed impossible for one constituted like herself, so thoughtful and affectionate, to pass through life and not look above and beyond it. She reverenced all she looked upon; the lowliest flower was a mystery to her mind; but, still, it spoke to her heart of the goodness of God. Ella had many suitors, but she loved one, and one only. They had grown up together; he was ever by her side, even in her childhood, when he watched every expression of her guileless face, and was eager to gratify her every wish, ere it was uttered. As she grew to womanhood, he regarded her as a holy and pure being, and the earnest wish of his heart was, that he might be worthy of her affection. All who looked upon the manly face of Charles Arnold, and who were acquainted with his former life, said, "He alone is worthy to be the husband of the beautiful Ella;" and the fond parents thought so too—and though they gave her away with tears, they felt he was worthy to be entrusted with their treasure. Such was the father and mother of our little Minnie, when they stood

before the altar, and plighted the marriage vow which was registered in Heaven. But how had that vow been kept? We shall see.

Soon after their marriage, Ella was called upon to witness the
departure of that dear mother, who had watched over her with such
sedulous care. It was a hard blow; but she endured it as only the
christian can bear up, under such overwhelming trials. Not many
months after, her father followed! A fever, that proved fatal to many,
deprived her of her last earthly parent. Poor Ella!—the death of her
father and mother had come upon her so suddenly and unexpected,
that she would have sunk under it, had it not been for the untiring
love and sympathy of her husband; and she blessed God, that he
had bestowed such a priceless blessing upon her. And, at that time,
he was worthy of her love. He possessed that intuitive sense of the
beautiful—that ready sympathy, which is rarely to be found in
man—united to a childlike submission to the will of his heavenly
Father, that you sometimes look in vain for, in the older and more
advanced christian. Charles Arnold was sincerity itself. But it was
fashionable, among the higher circles, to have wine on their tables,
and handed round when callers came. He had early imbibed a taste
for it, and was in the daily habit of drinking it; but never, for one
moment, did he think that he should become the *slave* of that habit.
He was a promising lawyer; but, as there were many of that profession, in his native city, he thought it best for them to remove to
the beautiful town of N. Ella bade farewell to the home of her childhood, and accompanied her husband, with a resigned heart. For a
few years, all was peace, in their happy dwelling. Little Minnie
came, to gladden their hearts with her winning smiles; and, three
years after, the little, prattling Charlie. But a change, (almost imperceptible, at first,) by degrees took place. Ella often perceived that
her husband's face was flushed, and his eyes were unusually bright;
but she laid it to over-exertion and excitement in his business. Very
soon, however, it became too apparent, and she could hide the
horrid truth from her heart no longer. I need not describe the agony
of that moment; it was far, far worse than death. Step by step, he
trode the downward path, and his fine mind each day became more
obtuse. For a time, he was invariably kind to his gentle wife and
winning children;—but what will the accursed alcohol not change?
They had lived a very retired life, as ill health had been her portion,
for the last few years; and now, in her utter desolation, she had none

to look to, unless she could look for comfort in her little Minnie, whose discerning eye had detected the change, and could bear it no longer; and the conversation ensued, with which our story commenced. Passing over a few years, in which his business was, at first, neglected, and finally given up entirely; their property was all gone, and extreme poverty had come upon them. Many a sleepless night, poor Ella passed in watching and waiting for her now wretched husband. Once in a while, he would revive a little, and would seem to have still the milk of human kindness in his heart. At such times, he would say, "Oh, Ella! if I could once go where rum was not, your husband would yet be restored to you; but I have lost all power over myself!" Then she formed the resolution of going to all the rum-sellers, to implore them to save her husband. She who had been so tenderly nurtured, was alone; with no servant; destitute of the bare necessaries of life, and in feeble health; for her continued watching had worn down a frame naturally delicate, to a mere shadow;—but what will not woman endure and suffer, for the husband of her youth? Behold her, then, wending her steps to the grog-shops! It was of no use—she might as well have appealed to the stones. Time rolled on, but brought no change to the sufferers: starvation often stared them in the face. The mother did all she could, and Minnie assisted. She had sent them to school, for she did not feel adequate to the task of teaching them; but the finger of scorn was continually pointed at them, even by the rumseller's sons and daughters—they, who lived in their splendid houses, that had been built with the groans and tears of the suffering thousands: and the mother could not bear that they should suffer this, when they had so much to endure at home; and she withdrew them from school. All the while, the heart of Minnie was almost bursting with suppressed emotion. She had endured the harsh treatment of her father, oh! how many times; and, although she felt a deathly sickness creep over her, and she trembled like an aspen, when she heard his step approach, still, she thought she could suffer all—every thing—rather than see her angel mother and her darling brother, the objects of his hatred. At such times, she would almost lose her reason, and she would exclaim constantly, "What can I do? Oh! my Father in Heaven, what can I do for my suffering Mother? Oh, show me some way to aid her!"

One night, after one of these bitter conflicts, she threw her little weary body on the pallet of straw—striving to think how she could crush the hydra-headed monster. She fell asleep, and dreamed that God had given her power to destroy every drop of spiritous liquor that was in the world—and it covered a space much farther than the eye could reach. And a lighted torch was handed her; and, as she touched it, the flames reached to heaven! Then she clapped her hands, and shouted for joy; and she called aloud, (and her voice floated all over the earth,)—Come, suffering mothers, and broken-hearted wives; come, desponding sisters, and despised children; come, and see the great conflagration. The monster is crushed; not another drop can be on this earth, whilst God reigns in Heaven! And they came, with their pale faces and sunken eyes, and experienced a joy they had not known for years. Suddenly, her ear was arrested by the most unaccountable sounds; they were like the wailings of the damned. She turned, astonished; for at that moment, she thought there was not a heart in the world, but was bounding for joy. There was a multitude of grim-visaged beings; and, to her eager inquiries, of who they were, it was shouted, on all sides,— "They are the rumsellers; their day is up. Woe! woe! to the defeated rumsellers." Then Minnie awoke, and found it all a dream. "Oh! (said she,) if this had been true, to what a different world should I have opened my eyes this morning!"—and tears fell fast on her pillow. But she thought the dream had a meaning. She believed that her earnest and oft-repeated inquiries of what she should do, had, at length, been answered, and that henceforth it was her duty to destroy all that it was in her power to get at. She never mentioned the subject to her mother; for she thought she would not see it in the same light that she herself did; but her resolution was taken. Ah! Minnie, herein was thy great mistake. Thou shouldst have consulted with that wise and good mother; and, surely, one who had ever been so dutiful and obedient, would have listened to her counsels. She would have taught thee that it is far nobler to endure affliction, than to do "evil" that good may come. It was an error of the head, not of the heart. Enthusiastic she was, to a degree that separated her from the children around her; and she had witnessed nothing but suffering, from a child; but revenge could not, for a moment, find a resting place in the heart of one so tremblingly alive to the sufferings of others. Physical prostration, and intense mental excitement, had produced a sort of monomania on this subject; and it would have been impossible, perhaps, to have convinced her that it was not the finger of God, that had pointed out her duty;

and it was this view of it, that gave that naturally timid girl, strength to perform that, which would have caused many a stout-hearted man to tremble. She was well acquainted with many places in the town, where it was kept; for, as she traversed it often, in search of fuel, to keep them from freezing, the fumes of the liquor she could trace for miles. One place, in particular, she remembered. It was a long red building, standing on a wharf; and she knew that it was filled with the deadly poison. She had several times been in it herself, when she saw children going in and out; and she was drawn thither, she knew not why. Once, when they had been repairing it, she ventured in, and asked permission to gather the chips that were lying around. She looked at the barrels, and thought, ["]if it had not been for rum, our home would have been as happy as we could have wished. My father would have been beloved and respected. I should have honored him, and looked up to him. He would have provided us with fuel, and I should not have been here; my poor mother would—" but her heart was too full, when she thought of her, and she hastened out of the building. It was owned by the wealthy Mr. N——, the wealthiest merchant in the town. She knew that he sold it to the rumseller, and they dealt it out to her father and to thousands of poor wretches beside. "This," said she, "shall be the place where I will commence. It is alone; no dwelling is near; no one can be injured by the flames." At night, when her mother slept for a while, that young girl crept from her bed; wrapped a shawl hastily around her, and, with the materials in her hand, stole forth. Her heart beat fast; but, at the same time, she was conscious that she was stronger than she had ever been before. She reached the spot; drew out the shavings, and placed them where she thought they would do best; then applied the match. She never looked behind till she reached the street that led to the room where her mother and brother were sleeping. Then she turned, and saw the flames rising; and it seemed to her that her dream was about to be realized. Just before she reached her home, the cry of *"Fire!"* fell on her ear. She ran faster; gained the door; glided in, and lay down on her bed. Her mother was asleep, but soon roused. Springing up, she exclaimed, "It is fire! where are you, my children?" Minnie answered, as calmly as she would have done at any other time, "We are here, dear mother. Do not be alarmed; we have nothing to fear." In the morning, there was not a trace of the building to be seen, save the blackened mass of burnt timber that was strewn over the ground.

It was effectual. Every drop of the *fire-water* was consumed. Several times, Minnie succeeded in carrying out her work of destruction; but she was, at last, detected! They rushed in, and tore her from her mother, who lay stretched upon a bed of sickness, and left her, as one dead. Charlie—a noble-hearted boy, who had now reached his thirteenth year—was distracted. He wanted to follow his sister, but could not think of leaving his apparently dying mother. He looked at her pale face, as she lay there in a swoon, unconscious of what was going on around, and, kissing her forehead, said. "Oh! my injured mother! thou hast ever preached forgiveness; but if they ill-treat my sister, it shall no longer be peace, but a sword."

It was near night when they took Minnie from her home, and conveyed her to prison. They thrust her into a narrow cell, and turned the key upon her. But she trembled not; she shed no tears. At that moment she felt that she could suffer even death itself. She was unconscious that it was dark around. At length she thought of her mother, and the flood-gates of her heart were opened, and tears rushed to her eyes. She dropped on her knees, and implored the Father of mercies to watch over that mother. "Oh! my God, (she said) thou wert near me in my dream; thou [will] not forsake me now. Whatever punishment they may see fit to inflict; may I bear it cheerfully—but they will not separate me from my mother; Oh, Father, they will not do that!" and the poor girl wept and prayed till morning. Then she fell into a troubled sleep, but was awakened by the sound of whispering voices, and the gentle pressure of a kindly hand rested upon her. She thought this, too, was a dream,— a dream that would be dispelled as the other blessed vision had, all too soon, vanished; but she was mistaken. They were friends, who had heard her strange story, and had wept and pondered over it, and had resolved to do all that lay in their power, to bind up the bruised reed, and make her prison life comfortable. They had read the heart of Minnie, and therefore had ministered to the wants of the sick and suffering family, first. These were the glad tidings that greeted Minnie on awakening. Her mother had been tenderly cared for; they had searched and found her wretched father; and the heart of Charlie had been comforted by the assurance that no harm should come to his dear sister, other than the separation that must necessarily continue for some time longer. Thus days, weeks, and months wore away, and found our Minnie still a convict in the prisoner's cell. But new friends were daily added, and she bore up bravely under all the crushing thoughts and feelings that oppressed her delicate and sensitive spirit. The family had been removed to a neat and comfortable cottage, and a good and efficient nurse had been procured to take care of them. A long and protracted fever, brought on by exposure, had completely prostrated her father, and brought him to the verge of the grave. Her mother was unable to leave her bed. The constant anxiety and yearning desires of her heart, retarded that progress toward health, she so earnestly coveted, so that she might once more look upon her darling; yet for that dear one's sake, she struggled hard to be patient. Each day their wants were abundantly supplied; and that blessed sympathy which gold cannot buy, was now hers, an ever present angel in their house of mourning. At length, the day of trial came, and Minnie was led out to face the multitude. The house was crowded, for it had created a great sensation throughout the neighboring towns, and they all thronged to see one who had dared so much. It was buzzed on all sides that it was the daughter of a drunkard, but they were astonished when they beheld Minnie. She was just turned fifteen; rather tall, but slender; nay, almost fragile in form. There was the noble dignity of mien, that had characterized her father, united with the exquisite grace and gentleness of the once beautiful Ella. Her hair was glossy, and of a rich brown color; her face was pale, but the features beautifully moulded; the mouth small, and the sweet expression of that mouth was never forgotten by those who had once seen her smile; the eyes were hazel, but there was a world of pity and beseeching tenderness in those soft, dark, liquid orbs, and a high, holy expression, that awed the beholder. No unbeliever in a future state, could look into the depths of those eyes, and not feel that there was a Heaven, and thither the poor, forsaken child of scorn was bound. The witnesses were examined; Minnie's counsel plead long and ably; he forgot all but the wrongs that had maddened and driven to the verge of insanity that delicate, tender hearted little being before him. He portrayed the agony that must have wrung the heart of one so constituted. He plead for her as he would have pleaded for his own sister; for he was young, and his heart had not yet become hardened by contact with the selfishness that is in the world. He spoke of her extreme youth; of her doubts and fears; of the intensity of her emotions; of the delicate heart-chord that vibrated to every wail of sorrow. He pictured the all absorbing thought that took full possession of her mind after her dream,—that it was a duty she was called upon to perform; that she could not turn aside from it, from the fear of consequences, without trampling upon the highest and holiest dictates of her spiritual nature. She knew that God had forbidden us to put the cup to our neighbor's lips; that we are commanded to feed the hungry, and clothe the naked; but they had been stripped of all they possessed in the world. Her broken hearted mother was constantly before her; and she remembered a time when that mother went forth a suppliant, imploring those men not to give her husband that, which would deprive him of his reason. She had asked the question,—what right had they to turn the morning of her mother's days into one long, dark, cheerless night? What right had they to reduce her and her little brother to beggary, and after they had covered them with rags, let their children point the finger of scorn at them? Then he drew a comparison between the sin of the dealers in the rum traffic, and those who were considered by law, criminals. All these things, said he, have they done, but they are respected; the law cannot touch them; nay, it is on their side; but if a half starved wretch takes but enough to satisfy his hunger, you straightway condemn him to imprisonment. If the angry, but kind hearted man, who would scorn to deprive children of their bread, commits a deed, in an unguarded moment, that his very soul abhors, and he would give worlds to undo; you condemn him to death, and think you have done a christian deed. Oh! he exclaimed, how much rather would I clasp the hand of such a man, dripping with blood, though it be, than come in contact with his, who deals out death every hour; death not only to the body but the soul, and feels no compunction! Throughout the whole of this speech, Minnie's eyes were riveted upon the speaker, with that intense and fixed gaze that showed the spirit, for the time being, had entirely lost sight of its earthly surroundings.

Then the counsel for the state arose with the intention of overthrowing all that had been said; but it was not an easy task, in this instance, for he, too, was young, and he had felt the truth of all the preceding remarks; but it was his profession. He had to look away from Minnie, and endeavored to take a practical view of the matter. He showed how absurd a thing it would be, for reasonable people to be beguiled by dreams and visions; that if an exception was made in her case, the country would be flooded with similar cases; that our lunatic asylums would be crowded by persons fancying they had certain missions to perform, that had been divinely communicated. But this part is too sad to dwell upon. Suffice it to say, that Minnie was found guilty, and sentenced to three years imprisonment. Before the judged had pronounced her doom, she was asked if she had any thing to say why sentence should not be passed upon her, and was commanded to rise. As she did so, a murmur ran through that crowded audience; the sympathies of all were excited in her behalf, except a few of the most hardened and selfish. It was with difficulty she could stand; for she had barely tasted food the day before, and the bitter night of suffering had almost deprived her of strength. She supported herself by leaning on the railing which hems the prisoner in; then she raised her eyes and gazed on the multitude. She wondered if there was one in the wide world, so desolate, so utterly forsaken as herself. Where was the father who should have been near, if danger had assailed her? There was breathless pause; the heads of all were bent forward, and the hearts of the sympathizing beat fast. It was evident she was suffering much. She gasped for breath. Some one near, put a glass of water to her lips; she made one or two efforts more to speak; then, raising her head, and pointing to her counsel, said, in a low, but distinct voice, "That gentleman has spoken truly, he has read my heart aright; I was unconscious of crime, I did it for poor humanity's sake. It did not seem to be myself, but a power superior, that controlled and guided my spirit. If I have sinned and trampled upon the laws of God and the land, then ought I to suffer the penalty. I will throw myself upon God's mercy, which is never withheld from his erring and repentant children; but from the experience of my short and sorrowful life, it would seem worse than useless to hope for any mercy from man." The last words were scarcely audible, and she sank down exhausted. As the officers approached Minnie, for the purpose of conveying her back to prison, there was a murmur of dissatisfaction among the crowd, and several sprang forward. In the tumult of strange noises, the terrified girl knew not where to look for help; but a kindly arm was thrown around her, and she was drawn out of the crowd. She had fainted, and many ladies sobbed aloud when they saw that pale, beautiful face borne along in the arms of the gray-headed gentleman; and hard visaged men brushed the tears from their cheeks. When Minnie opened her eyes, her head rested on the shoulder of the kind old man. He spoke in soothing tones and said, "Fear nothing, my poor child, I am going to be thy father." "Father, (said Minnie) I have no father." "I know it, but I will be thy father." "Where is my mother? my poor mother!—Oh! take me to her." He assured her that pleasure should soon be hers; that they would use every means in their power to have her sentence repealed. At that moment the carriage stopped, and Minnie was once more an inmate of the prisoner's cell.

The old gentleman was the wealthy Mr. N., whose property Minnie had first destroyed. He had been interested in the case, and had often assisted the family without their knowing from whence the aid came; but not until he looked upon Minnie, did the whole extent of their misery rise up before him. He visited her daily, and was engaged heart and soul in her cause. In the mean time, great changes were going on around them; the most influential men of the place rose in a body, and declared it was time to do something in the cause of Temperance.

The people of N. had been notorious for holding out against all reforms, and they had heretofore laughed at temperance pledges and tetotallers; but now they said,—we will have a "pledge,"—and they wrote one, and hundreds signed their names to that pledge— Mr. N. leading the way. Such a tremendous excitement was never known in the town of N. before. Some of the rum sellers even brought out their casks and turned the liquor into the streets. Many remembered the fine looking lawyer when he first came among them, and they said; "if he could fall, there is no safety for any one." Again it seemed as if Minnie's *dream* was about to be realized.

But to return to that suffering one. From the moment she entered the cell, though surrounded by weeping and kind-hearted beings, an apathy gradually stole over her, and in a few hours she seemed unconscious of the presence of any one. By night, the delirium of fever had fastened itself upon her prostrated frame; and her unconscious cries for her mother, for release from bondage, for rest and freedom from pain, were heart-rending to hear. Her mother had to be apprized of her condition, and Mr. N. set out to perform that painful duty; and painful, it was, indeed, to him. The kind hearted old man wept like a child. On that bed, lay one worthy to grace a court; for the true nobility of the soul will shine forth, let the out-ward surroundings be what they may. There was no alternative; the mother must go to her child, even if death should be the result. We must pass over that meeting. It was well, perhaps, that one was unconscious. Hours, days, and weeks passed, and the fever still raged. It was on the brain, and Minnie's life hung by a slender thread. Those long nights of bitter agony,—who can describe them? When the spirit is swayed to and fro, now on the verge of precipices with no power to retreat; now poised on loose fragments, high, high up, with no arm to snatch us from falling, and we sink down, down, our cries for help lost in the fathomless depth below; then the horrible sense of *suffocation*, when we struggle to free ourselves; to cry for aid; with the faculty of perception intensified tenfold! Oh! ye fathers, who tarry long at the wine cup, bringing disgrace and sorrow, not only to your own souls, but to the tender, hapless beings whose lives ye have invoked, come, look upon this picture! It is only one of a thousand, but it is a faithful transcript. We will not linger. Suffice it to say, that the time came, when the magnetism of the mother's touch, was distinguished from all others; when the mother's voice—

> "had power to quiet
> The restless pulse of care,
> And came like the benediction
> That follows after prayer."

The death-angel had passed by, and it was Minnie's destiny, (she who was born with the martyr spirit,) to live; to live, though, Promethian like, chained to a rock, with the vultures gnawing at her vitals,—she, meanwhile, striving to conceal the wounds, smiling sadly upon the loved ones, and speaking gently to all. But there was one now often near, who had watched and waited with the anxious mother; one whose presence had become dear to the youthful convalescent. She listened for the approaching footsteps, while a new world of joy sprung up in her heart, and irradiated that hitherto sad little face; and this new world of love transfigured every thing around her, causing a halo of peace to rest, even upon the walls of her prison. Arthur P., the young and promising lawyer, who had labored so earnestly in Minnie's cause, had found it impossible to banish from his mind, her form and face. In the midst of business, sleeping or waking, those tender, pleading eyes were ever before him. For a time, he struggled against what some would have deemed a weakness, but his nature was noble, and he was not ashamed to follow the dictates of his higher nature, when thus prompted. He resolved to see her, whose untoward fortunes had called forth his truest sympathies, and whose touching face, and guileless spirit, had taken his own soul captive. Thus, day after day found him by the side of the mother, tenderly nursing the sick, and watching with intense emotion, every change of that disease, which was to cause new buds of promise to spring up, or to dash those new and heaven inspiring hopes, suddenly to the earth! But the death-angel passed, as we said before, and Minnie lived and loved! Arthur's had been a thoughtful, reflecting mind, even from his boyhood; and he could not but feel, that Minnie was the instrument that God had raised up to strengthen those principles, to enlarge and sanctify those aspirations. Passing over long months of weariness and suspense, of "hope deferred, that maketh the heart sick;" the friends of Minnie at length succeeded in obtaining her release, and they bore her in triumph to her home. With a chastened heart, she knelt down, and, burying her face in her hands, sobbed out a prayer of gratitude to God, for freedom to roam over the green earth once more, and to be ever near the loved ones!

Those scenes, and the emotions they produced, were never effaced from her memory. Mr. N. had taken the necessary measures to make Minnie his adopted child, while she was yet a prisoner. He had no children of his own; and a prouder man was not in the town of N. than he, when he took Minnie by the hand, and imprinted a kiss on her fair young cheek, and called her, daughter. He never forgot the first time her friendless head rested upon his shoulder, when he was bearing her through the streets, all unconscious on whose bosom she leaned. The presence of Minnie imparted new life and strength to each drooping member of that little family; and she tended, with assiduous care, her now repentant father,—ministering to his wants, day and night. He was rejoiced to know, a change had taken place in the fortunes of his gentle wife and dear children; but remorse was like a vulture at his heart, and he could not be happy. It was hard, very hard for him to rise above his besetting sin; but his guardian angel was always near, even at midnight, to strengthen and encourage; and he would say, "You see, dear Minnie, what a slave I am, even with the fear of God before my eyes." He was desirous to put his name to the pledge, and did so. He shed tears of sorrow and repentance; and said, that if it was the will of God that he should remain in this world, still longer, he felt that he should lead a different life; but he could not retrieve the past! It was evident, however, that his hours were numbered. He lingered for a few months after Minnie's release; and then, Ella closed the eyes of her once idolized husband. Bitter tears she shed over him; for she remembered all that he had been to her in her youthful days. She thought of his sympathy and untiring love, when she was bereft of her parents; and of his tenderness, and joy, and delight, when their little Minnie was born; and how proud he was of his little Charlie. She dwelt upon his goodness and kindness to all around, until he became the slave of alcohol. She forgot those long years of suffering; or, if she thought of them, only pitied the poor slave of intemperance, the more. After Ella had looked upon her husband, for the last time, she turned to Minnie, and, clasping her to her heart, said, "My first-born darling! my precious one! thou hast been a blessing to us all. Thou didst err; but God has overruled that evil for our good. Little did I think, when I told thee that stern duties were before us, that thou would'st finally triumph so gloriously. I said thou would'st feel nothing but the thorns, but thou wilt be refreshed with the flowers; and surely thou hast richly deserved it!" Charles, the noble minded Charles, was ever an apostle of Temperance. He had suffered so much himself, that he could never forget the sufferings of others, particularly the children of intemperate parents. He had a house built, and thither he would have all poor, street drunkards carried. There they were fed and clothed, and when the mania came on, stimulants comparatively harmless, were given them instead; and he saved hundreds in this way.

Several years have elapsed since Minnie quitted her narrow cell, and the affianced lovers are of one heart and mind. They have striven to make life beautiful and sublime, by doing cheerfully the duty that lies nearest, and by being always active in every good word and work. Theirs was not the mad haste that would lead them to "sacrifice the palm-tree for the temporary draught of wine," as alas, thousands have done and are constantly doing. Arthur had but one purpose and aim in life, and the gentle, but heroic being was ever by his side, as an angel of patience and of hope—of endurance and trust!

The long, dark, starless night had vanished, and the morning star shone brightly in the heavens,—its pure, tender light, falling on all around. While the beholders were gazing upon it, it gradually disappeared from their view, obscured by the stronger light of the rising sun; for its mission was to usher in that glorious orb whose warmth should fertilize the earth, and whose bright beams, were to make glad the hearts of the sorrowing ones. Thus, slowly, and noiselessly drops the curtain, before the advent of the true marriage of Love and Wisdom.

Part 3

WOMEN'S ROLES

HARRIET BEECHER STOWE
1811–1896

B est known for her anti-slavery novel, *Uncle Tom's Cabin*, Stowe
grew up in a family long associated with organized religion (her
father, Lyman Beecher, and brothers, most notably Henry Ward
Beecher, were ministers) and continued the tradition by marrying
a minister, Calvin Stowe. Valuing education and supporting reform
efforts became a part of her life. Not surprisingly, her earliest writings addressed intemperance. Although not actively involved with
temperance organizations, she did write at least one public letter
praising women for their effectiveness in temperance work.

Alcohol and its abuse play important roles in *Uncle Tom's
Cabin*, the century's best-known novel. In the opening scene of the
novel, Stowe quickly reveals the nature of the slave trader Haley
and sets the tone for the rest of the novel. In quick succession, Haley
drinks wine, two glasses of brandy, and then more wine. Alcohol
is also implicated in the horrid activities at Simon Legree's planta-
tion. The wallpaper in Legree's home is "defaced, in spots, by slops
of beer and wine" (513); Legree also plies his henchmen with whiskey and attempts to get Emmeline to drink brandy against her will.
For Stowe, the heavenly home is the Quaker one, where alcohol is
never present.

Stowe wrote several explicitly temperance stories. The stories
demonstrate her belief in women's ability to bring about change.
They also illustrate the popularity of the topic and the many op-

portunities for publishing the temperance topic offered. For example, "The Coral Ring," which follows, was featured in an 1843 gift book, *The Christian Souvenir: An Offering for Christmas and The New Year* (ed. Isaac F. Shepard, Boston: H. B. Williams). In 1848, the same story was published in *Godey's Lady's Book,* and in 1853 the Scottish Temperance League published *The Coral Ring* under its own cover. In addition, Stowe included the story in her collection *The May Flower, and Miscellaneous Writings* (1855), as well as in a later collection, *Stories, Sketches and Studies.*

Stowe originally published another temperance story, "Let Every Man Mind His Own Business," in 1839 in the *New-York Evangelist* as "The Drunkard Reclaimed"; she later included the work in several gift books and eventually collected the story in *The May Flower, and Miscellaneous Writings.* The story demonstrates an ambivalence on the issue of wives abandoning alcoholic husbands. Caught between duty toward her children and duty toward her husband, the protagonist compromises, sending her children with her brother so that she may make a final successful effort to save her alcoholic husband from *"everlasting despair"* (174). Stowe is thus able to finesse both the divorce issue and concern about the damage inflicted upon children when women stay in a bad relationship. In 1853, she published other temperance stories in *Temperance Tales.*

Her contention that women, by their influence, can save men from the dangers of alcohol helps to establish temperance as a women's issue, since only women, it seems, have the power to effect change. "Betty's Bright Idea," another widely published temperance story, demonstrates the ability of a young, caring girl to assist the family of a drunkard and to help him overcome his problem. In "The Coral Ring," Stowe indicts a social system that wastes women's lives in "parlor ornamentation." Through Edward Ashton, she acknowledges young women's intelligence and capacity to provide valuable service; she proposes that they find meaningful purpose in helping the sick and poor or, if uncomfortable in such an environment, in other useful labor. Stowe encourages young women to use their influence—to lead young men in positive directions—but also to openly challenge authority figures who insult them. She further extends public reform work to women by suggesting that one whose only purpose is "pass[ing] her time in as amusing a way as she can" is "selfish" for not making better use of her power.

The Coral Ring

"There is no time of life in which young girls are so thoroughly selfish as from fifteen to twenty," said Edward Ashton, deliberately, as he laid down a book he had been reading, and leaned over the center table.

"You insulting fellow!" replied a tall, brilliant-looking creature, who was lounging on an ottoman hard by, over one of Dickens's last works.

"Truth, coz, for all that," said the gentleman, with the air of one who means to provoke a discussion.

"Now, Edward, this is just one of your wholesale declarations, for nothing only to get me into a dispute with you, you know," replied the lady. "On your conscience, now, (if you have one,) is it not so?"

"My conscience feels quite easy, cousin, in subscribing to that sentiment as my confession of faith," replied the gentleman, with provoking *sang froid*.

"Pshaw! it's one of your fusty old bachelor notions. See what comes, now, of your living to your time of life without a wife—disrespect for the sex, and all that. Really, cousin, your symptoms are getting alarming."

"Nay, now, Cousin Florence," said Edward, "you are a girl of moderately good sense, with all your nonsense. Now don't you (I know you *do*) think just so too?"

"Think just so too!—do you hear the creature?" replied Florence. "No, sir; you can speak for yourself in this matter, but I beg leave to enter my protest when you speak for me too."

"Well, now, where is there, coz, among all our circle, a young girl that has any sort of purpose or object in life, to speak of, except to make herself as interesting and agreeable as possible? to be admired, and to pass her time in as amusing a way as she can? Where will you find one between fifteen and twenty that has any serious regard for the improvement and best welfare of those with whom she is connected at all, or that modifies her conduct, in the least, with reference to it? Now, cousin, in very serious earnest, you have about as much real character, as much earnestness and depth of feeling, and as much good sense, when one can get at it, as any young lady of them all; and yet, on your conscience, can you say that you live with any sort of reference to any body's good, or to any thing but your own amusement and gratification?"

"What a shocking adjuration!" replied the lady; "prefaced, too, by a three-story compliment. Well, being so adjured, I must think to the best of my ability. And now, seriously and soberly, I don't see as I am selfish. I do all that I have any occasion to do for any body. You know that we have servants to do every thing that is necessary about the house, so that there is not occasion for my making any display of housewifery excellence. And I wait on mamma if she has a headache, and hand papa his slippers and newspaper, and find Uncle John's spectacles for him twenty times a day, (no small matter, that,) and then—"

"But, after all, what is the object and purpose of your life?"

"Why, I haven't any. I don't see how I can have any—that is, as I am made. Now, you know, I've none of the fussing, baby-tending, herb-tea-making recommendations of Aunt Sally, and divers others of the class commonly called *useful*. Indeed, to tell the truth, I think useful persons are commonly rather fussy and stupid. They are just like the boneset, and hoarhound, and catnip—very necessary to be raised in a garden, but not in the least ornamental."

"And you charming young ladies, who philosophize in kid slippers and French dresses, are the tulips and roses—very charming, and delightful, and sweet, but fit for nothing on earth but parlor ornaments."

"Well, parlor ornaments are good in their way," said the young lady, coloring, and looking a little vexed.

"So you give up the point, then," said the gentleman, "that you girls are good for—just to amuse yourselves, amuse others, look pretty, and be agreeable."

"Well, and if we behave well to our parents, and are amiable in the family—I don't know—and yet," said Florence, sighing, "I have often had a sort of vague idea of something higher that we might become; yet, really, what more than this is expected of us? what else can we do?"

"I used to read in old-fashioned novels about ladies visiting the sick and the poor," replied Edward. "You remember Coelebs in Search of a Wife?"

"Yes, truly; that is to say, I remember the story part of it, and the love scenes; but as for all those everlasting conversations of Dr. Barlow, Mr. Stanley, and nobody knows who else, I skipped those, of course. But really, this visiting and tending the poor, and all that, seems very well in a story, where the lady goes into a picturesque cottage, half overgrown with honeysuckle, and finds an emaciated, but still beautiful woman propped up by pillows. But come to the downright matter of fact of poking about in all these vile, dirty alleys, and entering little dark rooms, amid troops of grinning children, and smelling codfish and onions, and nobody knows what—dear me, my benevolence always evaporates before I get through. I'd rather pay any body five dollars a day to do it for me than do it myself. The fact is, that I have neither fancy nor nerves for this kind of thing."

"Well, granting, then, that you can do nothing for your fellow-creatures unless you are to do it in the most genteel, comfortable, and picturesque manner possible, is there not a great field for a woman like you, Florence, in your influence over your associates? With your talents for conversation, your tact, and self-possession, and ladylike gift of saying any thing you choose, are you not responsible, in some wise, for the influence you exert over those by whom you are surrounded?"

"I never thought of that," replied Florence.

"Now, you remember the remarks that Mr. Fortesque made the other evening on the religious services at church?"

"Yes, I do; and I thought then he was too bad."

"And I do not suppose there was one of you ladies in the room that did not think so too, but yet the matter was all passed over with smiles and with not a single insinuation that he had said any thing unpleasing or disagreeable."

"Well, what could we do? One does not want to be rude you know."

"Do! Could you not, Florence, you who have always taken the lead in society, and who have been noted for always being able to say and do what you please—could you not have shown him that those remarks were unpleasing to you, as decidedly as you certainly would have done if they had related to the character of your father or brother? To my mind, a woman of true moral feeling should consider herself as much insulted when her religion is treated with contempt as if the contempt were shown to herself. Do you not *know* the power which is given to you women to awe and restrain us in your presence, and to guard the sacredness of things which you treat as holy? Believe me, Florence, that Fortesque, infidel as he is, would reverence a woman with whom he dared not trifle on sacred subjects."

Florence rose from her seat with a heightened color, her dark eyes brightening through tears.

"I am sure what you say is just, cousin, and yet I have never thought of it before. I will—I am determined to begin, after this, to live with some better purpose than I have done."

"And let me tell you, Florence, in starting a new course, as in learning to walk, taking the first step is every thing. Now, I have a first step to propose to you."

"Well, cousin—"

"Well, you know, I suppose, that among your train of adorers you number Colonel Elliot?"

Florence smiled.

"And perhaps you do not know, what is certainly true, that, among the most discerning and cool part of his friends, Elliot is considered a lost man."

"Good Heavens! Edward, what do you mean?"

"Simply this: that with all his brilliant talents, his amiable and generous feelings, and his success in society, Elliot has not self-control enough to prevent his becoming confirmed in intemperate habits."

"I never dreamed of this," replied Florence. "I knew that he was spirited and free, fond of society, and excitable; but never suspected any thing beyond."

"Elliot has tact enough never to appear in ladies' society when he is not in a fit state for it," replied Edward; "but yet it is so."

"But is he really so bad?"

"He stands just on the verge, Florence; just where a word fitly spoke might turn him. He is a noble creature, full of all sorts of fine impulses and feelings; the only son of a mother who dotes on him, the idolized brother of sisters who love him as you love your brother, Florence; and he stands where a word, a look—so they be of the right kind—might save him."

"And why, then, do you not speak to him?" said Florence.

"Because I am not the best person, Florence. There is another who can do it better; one whom he admires, who stands in a position which would forbid his feeling angry; a person, cousin, whom I have heard in gayer moments say that she knew how to say any thing she pleased without offending any body."

"O Edward!" said Florence, coloring; "do not bring up my foolish speeches against me, and do not speak as if I ought to interfere in this matter, for indeed I cannot do it. I never could in the world, I am certain I could not."

"And so," said Edward, "you, whom I have heard say so many things which no one else could say, or dared to say—you, who have gone on with your laughing assurance in your own powers of pleasing, shrink from trying that power when a noble and generous heart might be saved by it. You have been willing to venture a great deal for the sake of amusing yourself and winning admiration; but you dare not say a word for any high or noble purpose. Do you not see how you confirm what I said of the selfishness of you women?"

"But you must remember, Edward, this is a matter of great delicacy."

"That word *delicacy* is a charming cover-all in all these cases, Florence. Now, here is a fine, noble-spirited young man, away from his mother and sisters, away from any family friend who might care for him, tempted, betrayed, almost to ruin, and a few words from you, said as a woman knows how to say them, might be his salvation. But you will coldly look on and see him go to destruction, because you have too much *delicacy* to make the effort—like the man that would not help his neighbor out of the water because he had never had the honor of an *introduction*."

"But, Edward, consider how peculiarly fastidious Elliot is—how jealous of any attempt to restrain and guide him."

"And just for that reason it is that *men* of his acquaintance cannot do any thing with him. But what are you women made with so much tact and power of charming for, if it is not to do these very things that we cannot do? It is a delicate matter—true; and has not Heaven given to you a fine touch and a fine eye for just such delicate matters? Have you not seen, a thousand times, that what might be resented as an impertinent interference on the part of a man, comes to us as a flattering expression of interest from the lips of a woman?"

"Well, but, cousin, what would you have me do? How would you have me do it?" said Florence, earnestly.

"You know that Fashion, which makes so many wrong turns and so many absurd ones, has at last made one good one, and it is now a fashionable thing to sign the temperance pledge. Elliot himself would be glad to do it, but he foolishly committed himself against it in the outset, and now feels bound to stand to his opinion. He has, too, been rather rudely assailed by some of the apostles of the new state of things, who did not understand the peculiar points of his character; in short, I am afraid that he will feel bound to go to destruction for the sake of supporting his own opinion. Now, if I should undertake with him, he might shoot me; but I hardly think there is any thing of the sort to be apprehended in your case. Just try your enchantments; you have bewitched wise men into doing foolish things before now; try, now, if you can't bewitch a foolish man into doing a wise thing."

Florence smiled archly, but instantly grew more thoughtful.

"Well, cousin," she said, "I will try. Though you are liberal in your ascriptions of power, yet I can put the matter to the test of experiment."

Florence Elmore was, at the time we speak of, in her twentieth year. Born of one of the wealthiest families in ———, highly educated and accomplished, idolized by her parents and brothers, she had entered the world as one born to command. With much native nobleness and magnanimity of character, with warm and impulsive feelings, and a capability of every thing high or great, she had hitherto lived solely for her own amusement, and looked on the whole brilliant circle by which she was surrounded, with all its various actors, as something got up for her special diversion. The idea of influencing any one, for better or worse, by any thing she ever said or did had never occurred to her. The crowd of admirers of the other sex, who, as a matter of course, were always about her, she regarded as so many sources of diversion; but the idea of feeling any sympathy with them as human beings, or of making use of her power over them for their improvement, was one that had never entered her head.

Edward Ashton was an old bachelor cousin of Florence's, who, having earned the title of oddity, in general society, availed himself of it to exercise a turn for telling the truth to the various young ladies of his acquaintance, especially to his fair cousin Florence. We remark, by the by, that these privileged truth tellers are quite a necessary of life to young ladies in the full tide of society, and we really think it would be worth while for every dozen of them to unite to keep a person of this kind on a salary, for the benefit of the whole. However, that is nothing to our present purpose; we must return to our fair heroine, whom we left, at the close of the last conversation, standing in deep revery, by the window.

"It's more than half true," she said to herself—"more than half. Here am I, twenty years old, and never have thought of any thing,

never done any thing, except to amuse and gratify myself; no purpose, no object; nothing high, nothing dignified, nothing worth living for! Only a parlor ornament—heigh ho! Well, I really do believe I could do something with this Elliot; and yet how dare I try?"

Now, my good readers, if you are anticipating a love story, we
must hasten to put in our disclaimer; you are quite mistaken in the
case. Our fair, brilliant heroine was, at this time of speaking, as
heart-whole as the diamond on her bosom, which reflected the light
in too many sparkling rays ever to absorb it. She had, to be sure,
half in earnest, half in jest, maintained a bantering, platonic sort
of friendship with George Elliot. She had danced, ridden, sung, and
sketched with him; but so had she with twenty other young men;
and as to coming to any thing tender with such a quick, brilliant,
restless, creature, Elliot would as soon have undertaken to senti-
mentalize over a glass of soda water. No; there was decidedly no
love in the case.

"What a curious ring that is!" said Elliot to her, a day or two
after, as they were reading together.

"It is a knight's ring," said she, playfully, as she drew it off and
pointed to a coral cross set in the gold, "a ring for the red-cross
knights. Come, now, I've a great mind to bind you to my service
with it."

"Do, lady fair," said Elliot, stretching out his hand for the ring.

An evening or two after, Elliot attended Florence to a party at
Mrs. B.'s. Every thing was gay and brilliant, and there was no lack
either of wit or win. Elliot was standing in a little alcove, spread with
refreshments, with a glass of wine in his hand. "I forbid it; the cup
is poisoned!" said a voice in his ear. He turned quickly, and Florence was at his side. Every one was busy, with laughing and talking around, and nobody saw the sudden start and flush that these
words produced, as Elliot looked earnestly in the lady's face. She
smiled, and pointed playfully to the ring; but after all, there was in
her face an expression of agitation and interest which she could not
repress, and Elliot felt, however playful the manner, that she was
in earnest; and as she glided away in the crowd, he stood with his
arms folded, and his eyes fixed on the spot where she disappeared.

"Is it possible that I am suspected—that there are things said
of me as if I were in danger?" were the first thoughts that flashed
through his mind. How strange that a man may appear doomed,
given up, and lost, to the eye of every looker on, before he begins

to suspect himself! This was the first time that any defined appre-
hension of loss of character had occurred to Elliot, and he was
startled as if from a dream.

"What the deuce is the matter with you, Elliot? You look as
solemn as a hearse!" said a young man near by.

"Has Miss Elmore cut you?" said another.

"Come, man, have a glass," said a third.

"Let him alone—he's bewitched," said a fourth. "I saw the spell
laid on him. None of us can say but our turn may come next."

An hour later, that evening, Florence was talking with her usual
spirit to a group who were collected around her, when, suddenly
looking up, she saw Elliot, standing in an abstracted manner, at one
of the windows that looked out into the balcony.

"He is offended, I dare say," she thought; "but what do I care?
For once in my life I have tried to do a right thing—a good thing. I
have risked giving offence for less than this, many a time." Still,
Florence could not but feel tremulous, when a few moments after,
Elliot approached her and offered his arm for a promenade. They
walked up and down the room, she talking volubly, and he answer-
ing yes and no, till at length, as if by accident, he drew her into the
balcony which overhung the garden. The moon was shining brightly,
and every thing without, in its placid quietness, contrasted strangely
with the busy, hurrying scene within.

"Miss Elmore," said Elliot, abruptly, "may I ask you, sincerely,
had you any design in a remark you made to me in the early part
of the evening?"

Florence paused, and though habitually the most practised and
self-possessed of women, the color actually receded from her cheek,
as she answered,—

"Yes, Mr. Elliot; I must confess that I had."

"And is it possible, then, that you have heard any thing?"

"I have heard, Mr. Elliot, that which makes me tremble for you,
and for those whose life, I know, is bound up in you; and, tell me,
were it well or friendly in me to know that such things were said,
that such danger existed, and not to warn you of it?"

Elliot stood for a few moments in silence.

"Have I offended? Have I taken too great a liberty?" said Florence gently.

Hither to Elliot had only seen in Florence the self-possessed,
assured, light-hearted woman of fashion; but there was a reality and

depth of feeling in the few words she had spoke to him, in this interview, that opened to him entirely a new view in her character.

"No, Miss Elmore," replied he, earnestly, after some pause; "I may be *pained*, offended I cannot be. To tell the truth, I have been thoughtless, excited, dazzled; my spirits, naturally buoyant, have carried me, often, too far; and lately I have painfully suspected my own powers of resistance. I have really felt that I needed help, but have been too proud to confess, even to myself, that I needed it. You, Miss Elmore, have done what, perhaps, no one else could have done. I am overwhelmed with gratitude, and I shall bless you for it to the latest day of my life. I am ready to pledge myself to any thing you may ask on this subject."

"Then," said Florence, "do not shrink from doing what is safe, and necessary, and right for you to do, because you have once said you would not do it. You understand me."

"Precisely," replied Elliot; "and you shall be obeyed."

It was not more than a week before the news was circulated that even George Elliot had signed the pledge of temperance. There was much wondering at this sudden turn among those who had known his utter repugnance to any measure of the kind, and the extent to which he had yielded to temptation; but few knew how fine and delicate had been the touch to which his pride had yielded.

LOUISA MAY ALCOTT
1832–1888

Louisa May Alcott is best known for *Little Women* and the series that continued the story of the March family. Louisa and her three sisters were encouraged to develop their talents, and all became respected for their work. Louisa's talent, writing, helped to support her family, especially after the success of *Little Women*.

Alcott was nurtured in a tradition of reform. Her parents supported abolition and participated in numerous other reform efforts. They took part in communal living and were primarily vegetarians. The Alcotts also boycotted products of slave labor and promoted numerous innovative educational reforms. Louisa herself participated actively in the temperance movement, serving as corresponding secretary of the Concord, Massachusetts, WCTU in 1883.

Such support for reform appears throughout Alcott's works. In *Little Women*, Alcott depicts the problems Meg must confront when she is enticed to drink champagne at a ball; later, Meg takes a stand against intoxicating beverages when she decides that her wedding will be alcohol free. Alcott makes reference to temperance in nearly all her novels. She titles a chapter in *Jack and Jill* "Good Templars," devoting the entire chapter to Frank and Jack's participation in the temperance cause. In *Jo's Boys*, danger associated with alcohol threatens each of Jo's sons at one time or another; Rose, in *Rose in Bloom*, exacts a promise from Charlie that he will not drink, but Charlie takes a final fling with champagne and is subsequently thrown from his horse and dies; and *Little Men*'s Mr. Bhaer openly opposes drinking, gambling, and swearing.

Written in 1876, not long after the founding of the Woman's Christian Temperance Union, "Silver Pitchers," appearing in *Silver Pitchers: and Independence, a Centennial Love Story* (Boston: Roberts Brothers), is a specifically temperance story. Alcott dismisses women's inability to make a difference "because I am only a girl." She demonstrates the many and far-reaching impacts three young women have on a community. Alcott insists that women should "use our youth, our beauty, our influence for something nobler than merely pleasing men's eyes, or playing with their hearts."

Priscilla's "crusade," "in the only way we girls can do it," seems to offer a means of participation by girls and young women. More mature women generally led the public protests that had erupted across the nation. The Woman's Crusade (1873–74) was recent history at the time of the story's publication, and Priscilla's suggestion that girls "can't preach and pray in streets and bar-rooms" recalls the recent activity of tens of thousands of women in just such demonstrations. Alcott provides suggestions for younger women who might wish to take part in the temperance cause.

Silver Pitchers

Chapter I. How It Began

"We can do nothing about it except show our displeasure in some proper manner," said Portia, in her most dignified tone.

"I should like to cut them all dead for a year to come; and I'm not sure that I won't!" cried Pauline, fiercely.

"We *ought* to make it impossible for such a thing to happen again, and I think we *might*," added Priscilla, so decidedly that the others looked at her in surprise.

The three friends sat by the fire "talking things over," as girls love to do. Pretty creatures, all of them, as they nestled together on the lounge in dressing-gowns and slippers, with unbound hair, eyes still bright with excitement, and tongues that still wagged briskly.

Usually the chat was of dresses, compliments, and all the little adventures that befall gay girls at a merry-making. But to-night something of uncommon interest absorbed the three, and kept them talking earnestly long after they should have been asleep.

Handsome Portia looked out from her blonde locks with a disgusted expression, as she sipped the chocolate thoughtful mamma had left inside the fender. Rosy-faced Pauline sat staring indignantly at the fire; while in gentle Priscilla's soft eyes the shadow of a real sorrow seemed to mingle with the light of a strong determination.

Yes, something had happened at this Thanksgiving festival which much offended the three friends, and demanded grave consideration on their part; for the "Sweet P's," as Portia, Pris, and Polly were called, were the belles of the town. One ruled by right of beauty and position, one by the power of a character so sweet and strong that its influence was widely felt, and one by the wit and winsomeness of a high yet generous spirit.

It had been an unusually pleasant evening, for after the quilting bee in the afternoon good Squire Allen had given a bountiful supper, and all the young folks of the town had joined in the old-fashioned games, which made the roof sing with hearty merriment.

All would have gone well if some one had not privately introduced something stronger than the cider provided by the Squire,— a mysterious and potent something, which caused several of the young men to betray that they were decidedly the worse for their libations.

That was serious enough; but the crowning iniquity was the putting of brandy into the coffee, which it was considered decorous for the young girls to prefer instead of cider.

Who the reprobates were remained a dead secret, for the young men laughed off the dreadful deed as a joke and the Squire apologized in the handsomest manner.

But the girls felt much aggrieved and would not be appeased, though the elders indulgently said, "Young men will be young men," even while they shook their heads over the pranks played and the nonsense spoken under the influence of the wine that had been so slyly drank.

Now what should be done about it? The "Sweet P's" knew that their mates would look to them for guidance at this crisis, for they were the leaders in all things. So they must decide on some line of conduct for all to adopt, as the best way of showing their disapproval of such practical jokes.

When Pris spoke, the others looked at her with surprise; for there was a new expression in her face, and both asked wonderingly, "How?"

"There are several ways, and we must decide which is the best. One is to refuse invitations to the sociable next week."

"But I've just got a lovely new dress expressly for it!" cried Portia, tragically.

"Then we might decline providing any supper," began Pris.

"That wouldn't prevent the boys from providing it, and I never could get through the night without a morsel of something!" exclaimed Polly, who loved to see devoted beings bending before her, with offerings of ice, or struggling manfully to steer a glass of lemonade through a tumultuous sea of silk and broadcloth, feeling well repaid by a word or smile from her when they landed safely.

"True, and it *would* be rather rude and resentful; for I am sure they will be models of deportment next time," and gentle Pris showed signs of relenting, though that foolish joke had cost her more than either of the others.

For a moment all sat gazing thoughtfully at the fire, trying to devise some awful retribution for the sinners, no part of which should fall upon themselves. Suddenly Polly clapped her hands, crying with a triumphant air,—

"I've got it, girls! I've got it!"

"What? How? Tell us quick!"

"We *will* refuse to go to the first sociable, and that will make a tremendous impression, for half the nice girls will follow our lead, and the boys will be in despair. Every one will ask why we are not there; and what can those poor wretches say but the truth? Won't that be a bitter pill for my lords and gentlemen?"

"It will certainly be one to us," said Portia, thinking of the "heavenly blue dress" with a pang.

"Wait a bit; our turn will come at the next sociable. To this we can go with escorts of our own choosing, or none at all, for they are free and easy affairs, you know. So we need be under no obligation to any of those sinners, and can trample upon them as much as we please."

"But how about the games, the walks home, and all the pleasant little services the young men of our set like to offer and we to receive?" asked Portia, who had grown up with these "boys," as Polly called them, and found it hard to turn her back on the playmates who had now become friends or lovers.

"Bless me! I forgot that the feud might last more than one evening. Give me an idea, Pris," and Polly's triumph ended suddenly.

"I will," answered Pris, soberly; "for at this informal sociable we can institute a new order of things. It will make a talk, but I think we have a right to do it, and I'm sure it will have a good effect, if we only hold out, and don't mind being laughed at. Let us refuse to associate with the young men whom we know to be what is called 'gay,' and accept as friends those of whose good habits we are sure. If they complain, as of course they will, we can say their own misconduct made it necessary and there we have them."

"But, Pris, who ever heard of such an idea? People will say all sorts of things about us!" said Portia, rather startled at the proposition.

"Let them! I say it's a grand plan, and I'll stand by you, Pris, through thick and thin!" cried Polly, who enjoyed the revolutionary spirit of the thing.

"We can but try it, and give the young men a lesson; for, girls, matters are coming to a pass, when it is our *duty* to do something. I cannot think it is right for us to sit silent and see these fine fellows getting into bad habits because no one dares or cares to speak out, though we gossip and complain in private."

"Do you want us to begin a crusade?" asked Portia, uneasily.

"Yes, in the only way we girls can do it. We can't preach and pray in streets and bar-rooms, but we may at home, and in our own little world show that we want to use our influence for good. I know that you two can do any thing you choose with the young people in this town, and it is just that set who most need the sort of help you can give, if you will."

"*You* have more influence than both of us put together; so don't be modest, Pris, but tell us what to do and I'll do it, even if I'm hooted at," cried warm-hearted Polly, won at once.

"You must do as you think right; but *I* have made up my mind to protest against wine-drinking in every way I can. I know it will cost me much, for I have nothing to depend upon but the good opinion of my friends; nevertheless, I shall do what seems my duty, and I may be able to save some other girl from the heart-aches I have known."

"You won't lose our good opinion, you dear little saint! Just tell us how to begin and we will follow our leader," cried both Portia and Polly, fired with emulation by their friend's quiet resolution.

Pris looked from one to the other, and seeing real love and confidence in their faces, was moved to deepen the impression she had made, by telling them the sad secret of her life. Pressing her hands tightly together, and drooping her head, she answered in words that were the more pathetic for their brevity,—

"Dear girls, don't think me rash or sentimental, for I *know* what I am trying to do, and you will understand my earnestness better when I tell you that a terrible experience taught me to dread this appetite more than death. It killed my father, broke mother's heart, and left me all alone."

As she paused, poor Pris hid her face and shrank away, as if by this confession she had forfeited her place in the respect of her mates. But the girlish hearts only clung the closer to her, and proved the sincerity of their affection by sympathetic tears and tender words, as Portia and Polly held her fast, making a prettier group than the marble nymphs on the mantelpiece; for the Christian graces quite outdid the heathen ones.

Polly spoke first, and spoke cheerfully, feeling, with the instinct of a fine nature, that Priscilla's grief was too sacred to be talked about, and that they could best show their appreciation of her confidence by proving themselves ready to save others from a sorrow like hers.

"Let us be a little society of three, and do what we can. I shall begin at home, and watch over brother Ned; for lately he has been growing away from me, somehow, and I'm afraid he is beginning to be 'gay.' I shall get teased unmercifully; but I won't mind if I keep him safe."

"I have no one at home to watch over but papa, and he is in no danger, of course; so I shall show Charley Lord that I am not pleased with him," said Portia, little dreaming where her work was to be done.

"And you will set about reforming that delightful scapegrace, Phil Butler?" added Polly, peeping archly into the still drooping face of Pris.

"I have lost my right to do it, for I told him to-night that love and respect must go together in my heart," and Pris wiped her wet eyes with a hand that no longer wore a ring.

Portia and Polly looked at one another in dismay, for by this act Pris proved how thoroughly in earnest she was.

Neither had any words of comfort for so great a trouble, and sat silently caressing her, till Pris looked up, with her own serene smile again, and said, as if to change the current of their thoughts,—

"We must have a badge for the members of our new society, so let us each wear one of these tiny silver pitchers. I've lost the mate to mine, but Portia has a pair just like them. You can divide, then we are all provided for."

Portia ran to her jewel-case, caught up a pair of delicate filigree ear-rings, hastily divided a narrow velvet ribbon into three parts, attached to each a silver pitcher, and, as the friends smilingly put on these badges, they pledged their loyalty to the new league by a silent good night kiss.

Chapter II. A Declaration of Independence

Great was the astonishment of their "set" when it was known that the "Sweet P's" had refused all invitations to the opening sociable.

The young men were in despair, the gossips talked themselves hoarse discussing the affair, and the girls exulted; for, as Polly predicted, the effect of their first step was "tremendous."

When the evening came, however, by one accord they met in Portia's room, to support each other through that trying period. They affected to be quite firm and cheerful; but one after the other broke down, and sadly confessed that the sacrifice to principle was harder than they expected. What added to their anguish was the fact that the Judge's house stood just opposite the town-hall, and every attempt to keep away from certain windows proved a dead failure.

"It is so trying to see those girls go in with their dresses bundled up, and not even know what they wear," mourned Portia, watching shrouded figures trip up the steps that led to the paradise from which she had exiled herself.

"They must be having a capital time, for every one seems to have gone. I wonder who Phil took," sighed Pris, when at length the carriages ceased to roll.

"Girls! I wish to be true to my vow, but if you don't hold me I shall certainly rush over there and join in the fun, for that music is too much for me," cried Polly, desperately, as the singing began.

It was an endless evening to the three pretty pioneers, though they went early to bed, and heroically tried to sleep with that distracting music in their ears. Slumber came at last, but as the clocks were striking twelve a little ghost emerged from Portia's room, and gliding to the hall window vanished among the heavy damask curtains.

Presently another little ghost appeared from the same quarter, and stealing softly to the same window was about to vanish in the same capacious draperies, when a stifled cry was heard, and Portia, the second sprite, exclaimed in an astonished whisper,—

"Why, Pris, are you here, too? I saw Polly creep away from me, and came to take her back. How dare you go wandering about and startling me out of my wits in this way?"

"I was only looking to see if it was all over," quavered Pris, meekly emerging from the right-hand curtain.

"So was I!" laughed Polly, bouncing out from the left-hand one.

There was a sound of soft merriment in that shadowy hall for a moment, and then the spirits took a look at the world outside, for the moon was shining brightly. Yes, the fun was evidently over, for the lamps were being extinguished, and several young men stood on the steps exchanging last words. One wore a cloak theatrically thrown over the shoulder, and Polly knew him at once.

"That's Ned! I *must* hear what they are saying. Keep quiet and I'll listen," she whispered, rolling herself in the dark folds of the curtain and opening the window a crack, so that a frosty breeze could blow freely into her left ear.

"You'll get your death," murmured Portia, shivering in her quilted wrapper.

"O, never mind!" cried Pris, who recognized the tallest man in the group, and was wild to catch a word from "poor Phil."

"They think they've done a fine thing; but, bless their little hearts, we'll show that we can do without them by not asking them to the next sociable, or taking notice of them if they go. That will bring them round without fail," said one masculine voice, with a jolly laugh.

"Many thanks for letting us know your plots, Mr. Lord. Now we can arrange a nice little surprise for *you*," and Portia made a scornful curtsey in the dark.

"Faith! I don't blame the girls much, for that was a confoundedly ungentlemanly trick of yours, and I'll thank you not to lay any of the blame of it on me; I've got as much as I can carry without that," said the tall figure, stalking away alone.

"I'm *so* glad to know that Phil had nothing to do with it!" breathed Pris, gratefully.

"Come on, Charley! I must get home as soon as possible, or Polly will be down on me, for she has taken a new tack lately, and holds forth on the error of my ways like a granny."

"Won't I give Ned an extra lecture for that speech, the rascal!"

and Polly shook a small fist at him as her brother passed under the window, blissfully unconscious of the avenging angels up aloft.

"'Tis well; let us away and take sweet counsel how we may annihilate them," added Polly, melodramatically, as the three ghosts vanished from the glimpses of the moon.

Every one turned out to the sociables, for they were town affairs, and early hours, simple suppers, and games of all sorts, made it possible for old and young to enjoy them together.

On the night of the second one there was a goodly gathering, for the public rebuke administered to the young men had made a stir, and everybody was curious to see what the consequences would be when the parties met.

There was a sensation, therefore, when a whisper went around that the "Sweet P's" had come, and a general smile of wonder and amusement appeared when the girls entered, Portia on the arm of her father, Polly gallantly escorted by her twelve-year-old brother Will, and Pris beside Belinda Chamberlain, whose five feet seven made her a capital cavalier.

"Outwitted!" laughed Charley Lord, taking the joke at once as he saw Portia's gray-headed squire.

"I *knew* Polly was plotting mischief, she has been so quiet lately," muttered Ned, eying his little brother with lofty scorn.

Phil said nothing, but he gave a sigh of relief on seeing that Pris had chosen an escort of whom it was impossible to be jealous.

The Judge seldom honored these gatherings, but Portia ruled papa, and when she explained the peculiar state of things, he had heroically left his easy chair to cast himself into the breach.

Master Will was in high feather at his sudden promotion, and bore himself gallantly, though almost as much absorbed by his wristbands as Mr. Toots; for Polly had got him up regardless of expense, with a gay tie, new gloves and, O, crowning splendor! a red carnation in his button-hole.

Buxom Belinda was delighted with the chance to play cavalier, and so get her fair share of all the fun going, for usually she stood in a corner smiling at an unappreciative world, like a patient sunflower.

The faces of the young men were a study as the games began, and the three girls joined in them with the partners they had chosen.

"The Judge is evidently on his mettle, but he can't stand that sort of thing long, even to please Portia; and then her Majesty will have to give in, or condescend to some one out of her set," thought Charley Lord, longing already to be taken into favor again.

The Sweet P's had come. From Louisa May Alcott, *Silver Pitchers, and Independence, a Centennial Love Story.* Boston: Little, Brown, 1908, p. 15.

"Polly will have to come and ask me to lead, if she wants to sing her favorite songs; for I'll be hanged if I do it till she has humbled herself by asking," said Ned, feeling sure that his sister would soon relent.

"If it was any one but Belinda, I don't think I could stand it," exclaimed Phil, as he watched his lost sweetheart with wistful eyes; for, though he submitted to the sentence which he knew he deserved, he could not relinquish so much excellence without deep regret.

But the young men underrated the spirit of the girls, and over-rated their own strength. The "Sweet P's" went on enjoying them-selves, apparently quite indifferent to the neglect of their once de-voted friends. But to the outcasts it was perfectly maddening to see stately Portia promenading with stout Major Quackenboss, who put his best foot foremost with the air of a conquering hero; also to behold sweet Pris playing games with her little pupils in a way that filled their small souls with rapture. But the most aggravating spectacle of all was captivating Polly, chatting gayly with young Farmer Brown, who was evidently losing both head and heart in the light of her smiles.

"It's no use, boys; I *must* have one turn with Portia, and you may hang me for a traitor immediately afterward," cried Charley at last, recklessly casting both pride and promise to the winds.

"O, very well; if you are going to give in, we may as well all eat humble pie 'together,'" and Ned imitated his weak-minded friend, glad of an excuse to claim the leadership of the little choir who led off the weekly "sing."

Phil dared not follow their example as far as Pris was concerned, but made his most elegant bow to Belinda, and begged to have the honor of seeing her home. His chagrin may be imagined when the lofty wall-flower replied, with a significant emphasis that made his face burn,—

"No, thank you. I need a very *steady* escort, for I shouldn't take a fall into a snow-bank as lightly as Pris did not long ago."

Charley met with a like fate at Portia's hands, for she outraged established etiquette by coldly declining his meek invitation to promenade, and two minutes later graciously accepting that of an unfashionable young man, who was known to belong to a temper-ance lodge.

But Ned's repulse was the most crushing of all, for in reply to his condescending hint,—

"I suppose people won't be satisfied unless we give them our favorites, hey, Polly?" he received a verbal box on the ear in the sharp answer,—

"We don't want *you*, for I intend to lead myself, and introduce a new set of songs which won't be at all to your taste."

Then, to his utter amazement and confusion, Miss Polly began to sing one of the good old temperance songs, the burden whereof was,—

> "O, that will be joyful, joyful, joyful,
>   O, that will be joyful,
>   When young men drink no more!"

It was taken up all over the hall, and the chorus rang out with an energy that caused sundry young men to turn red and dodge behind any capacious back they could find, for every one understood Polly's motive, and looked approvingly upon her as she stood singing, with an occasional quiver in the voice that usually was as clear and sweet as a blackbird's.

This unexpected manoeuvre on the part of the fair enemy produced direful perplexity and dismay in the opposing camp, wither the discomfited trio fled with tidings of their defeat. None of them dared try again in that quarter, but endeavored to console themselves by flirting wildly with such girls as still remained available, for, sad to relate, many of the most eligible took courage and followed the example of the "Sweet P's." This fact cast added gloom over the hapless gentlemen of the offending set, and caused them to fear that a social revolution would follow what they had considered merely a girlish freak.

"Shouldn't wonder if they got up a praying-band after this," groaned Ned, preparing himself for the strongest measures.

"Portia had better lead off, then, for the first time I indulged too freely in the 'rosy' was at her father's house," added Charley, laying all the blame of his expulsion from Eden upon Eve, like a true Adam.

"Look here, boys, we ought to thank, not blame them, for they want to help us, I'm sure, and some of us need help, God knows!" sighed Phil, with a look and tone that made his comrades forget their pique in sudden self-reproach; for not one of them could deny his words, or help feeling that the prayers of such innocent souls would avail much.

Chapter III. What Portia Did

"I know your head aches, mamma, so lie here and rest while I sit in my little chair and amuse you till papa comes in."

As Portia bent to arrange the sofa-cushions comfortably, the tiny silver pitcher hanging at her neck swung forward and caught her mother's eye.

"Is it the latest fashion to wear odd ear-rings instead of lockets?" she asked, touching the delicate trinket with an amused smile.

"No, mamma, it is something better than a fashion; it is the badge of a temperance league that Pris, Polly, and I have lately made," answered Portia, wondering how her mother would take it.

"Dear little girls! God bless and help you in your good work!" was the quick reply, that both surprised and touched her by its fervency.

"Then you don't mind, or think us silly to try and do even a very little toward curing this great evil?" she asked, with a sweet seriousness that was new and most becoming to her.

"My child, I feel as if it was a special providence," began her mother, then checked herself and added more quietly, "Tell me all about this league, dear, unless it is a secret."

"I have no secrets from you, mother," and nestling into her low chair Portia told her story, ending with an earnestness that showed how much she had the new plan at heart.

"So you see Polly is trying to keep Ned safe, and Pris prays for Phil; not in vain, I think, for he has been very good lately, they tell me. But *I* have neither brother nor lover to help, and I cannot go out to find any one, because I am only a girl. Now what *can* I do, mamma, for I truly want to do my share?"

The mother lay silent for a moment, then, as if yielding to an irresistible impulse, drew her daughter nearer, and whispered with lips that trembled as they spoke,—

"You can help your father, dear."

"Mamma, what can you mean?" cried Portia, in a tone of indignant surprise.

"Listen patiently, child, or I shall regret that your confidence inspired me with courage to give you mine. Never think for one moment that I accuse my husband of anything like drunkenness. He has always taken his wine like a gentleman, and never more than was good for him till of late. For this there are many excuses; he

is growing old, his life is less active than it was, many of the pleasures he once enjoyed fail now, and he has fallen into ways that
harm his health."

"I know, mama; he doesn't care for company as he used to, or
business, either, but seems quite contented to sit among his papers
half the morning, and doze over the fire half the evening. I've wondered at it, for he is not really old, and looks as hale and handsome
as ever," said Portia, feeling that something hovered on her mother's
lips which she found it hard to utter.

"You are right; it is *not* age alone that makes him so unlike his
once cheerful, active self; it is—bend lower, dear, and never breathe
to any one what I tell you now, only that you may help me save
your father's life, perhaps."

Startled by the almost solemn earnestness of these words, Portia
laid her head upon the pillow, and twilight wrapt the room in its
soft gloom, as if to shut out all the world, while the mother told
the daughter the danger that threatened him whom they both so
loved and honored.

"Papa has fallen into the way of taking more wine after dinner
than is good for him. He does not know how the habit is growing
upon him, and is hurt if I hint at such a thing. But Dr. Hall warned
me of the danger after papa's last ill turn, saying that at his age and
with his temperament apoplexy would be sure to follow over-in-
dulgence of this sort."

"O mamma, what can I do?" whispered Portia, with a thrill,
as the words of Pris returned to her with sudden force, "It killed
my father, broke mother's heart, and left me all alone."

"Watch over him, dear, amuse him as you only can, and wean
him from this unsuspected harm by all the innocent arts your daugh-
terly love can devise. I have kept this to myself, because it is hard
for a wife to see any fault in her husband; still harder for her to
speak of it even to so good a child as mine. But my anxiety unfits
me to do all I might, so I need help; and of whom can I ask it but
of you? My darling, make a little league with mother, and let us
watch and pray in secret for this dear man who is all in all to us."

What Portia answered, what comfort she gave, and what further confidences she received, may not be told, for this household
covenant was too sacred for report. No visible badge was assumed,
no audible vow taken, but in the wife's face, as it smiled on her

husband that night, there was a tenderer light than ever, and the kiss that welcomed papa was the seal upon a purpose as strong as the daughter's love.

Usually the ladies left the Judge to read his paper and take his wine in the old-fashioned way, while they had coffee in the drawing-room. As they rose, Portia saw the shadow fall upon her mother's face, which she had often seen before, but never understood till now; for *this* was the dangerous hour, this the moment when the child must stand between temptation and her father, if she could.

That evening, very soon after the servant had cleared the table of all but the decanters, a fresh young voice singing blithely in the parlor made the Judge put down his glass to listen in pleased surprise.

Presently he stepped across the hall to set both doors open, saying, in a half-reproachful tone,—

"Sing away, my lark, and let papa hear you, for he seldom gets a chance now-a-days."

"Then he must stay and applaud me, else I shall think that speech only an empty compliment," answered Portia, as she beckoned with her most winsome smile.

The Judge never dreamed that his good angel spoke; but he saw his handsome girl beaming at him from the music stool, and strolled in, meaning to go back when the song ended.

But the blue charmer in the parlor proved more potent than the red one in the dining-room, and he sat on, placidly sipping the excellent coffee, artfully supplied by his wife, quite unconscious of the little plot to rob him of the harmful indulgence which too often made his evenings a blank, and his mornings a vain attempt to revive the spirits that once kept increasing years from seeming burdensome.

That was the beginning of Portia's home mission; and from that hour she devoted herself to it, thinking of no reward, for such "secret service" could receive neither public sympathy nor praise.

It was not an easy task, as she soon found, in spite of the stanch and skillful ally who planned the attacks she dutifully made upon the enemy threatening their domestic peace.

When music ceased to have charms, and the Judge declared he *must* get his "forty winks" after dinner, Portia boldly declared that she would stay and see that he had them comfortably. So papa laughed and submitted, took a brief nap, and woke in such good-humor that he made no complaint on finding the daughter replacing the decanter.

This answered for a while; and when its efficacy seemed about to fail, unexpected help appeared; for mamma's eyes began to trouble her, and Portia proposed that her father should entertain the invalid in the evening, while she served her through the day.

This plan worked capitally, for the Judge loved his good wife almost as much as she deserved, and devoted himself to her so faithfully that the effort proved a better stimulant than any his well-stocked cellar could supply.

Dr. Hall prescribed exercise and cheerful society for his new patient, and in seeing that these instructions were obeyed the Judge got the benefit of them, and found no time for solitary wine-bibbing.

"I do believe I'm growing young again, for the old dulness is quite gone, and all this work and play does not seem to tire me a bit," he said, after an unusually lively evening with the congenial guests Portia took care to bring about him.

"But it must be very stupid for you, my dear, as we old folks have all the fun. Why don't you invite the young people here oftener?" he added, as his eye fell on Portia, gazing thoughtfully into the fire.

"I wish I dared tell you why," she answered wistfully.

"Afraid of your old papa?" and he looked both surprised and grieved.

"I won't be, for you are the kindest father that ever a girl had, and I know you'll help me, as you always do, papa. I don't dare ask my young friends here because I'm not willing to expose some of them to temptation," began Portia, bravely.

"What temptation? This?" asked her father, turning her half-averted face to the light, with a smile full of paternal pride.

"No, sir; a far more dangerous one than ever I can be."

"Then I should like to see it!" and the old gentleman looked about him for this rival of his lovely daughter.

"It is these," she said, pointing to the bottles and glasses on the sideboard.

The Judge understood her then, and knit his brows, but before he could reply Portia went steadily on, though her cheeks burned, and her eyes were bent upon the fire again.

"Father, I belong to a society of three, and we have promised to do all we can for temperance. As yet I can only show bravely the faith that is in me; therefore I can never offer any friend of mine a drop of wine, and so I do not ask them here, where it would seem most uncourteous to refuse."

"I trust no gentleman ever had cause to reproach me for the hospitality I was taught to show my guests," began the Judge in his most stately manner.

But he got no further, for a soft hand touched his lips, and Portia answered sorrowfully,—

"One man has, sir; Charley Lord says the first time he took too much was in this house, and it has grieved me to the heart, for it is true; O, papa, never let any one have the right to say that again of us! Forgive me if I seem undutiful, but I *must* speak out, for I want my dear father to stand on my side, and set an example which will make me even fonder and prouder of him than I am now."

As Portia paused, half frightened at her own frankness, she put her arms about his neck, and hid her face on his breast, still pleading her cause with the silent eloquence so hard to resist.

The judge made no reply for several minutes, and in that pause many thoughts passed through his mind, and a vague suspicion that had haunted him of late became a firm conviction. For suddenly he seemed to see his own weakness in its true light, to understand the meaning of the watchful love, the patient care that had so silently and helpfully surrounded him; and in Portia's appeal for younger men he read a tender warning to himself.

He was a proud man, but a very just one; and though a flush of anger swept across his face at first, he acknowledged the truth of the words that were so hard to speak.

With his hand laid fondly on the head that was half-hidden, lest a look should seem to reproach him, this brave old gentleman proved that he loved his neighbor better than himself, and honestly confessed his own shortcomings.

"No man shall ever say again that *I* tempted him."

Then as Portia lifted up a happy face, he looked straight into the grateful eyes that dimmed with sudden tears, and added tenderly,—

"My daughter, I am not too proud to own a fault, nor, please God, too old to mend it."

Chapter IV. What Polly Did

Since their mother's death, Polly had tried to fill her place, and take good care of the boys. But the poor little damsel had a hard time of it sometimes; for Ned, being a year or two older, thought it his duty to emancipate himself from petticoat government as rapidly as possible, and to do as he pleased, regardless of her warnings or advice.

Yet at heart he was very fond of his pretty sister. At times he felt strongly tempted to confide his troubles and perplexities to her, for since the loss of his mother he often longed for a tender, helpful creature to cheer and strengthen him.

Unfortunately he had reached the age when boys consider it "the thing" to repress every sign of regard for their own womenfolk, sisters especially; so Ned barricaded himself behind the manly superiority of his twenty years, and snubbed Polly.

Will had not yet developed this unpleasant trait, but his sister expected it, and often exclaimed, despairingly, to her bosom friends,—

"When *he* follows Ned's example, and begins to rampage, what *will* become of me?"

The father—a learned and busy man—was so occupied by the duties of his large parish, or so absorbed in the abstruse studies to which his brief leisure was devoted, that he had no time left for his children. Polly took good care of him and the house, and the boys seemed to be doing well, so he went his way in peace, quite unconscious that his eldest son needed all a father's care to keep him from the temptations to which a social nature, not evil propensities, exposed him.

Polly saw the danger, and spoke of it; but Mr. Snow only answered absently,—

"Tut, tut, my dear; you are over-anxious, and forget that young men all have a few wild oats to sow."

While Ned silenced her with that other familiar and harmful phrase, "I'm only seeing life a bit, so don't you fret, child," little dreaming that such "seeing life" too often ends in seeing death.

So Polly labored in vain, till something happened which taught them all a lesson. Ned went on a sleighing frolic with the comrades whom of all others his sister dreaded most.

"Do be careful and not come home as you did last time, for father will be in, and it would shock him dreadfully if I shouldn't be able to keep you quiet," she said anxiously.

"You little granny, I wasn't tipsy, only cheerful, and that scared you out of your wits. I've got my key, so don't sit up. I hate to have a woman glowering at me when I come in," was Ned's ungracious reply; for the memory of that occasion was not a pleasant one.

"If a woman had not been sitting up, you'd have frozen on the door-mat, you ungrateful boy," cried Polly, angrily.

Ned began to whistle, and was going off without a word when Polly's loving heart got the better of her quick temper, and, catching up a splendid tippet she had made for him, she ran after her brother. She caught him just as he opened the front door, and, throwing both her arms and her gift about his neck, said, with a kiss that produced a sensation in the sleigh-full of gentlemen at the gate,—

"Ah, do be friends, for I can't bear to part so."

Now if no one had been by, Ned would have found that pleasant mingling of soft arms and worsted a genuine comforter; but masculine pride would not permit him to relent before witnesses, and the fear of being laughed at by "those fellows" made him put both sister and gift roughly aside, with a stern,—

"I won't be molly-coddled! Let me alone and shut that door!"

Polly did let him alone, with a look that haunted him, and shut the door with a spirited bang, that much amused the gentlemen.

"I'll never try to do anything for Ned again! It's no use, and he may go to the bad for all I care!" said Polly to herself, after a good cry.

But she bitterly repented that speech a few hours later, when her brother was brought back, apparently dead, by such of the "cheerful" party as escaped unhurt from a dangerous upset.

There was no concealing this sad home-coming from her father, though poor Ned was quiet enough now, being stunned by the fall, which had wounded his head and broken his right arm.

It *was* a shock, both to the man and the minister; and, when the worst was over, he left Polly to watch her brother, with eyes full of penitential tears, and went away, to reproach himself in private for devoting to ancient Fathers the time and thought he should have given to modern sons.

Ned was very ill, and when, at last, he began to mend, his helplessness taught him to see and love the sweetest side of Polly's character; for she was in truth his right hand, and waited on him with a zeal that touched his heart.

Not one reproach did she utter, not even by a look did she recall past warnings, or exult in the present humiliation which proved how needful they had been. Everything was forgotten except the fact that she had the happy privilege of caring for him almost as tenderly as a mother.

Not quite, though, and the memory of her whose place it was impossible to fill seemed to draw them closer together; as if the silent voice repeated its last injunctions to both son and daughter, "Take care of the boys, dear;" "Be good to your sister, Ned."

"I've been a regular brute to her, and the dear little soul is heaping coals of fire on my head by slaving over me like an angel," thought the remorseful invalid, one day, as he lay on the sofa, with a black patch adorning his brow, and his arm neatly done up in splints.

Polly thought he was asleep, and sat quietly rolling bandages till a head popped in at the door, and Will asked, in a sepulchral whisper,—

"I've got the book Ned wanted. Can I come and give it to you?"

Polly nodded, and he tiptoed in to her side, with a face so full of good-will and spirits that it was as refreshing as a breath of fresh air in that sick room.

"Nice boy! he never forgets to do a kindness and be a comfort to his Polly," she said, leaning her tired head on his buttony jacket, as he stood beside her.

Will wasn't ashamed to show affection for "his Polly," so he patted the pale cheeks with a hand as red as his mittens, and smiled down at her with his honest blue eyes full of the protecting affection it was so pleasant to receive.

"Yes, *I'm* going to be a tiptop boy, and never make you and father ashamed of me, as you were once of somebody we know. Now don't you laugh, and I'll show you something; it's the best I could do, and I wanted to prove that I mean what I say; truly, truly, wish I may die if I don't."

As he spoke, Will pulled out of his vest-pocket a little pewter cream-pot, tied to a shoe-string, and holding it up said, with a funny mixture of boyish dignity and defiance,—

"I bought it of Nelly Hunt, because her tea-set was half smashed up. Folks may laugh at my badge, but I don't care; and if you won't have me in your society I'll set up all alone, for I'm going into the temperance business, any way!"

Polly hugged him on the spot, and made his youthful countenance glow with honest pride by saying solemnly,—

"William G. Snow, I consider our league honored by the addition of so valuable a member; for a boy who can bear to be laughed at, and yet stick to his principles, is a treasure."

"The fellows *do* laugh at me, and call me 'Little Pitcher;' but I'd rather be that than 'Champagne Charlie,' as Ned called Mr. Lord," said Will, stoutly.

"Bless the little pitchers!" cried Polly, enthusiastically surveying both the pewter pot and its wearer.

A great tear was lying on her cheek, checked in its fall by the dimple that came as she looked at her brother's droll badge. Will caught it dexterously in the tiny cup, saying, with a stifled laugh,—

"Now you've baptized it, Polly, and it's as good as silver; for your tear shines in there like a great big diamond. Wonder how many it would take to fill it?"

"You'll never make me cry enough to find out. Now go and get my little silver chain, for that dear pewter pot deserves a better one than an old shoe-string," said Polly, looking after him with a happy face, as the small youth gave an ecstatic skip and was off.

"I'm afraid we've waked you up," she added, as Ned stirred.

"I was only day-dreaming; but I mean this one shall come true," and Ned rose straight up, with an energy that surprised his sister.

"Come and have your lunch, for it's time. Which will you take, Mrs. Neal's wine-jelly or my custard?" asked Polly, settling him in his big chair.

To her astonishment, Ned pitched the little mould of amber jelly into the fire, and tried to eat the custard with his left hand.

"My dear boy, have you lost your senses?" she ejaculated.

"No; I've just found them," he answered with a flash of the eye, that seemed to enlighten Polly without more words.

Taking her usual seat on the arm of the chair, she fed her big nursling in silence, till a sigh made her ask tenderly,—

"Isn't it right? I put in lots of sugar because you like it sweet."

"All the sugar in the world won't sweeten it to me, Polly; for there's a bitter drop at the bottom of all my cups. Will said your tear shone like a diamond in his little pitcher, and well it might. But you can't cry happy tears over me, though I've made you shed enough sad ones to fill the big punch-bowl."

Ned tried to laugh, but somehow the custard choked him; and Polly laid the poor, cropped head on her shoulder for a minute, saying softly,—

"Never mind, dear, I wouldn't think about the old troubles now."

She got no farther, for with a left-handed thump that made all the cups dance wildly on the table, Ned cried out,—

"But I *will* think about the old troubles, for I don't intend to have any new ones of that sort! Do you suppose I'll see that snip of a boy standing up for what is right, and not have the pluck to do the same? Do you suppose I'll make my own father ashamed of me more than once? Or let the dearest little girl in the world wear herself out over me, and I not try to thank her in the way she likes best? Polly, my dear, you can't be as proud of your elder brother as you are of the younger, but you shall never have cause to blush for him again; *never,* sir, *never!*"

Ned lifted his hand for another emphatic thump, but changed his mind, and embraced his sister as closely as one arm could do it.

"I ought to have a badge if I'm going to belong to your select society; but I don't know any lady who will give me an ear-ring or a cream-pot," said Ned, when the conversation got round again to the cheerful side of the question.

"I'll give you something better than either," answered Polly, as she transferred a plain locket from her watch-guard to the one lying on the table.

Ned knew that a beloved face and a lock of gray hair were inside; and when his sister added, with a look full of sweet significance, "For her sake, dear," he answered manfully,—

"I'll try, Polly!"

Chapter V. What Pris Did

Priscilla, meantime, was racking her brain to discover how she could help Philip; for since she had broken off her engagement no one spoke of him to her, and she could only judge of how things were going with him by what she saw and heard as she went about her daily task.

Pris kept school, and the road which she must take twice a day led directly by the office where Phil was studying medicine with old Dr. Buffum. Formerly she always smiled and nodded as she passed, or stopped to chat a moment with the student, who usually chanced to be taking a whiff of fresh air at that instant. Little notes flew in and out, and often her homeward walk was cheered by a companion, who taught the pretty teacher lessons she found it very easy to learn.

A happy time! But it was all over now, and brief glimpses of a brown head bent above a desk near that window was the only solace poor Pris had. The head never turned as she went by, but she felt sure that Phil knew her step, and found that moment, as she did, the hardest of the day.

She longed to relent, but dared not yet. He longed to show that he repented, but found it difficult without a sign of encouragement. So they went their separate ways, seldom meeting, for Phil stuck to his books with dogged resolution, and Pris had no heart for society.

Of course the affair was discussed with all the exasperating freedom of a country town, some blaming Pris for undue severity, some praising her spirit, and some friends,—not gossips,—predicting that both would be the better for the trial, which would not separate them long. Of this latter class were Portia and Polly, who felt it their duty to lend a hand when matters reached a certain point.

"Pris, dear, may I tell you something that I think you'd be glad to know?" began Polly, joining her friend one afternoon, as she went home weary and alone.

"*You* may tell me any thing," and Pris took her arm as if she felt the need of sympathy.

"You know Dr. Buffum let Phil help with Ned, so we have seen a good deal of him, and that is how I found out what I've got to tell you."

"He spoke of me, then?" whispered Pris, eagerly.

"Not a word till Ned made him. My boy is fond of your boy, and they had confidences which seem to have done them good. Of course Ned didn't tell me all about it, as *we* tell things (men never do, they are so proud and queer), but he said this,—

"'Look here, Polly, you must be very kind to Phil, and stand by him all you can, or he will go down. He is doing his best, and will hold on as long as he can, but a fellow *must* have comfort and encouragement of some sort, and if he don't get the right kind he'll try the wrong.'"

"O Polly! you will stand by him?"

"I have; for I just took Phil in a weakish moment, and found out all I wanted to know. Ned is right and you are wrong, Pris,—not in giving back the ring, but in seeming to cast him off entirely. He does not deserve that, for he was not to blame half so much as you think. But he won't excuse himself, for he feels that you are unjust; yet he loves you dearly, and you could do any thing with him, if you chose."

"I do choose, Polly; but how *can* I marry a man whom I cannot trust?" began Pris, sadly.

"Now, my child, I'm going to talk to you like a mother, for I've had experience with boys, and I know how to manage them," interrupted Polly, with such a charmingly maternal air that Pris laughed in spite of her trouble. "Be quiet and listen to the words of wisdom," continued her friend, seriously.

"Since I've taken care of Ned, I've learned a great deal, for the poor lad was so sick and sorry he couldn't shut his heart against me any more. So now I understand how to help and comfort him, for hearts are very much alike, Pris, and all need lots of love and patience to keep them good and happy. Ned told me his troubles, and I made up my mind that as *we* don't have so many temptations as boys, we should do all we can to help them, and make them the sort of men we can both love and trust."

"You are right, Polly. I've often thought how wrong it is for us to sit safe and silent while we know things are going wrong, just because it isn't considered proper for us to speak out. Then when the harm is done we are expected to turn virtuously away from the poor soul we might perhaps have saved if we had dared. God does not do so to us, and we ought not to do so to those over whom we have so much power," said Pris, with a heart full of sad and tender memories.

"We won't!" cried Polly, firmly. "We began in play, but we will go on in earnest, and use our youth, our beauty, our influence for something nobler than merely pleasing men's eyes, or playing with their hearts. We'll help them to be good, and brave, and true, and in doing this we shall become better women, and worthier to be loved, I know."

"Why, Polly, you are quite inspired!" and Pris stopped in the snowy road to look at her.

"It isn't all *my* wisdom. I've talked with father as well as Ned and Phil, and they have done me good. I've discovered that confidence is better than compliments, and friendship much nicer than flirting; so I'm going to turn over a new leaf, and use my good gifts for higher ends."

"Dear thing, what a comfort you are!" said Pris, pressing Polly's hands, and looking into her bright face with grateful eyes. "You have given me courage to do my duty, and I'll follow your example as fast as I can. Don't come any farther, please: I'd better be alone when I pass Phil's window, for I'm going to nod and smile, as I used to in the happy time. Then he will see that I don't cast him off and leave him to 'go down' for want of help, but am still his friend until I dare be more."

"Now, Pris, that's just lovely of you, and I know it will work wonders. Smile and nod away, dear, and try to do your part, as I'm trying to do mine."

For an instant the little gray hat and the jaunty one with the scarlet feather were bent close together; but what went on under the brims, who can say? Then Polly trotted off as fast as she could go, and Pris turned into a certain street with a quicker step and a brighter color than she had known for weeks.

She was late, for she had lingered with Polly, and she feared that patient watcher at the window would be gone. No; the brown head was there, but it lay wearily on the arms folded over a big book, and the eyes that stared out at the wintry sky had something tragic in them.

Poor Phil did need encouragement, and was in the mood to take the worst sort if the best failed him, for life looked very dark just then, and solitude was growing unbearable.

Suddenly, between him and the ruddy sunset a face appeared,— the dearest and the loveliest in the world to him. Not half averted now, nor set straightforward, cold and quiet as a marble countenance, but bent toward him, with a smile on the lips, and a wistful look in the tender eyes that made his heart leap up with sudden hope. Then it vanished; and when he sprung to the window nothing could be seen but the wave of a well-known cloak, fluttering round the corner.

But Priscilla's first effort was a great success; for the magic of a kind look glorified the dingy office, and every bottle on the shelves might have been filled with the elixir of life, so radiant did Phil's face become. The almost uncontrollable desire to rush away and recklessly forget his loneliness in the first companionship that offered was gone now, for a happy hope peopled his solitude with helpful thoughts and resolutions; the tragic look left the eyes, that still saw a good angel instead of a tempting demon between them and the evening sky; and when Phil shut up the big book he had been vainly trying to study, he felt that he had discovered a new cure for one of the sharpest pains the heart can suffer.

Next morning Pris unconsciously started for school too soon, so when she passed that window the room was empty. Resolved that Phil should not share her disappointment, she lifted the sash and dropped a white azalea on his desk. She smiled as she did it, and then whisked away as if she had taken instead of left a treasure. But the smile remained with the flower, I think, and Phil found it there when he hurried in to discover this sweet good-morning waiting for him.

He put it in the wine-glass which he had sworn never should be filled again with any thing but water, and sitting down before it listened to the little sermon the flower preached; for the delicate white azalea was Pris to him, and the eloquence of a pure and tender heart flowed from it, working miracles. One of them was that when sunset came it shone on two faces at the window, and the little snow-birds heard two voices breaking a long silence.

"God bless you, Pris."

"God help you, Phil!"

That was all, but from that hour the girl felt her power for good, and used it faithfully; and from that hour the young man worked bravely to earn the respect and confidence without which no love is safe and happy.

"We are friends now," they said, when they were seen together again; and friends they remained, in spite of shrugs and smiles, ill-natured speeches and more than one attempt to sow discord between them, for people did not understand the new order of things.

"I trust him" was the only answer Pris gave to all warnings and criticisms.

"I *will* be worthy of her," the vow that kept Phil steady in spite of the ridicule that is so hard to bear, and gave him courage to flee from the temptation he was not yet strong enough to meet face to face.

Portia and Polly stood by them stanchly; for having made her father's house a safe refuge, Portia offered Phil all the helpful influences of a happy home. Polly, with Ned to lend a hand, gave his comrade many a friendly lift; and when it was understood that the Judge, the minister, and the "Sweet P's" indorsed the young M.D., no one dared cast a stone at him.

All this took time, of course, but Phil got his reward at last, for one night a little thing happened which showed him his own progress, and made Pris feel that she might venture to wear the ring again.

At a party Phil was graciously invited to take wine with a lady, and refused. It was a very hard thing to do, for the lady was the hostess, a handsome woman, and the mother of a flock of little children, who all preferred the young doctor to the old one; and, greatest trial of all, several of his most dreaded comrades stood by to laugh at him, if he dared to let principle outweigh courtesy.

But he did it, though he grew pale with the effort to say steadily,—

"Will Mrs. Ward pardon me if I decline the honor? I am—"

There he stopped and turned scarlet, for a lie was on his lips,— a lie so much easier to tell than the honest truth that many would have forgiven its utterance at that minute.

His hostess naturally thought ill health was his excuse, and pitying his embarrassment, said, smiling,—

"Ah! you doctors don't prescribe wine for your own ailments as readily as for those of your patients."

But Phil, angry at his own weakness, spoke out frankly, with a look that said more than his words,—

"I cannot even accept the kind excuse you offer me, for I am not ill. It may be my duty to order wine sometimes for my patients, but it is also my duty to prescribe water for myself."

A dreadful little pause followed that speech; but Mrs. Ward understood now, and though she thought the scruple a foolish one, she accepted the apology like a well-bred woman, and, with a silent bow that ended the matter, turned to other guests, leaving poor Phil to his fate.

Not a pleasant one, but he bore it as well as he could, and when his mates left him stranded in a corner, he said, half aloud, with a long breath, as if the battle had been a hard one,—

"Yes, I suppose I *have* lost my best patient, but I've kept my own respect, and that ought to satisfy me."

"Let me add mine, and wish you health and happiness, dear Phil," said a voice behind him, and turning quickly he saw Pris standing there with two goblets of water, and a smile full of love and pride.

"You know what that toast means for me?" he whispered, with sudden sunshine in his face, as he took the offered glass.

"Yes; and I drink it with all my heart," she answered, with her hand in his.

Chapter VI. How It Ended

The leaven dropped by three girls in that little town worked so slowly that they hardly expected to do more than "raise their own patty-cakes," as Polly merrily expressed it. But no honest purpose is ever wasted, and by-and-by the fermentation began.

Several things helped it amazingly. The first of these was a temperance sermon, preached by Parson Snow, which produced a deep impression, because in doing this he had the courage, like Brutus, to condemn his own son. The brave sincerity, the tender earnestness of that sermon, touched the hearts of his people as no learned discourse had ever done, and bore fruit that well repaid him for the effort it cost.

It waked up the old people, sat the young ones to thinking, and showed them all that they had a work to do. For those who were down felt that they might be lifted up again, those who were trifling ignorantly or recklessly with temptation saw their danger, and those who had longed to speak out now dared to do it because he led the way.

So, warned by the wolf in his own fold, this shepherd of souls tried to keep his flock from harm, and, in doing it, found that his Christianity was the stronger, wiser, and purer for his humanity.

Another thing was the fact that the Judge was the first to follow his pastor's example, and prove by deeds that he indorsed his words. It was hard for the hospitable old gentleman to banish wine from his table, and forego the pleasant customs which long usage and many associations endeared to him; but he made his sacrifice handsomely, and his daughter helped him.

She kept the side-board from looking bare by filling the silver tankards with flowers, offered water to his guests with a grace that made a cordial of it, and showed such love and honor for her father that he was a very proud and happy man.

What the Judge did was considered "all right" by his neighbors, for he was not only the best-born, but the richest man in town, and with a certain class these facts had great weight. Portia knew this, and counted on it when she said she wanted him on her side; so she exulted when others followed the new fashion, some from principle, but many simply because he set it.

At first the young reformers were disappointed that every one was not as enthusiastic as themselves, and as ready to dare and do for the cause they had espoused. But wiser heads than those on their pretty shoulders curbed their impetuosity, and suggested various ways of gently insinuating the new idea, and making it so attractive that others would find it impossible to resist; for sunshine often wins when bluster makes us wrap our prejudices closer around us, like the traveller in the fable.

Portia baited *her* trap with Roman parties,—for she had been abroad,—and made them so delightful that no one complained when only cake and tea was served (that being the style in the Eternal City), but went and did likewise.

Artful Polly set up a comic newspaper, to amuse Ned, who was an invalid nearly all winter, and in it freed her mind on many subjects in such a witty way that the "Pollyanthus," as her brother named it, circulated through their set, merrily sowing good seed; for young folks will remember a joke longer than a sermon, and this editor made all hers tell.

Pris was not behindhand in her efforts, but worked in a different way, and got up a branch society among her little pupils, called "The Water Babies." That captivated the mothers at once, and even the fathers found it difficult to enjoy their wine with blue eyes watching them wistfully over the rims of silver mugs; while the few topers of the town hid themselves like night-birds flying from the sun, when, led by their gentle General, that little army of innocents marched through the streets with banners flying, blithe voices singing, rosy faces shining, and childish hearts full of the sweet delusion that *they* could save the world.

Of course the matrons discussed these events at the sewing-circle, and much talk went on of a more useful sort than the usual gossip about servants, sickness, dress, and scandal.

Mrs. Judge waxed eloquent upon the subject, and, being president, every one listened with due respect. Mrs. Ward seconded all her motions, for this lady had much surprised the town, not only by installing Phil as family physician, but by coming out strong for temperance. Somebody had told her all about the girls' labor of love, and she had felt ashamed to be outdone by them; so, like a conscientious woman, she decided to throw her influence into the right scale, take time by the forelock, and help to make the town a safer place for her five sons to grow up in than it was then.

These two leading ladies kept the ball rolling so briskly that others were soon converted and fell into rank, till a dozen or so were heartily in earnest. And then the job was half done; for in a great measure women make society what they choose to have it.

"We are told that home is our sphere, and advised to keep in it; so let us see that it is what it should be, and then we shall have proved our fitness for larger fields of labor, if we care to claim them," said Mrs. Judge, cutting out red flannel with charitable energy on one occasion.

"Most of us will find that quite as much as we can accomplish, I fancy," answered Mrs. Ward, thinking of her own riotous lads, who were probably pulling the house about their ears, while she made hoods for Mr. Flanagan's bare-headed lasses.

"'Pears to me we hain't no call to interfere in other folks's affairs. This never was a drinkin' town, and things is kep' in fustrate order, so *I* don't see the use of sech a talk about temperance," remarked Miss Simmons, an acid spinster, whose principal earthly wealth consisted of a choice collection of cats.

"If your tabbies took to drinking, you *would* see the use, I'm sure," laughed Polly, from the corner, which was a perfect posy-bed of girls.

"Thank goodness, *I've* no men folks to pester myself about," began Miss Simmons, with asperity.

"Ah, but you should; for if you refuse to make them happy, you ought at least to see that they console themselves in ways which can work them no further woe," continued Polly, gravely, though her black eyes danced with fun.

"Well, that wouldn't be no more than fair, I'm free to confess; but, sakes alive, I couldn't attend to 'em all!" said Miss Simmons, bridling with a simper that nearly upset the whole bevy of girls.

"Do make the effort, and help us poor things who haven't had your experience," added Pris, in her most persuasive voice.

"I declare I will! I'll have Hiram Stebbins in to tea; and when he's as good-natured as muffins and pie can make him, I'll set to and see if I can't talk him out of his attachment to that brandy bottle," cried Miss Simmons, with a sudden yearning towards the early sweetheart, who had won, but never claimed her virgin affections.

"I think you'll do it; and, if so, you will have accomplished what no one else could, and you shall have any prize you choose," cried Portia, smiling so hopefully that the faded old face grew almost young again, as Miss Simmons went home with something better to do than tend her tabbies.

"We've bagged that bird," said Polly, with real satisfaction.

"That's the way we set people to work," added Portia, smiling.

"She will do what we can't, for her heart is in it," said Pris, softly; and it was pleasant to see the blooming girls rejoice that poor old Hiram was in a fair way to be saved.

So the year went round, and Thanksgiving came again, with the home jollity that makes a festival throughout the land. The day would not be perfect if it did not finish with a frolic of some sort, and for reasons of their own the young gentlemen decided to have the first sociable of the year an unusually pleasant one.

"Everybody is going, and Ned says the supper is to be water-ice and ice-water," said Polly, taking a last look at herself in the long mirror, when the three friends were ready on that happy evening.

"I needn't sigh now over other girls' pretty dresses, as I did last year," and Portia plumed herself like a swan, as she settled Charley's roses in her bosom.

"And I needn't wonder who Phil will take," added Pris, stopping, with her glove half on, to look at the little ring back again from its long banishment in somebody's waistcoat pocket.

Never had the hall looked so elegant and gay, for it was charmingly decorated; couches were provided for the elders, mirrors for the beauties, and music of the best sounded from behind a thicket of shrubs and flowers. Every one seemed in unusually good spirits; the girls looked their loveliest, and the young men were models of propriety; though a close observer might have detected a suspicious twinkle in the eyes of the most audacious, as if they plotted some new joke.

The girls saw it, were on the watch, and thought the secret was out when they discovered that the gentlemen of their set all wore tiny pitchers, hanging like order from the knots of sweet-peas in their button-holes. But, bless their innocent hearts! that was only a ruse, and they were taken entirely by surprise when just before supper, the band struck up,

"Drink to me only with thine eyes;"

and every one looked smilingly at the three girls who were standing together near the middle of the hall.

They looked about them in pretty confusion, but in a moment beheld a spectacle that made them forget themselves; for the Judge, in an impressive white waistcoat, marched into the circle gathered about them, made a splendid bow, and said, with a smile that put the gas to shame,—

"Young ladies! I am desired by the gentlemen now present to beg your acceptance of a slight token of their gratitude, respect, and penitence. As the first man who joined the society which has proved a blessing to our town, Mr. William Snow will now have the honor of presenting the gift."

Then appeared Mr. William Snow, looking as proud as a peacock; and well he might, for on the salver which he bore stood a stately silver pitcher. A graceful little Hebe danced upon the handle, three names shone along the fretted brim, and three white lilies rose from the slender vase,—fit emblems of the maiden founders of the league.

Arriving before them, Master Will nearly upset the equilibrium of his precious burden in attempting to make a bow equal to the Judge's; but recovered himself gallantly, and delivered the following remarkable poem, which the public was expected to believe an emanation of his own genius:—

> "Hebe poured the nectar forth
>   When gods of old were jolly,
> But graces three *our* goblets fill,
>   Fair Portia, Pris and Polly.
> Their draughts make every man who tastes
>   Happier, better, richer;
> So here we vow ourselves henceforth
>   Knights of the Silver Pitcher."

ELIZABETH FRIES LUMMIS ELLET
1812–1877

Elizabeth F. Ellet was one of the best-known writers of her day. Much of her life was dedicated to recovering and celebrating the lives of important and exemplary women. In her most popular work, her two-volume (and finally three-volume) *Women of the American Revolution,* Ellet demonstrated women's contributions to national independence. She wrote other works about women: *Pioneer Women of the West* (1852), *The Queens of American Society* (1867), and *The Court Circles of the Republic* (1869). She also wrote books about women artists, women pioneers in various areas, and heroic women as well as biographies about individual women. Ellet was a prolific contributor to popular periodicals and gift books, sometimes acting as editor. In addition, she wrote articles for such publications as the *North American Review, American Quarterly Review,* and *Southern Quarterly Review.*

In "A Country Recollection, or, The Reformed Inebriate" (in *The Adopted Daughter and other Tales,* ed. Alice Cary [Philadelphia: J. B. Smith & Co., 1859]), Ellet attests to the influence Jane has over Walter, but she complicates the notion of influence beyond those presented by Alcott and Stowe. She introduces "A Country Recollection" with an idyllic setting typical of fictional happily-ever-after marriages and then contrasts it with the reality of life for wives of drunkards. "A Country Recollection" embodies other features of women's temperance fiction as well. Ellet incorporates numerous responses to the standard arguments for maintaining the traditional place for women. For example, Jane's education is not detrimental to her duties as housekeeper and mother; indeed, she is superior in such efforts. And the suggestion that by leaving the home she is "expos[ing] herself in this ridiculous manner" is undercut by the far more asinine behavior of her husband. Here, also, is a "common story." Jane's story could be that of any reader. And, like many wives in such fiction, Jane blooms in her single life after leaving her husband; in fact, she supports herself and her children in a comfortable fashion.

Jane's influence does help to save Walter, but only years after she has left him and while he is incarcerated. Significantly, her influence is successful only because he is safely imprisoned where he has nothing to do but read the tracts and Bible she brings and where "he could not now as formerly, rail at or punish her."

A Country Recollection, or, The Reformed Inebriate

It is many years since I was in a certain neighborhood among the mountains of New Jersey, where the richest cultivation enhances the beauty of scenery unusually fine, though not wild or bold enough for sublimity. It was a valley somewhat extensive, bordered on the south by abrupt and very high hills, wooded to their summit; except a small strip of cultivated land near their base, and terminating on the north side in sloping uplands covered with the wealth of harvest. A quiet stream murmured through the meadows, now narrowed between high banks, now expanding into a lakelet, near which stood a flour-mill. The house where I passed some days, at this time, had lawns sloping down to the stream; and I remember there flourished three large drooping willows, which I hoped might always escape the axe, and grow old, as guardians of the crystal waters. Their exact locality was fixed in my memory by the circumstance, that over their tops might be seen a cottage, situated on the side of the mountain, just in the verge of the woods, and about half a mile distant. The loneliness of its situation gave it something of romance; and I observed then, that what had once been a garden was choked with tall weeds and briers, and that a rude screen of boards had been built directly in front of the cottage, so as to shut out all view of the neighboring dwellings. This strange precaution seemed misanthropical; or, was it adopted for the purpose of concealing from curious eyes what might pass within door? To my inquiry who occupied that hermit's hut, the reply was "Walter B——."

"The B—— who married Jane S——?"

"The same."

Her name called up distant recollections. I had seen Miss S. once at a rustic ball. She was a country beauty; rather better educated than most of the damsels who were her companions. Indeed, her father used to complain that she spent too much time in reading. His idea was, that after a girl had left school, and completed her education, she had nothing more to do with books. But he rarely interfered except by a little grumbling, with her pursuits, especially as his house was always in the best order and his dinners excellent. Jane was a choice housekeeper, and her leisure hours she spent as pleased herself—not heeding her father's ominous shake of the head, when he saw her earnestly devouring a book, or noticed the shelves filled with books in her little chamber. "She will leave off such follies when she marries," was his consolatory remark; and in truth, when the indulged girl did marry, whether she gave up her reading or not, she did not suffer it to interfere with her household duties. She was the most exemplary wife and mother in the country; and all her neighbors predicted happiness from her union with young B. His father had left him a small farm, well stocked, with a house large enough for comfort and even elegance; and few men began life with better prospects of contentment. Walter was active and ambitious, and wanted to secure something more than a competency for old age. My acquaintance with the young couple had left them thus, and I was naturally somewhat surprised to find them living in a home of so little pretension.

"The only marvel about it," said the friend to whom I expressed my wonder, "is, that they have a home at all. When Walter took to drink, his stock went first, and then his farm was neglected, till at last, when sold to pay his debts it brought less than half its value."

Alas! it was the common story of the intemperate man; first moderate indulgence in frequent convivial meetings with his friends; then occasional excess that unfitted him for work for days, during which time he would vow and resolve and pledge his word to his wife that each should be the last, followed by more frequent returnings to the same excess, till the doom of the victim was sealed, and the very friends who had led him into vice abandoned him in disgust.

Since the desertion of his boon companions, Walter had become gloomy and sullen; a mood which, under the excitement he now every day sought, gave place to a wild and savage ferocity. The little children ran from him if they saw him on the road; and it was rumored that his wretched home too frequently witnessed his cruel brutality toward his unoffending wife. But he soon removed to this retired cottage on the mountain, and the screen of boards he built, effectually excluded all observation.

I listened to this melancholy history with the deepest sympathy for the unfortunate girl, now a helpless mother. She had sought no assistance from the neighbors, and few visited her, partly because they dreaded her husband, partly because she herself did not encourage them. But some compassionate persons sent her provisions from time to time.

While I looked at the little dwelling which was now the scene of so much misery, with an aching heart for the countless victims of this dreadful vice, a bright flash suddenly shot up from the roof of the hut, while at the same time a column of smoke poured from the chimney and upper windows. At the same moment a female figure rushed from behind the screen before mentioned, clasping an infant to her breast, and dragging along a child of about four years of age, and rapidly descended the slope of the mountain. Not many paces behind, her husband followed, calling upon her with shouts and execrations to return; but his evident intoxication rendered it impossible for him to equal the speed of his flying wife; and well was it for her, for a large knife was in his hand, which he brandished with frightful menaces. In less time than it would take to narrate what passed, several of the neighbors had run to meet her. Just as she reached the stream, through which she rushed with both children in her arms, then sank exhausted on the bank, they crowded round her with eager offers of assistance.

B. now came up, heedless of the men and women who regarded him with looks of fear and horror. He had dropped the knife, but had not changed his threatening tone; and with shocking imprecations he ordered his wife to "get up, and come home this instant." The poor woman uttered no reply, indeed she was hardly capable of speech; but the miller, a sturdy man, answered for her that she should go no more to the home of a villain who had nearly killed her. These words provoked B. to unbounded fury; he rushed upon the man who had spoken them, with such violence as to throw him off his guard, and would have strangled him but for the interference of others. When he found himself overpowered by superior strength, he revenged himself by the most fearful curses, vented especially on his poor wife, whom again, with abusive epithets, he ordered to go home, and not expose herself in this ridiculous manner.

"No, Walter," said his wife, rising at last, and confronting him with pale but determined face; "no—I will *not* return to you. I could have borne, as I have long done, your harshness and violence towards me, but you have this day raised your hand against the lives of these children; and, as it is my duty before God to protect *them,* I leave you for ever!"

Whatever reply the drunkard might have made, it was drowned in the indignant clamors of the by-standers, and he was dragged off to gaol. His wife was cared for by her sympathizing female acquaintance, and soon provided with a permanent situation, where, by the labor of her hands, she could support herself and her little ones. And soon, very soon, did her changed appearance bear witness to the improvement. She became contented and even cheerful; and the playful caresses of her children beguiled her of many sad thoughts.

When B. awoke from his intoxication in prison, the recollection of what he had done overwhelmed him with shame and remorse. He sent for one of his neighbors, and entreated him to go, on his part, to his injured wife, supplicate her forgiveness, and pledge the most solemn promises of future amendment. Jane wept much; she forgave him from her heart, as she prayed God he might be forgiven; but she could not, dared not trust his oft-violated word, and sacrifice her children. Her determination was fixed; and for weeks together, though with a bleeding heart, she returned the same answer to the entreaties of her repentant husband, she dared not even see him lest her resolution might be shaken.

When at last B. was discharged from gaol, full of indignation at what he termed the cruel obstinacy of his wife, he made no effort to see her or the children; but—after shutting himself up a month or two in the cottage, which had been saved, by timely attention, from being burned the night of Jane's escape—he departed, none knew whither. He left a reproachful letter to his wife, professing himself driven to desperation by her desertion, and laying on her the blame of his future crimes. No furniture of any value was found in the house, the greater part having been disposed of to procure food and—liquor.

Two years after this occurrence, (I have the particulars from a friend.) a crowd was assembled round the gaol in the little town of ———. A murder, under the most appalling circumstances, had been committed in the neighborhood; a man to whom suspicion attached had been arrested, and after strict examination committed for trial. Particulars that had transpired, left no doubt of his guilt on the minds of the people; and it was with suppressed execrations that the multitude followed the suspected felon to prison. When he disappeared from their sight within the gloomy walls, the popular rage broke out in groans and murmurs. One woman, young and interesting in appearance, who had listened with undisguised eagerness to a knot of idlers discussing the case, walked away when they ended their conference, and presenting herself at the door of the magistrate, who had conducted the examination, asked leave to speak with him. It was the wife of B. She had seen her husband led to gaol, loaded with the most terrible suspicions, and she came to have her worst fears allayed or confirmed.

The magistrate soothed her by assuring her that the evidence against B., though strong, was only circumstantial, and by no means absolutely proved his guilt. It was impossible to say what might be the event of the trial; but there was ground for hope. Poor Jane clung to this hope. "Oh, sir," sobbed she, "if he is guilty and must die, it is I who have murdered him! I deserted him, when all the world cast him out!"

When the unhappy wife returned home it was to give way to the bitter anguish of remorse; to weep and sob all night as if her heart would break. "How have I been able to kneel, night and morning, to ask pardon of God," she cried to herself, "when I refused my aid to save a fellow-being from destruction!" And yet—these little ones—and she hung over her sleeping children; the fair boy, with bright cheek, shaded by his clustering curls; and the sweet dark-eyed girl, so like him, before excess had marred his manly beauty! *Could* she have brought these innocent ones into wretchedness; perhaps guilt? Had she not done right to snatch them from ruin, even by abandoning their father? She knelt once more, and prayed for guidance, for discernment of the right; and her mind was calmed.

The next day before noon, the gaol was again visited by groups of idlers, gazing into the window of B.'s cell, which looked upon the street. It might be that the prisoner was maddened by their taunts and derision; he was leaping about with frantic gestures, clapping his hands and laughing immoderately, or thrusting his face between the bars to grin defiance at his tormentors. Suddenly a woman, her face concealed by a drooping bonnet and thick veil, glided through the crowd, and reaching up to the window offered a parcel to the prisoner. He grasped it eagerly, with a wistful look, but the woman did not stay to be recognized. It was observed, as she hastened away that her steps tottered, and she held down her head apparently overcome by emotion. Well might the fearfully changed countenance of the accused appall one who had known him in better days.

The parcel contained a portion of food more palatable than is usually allowed to prisoners, and a small pocket Bible—the book B. had once prized—the gift of his dying mother. His name was written on the first page in her hand. Many times in the week, always at dusk, did the same compassionate visitor stand at the grated window, and offer food or books to the prisoner, who was evidently affected by the kind attention. He ceased his idiotic dancing and laughing; he answered nothing more to the upbraidings of vagrants without, and those who looked into his window saw him most frequently seated quietly at the table reading, or with his head on his hand in deep thought. With thankfulness unspeakable, Jane saw this change; but her joy was dashed with sadness, when on one of her visits the prisoner besought her, with piteous entreaty, to bring him a bottle of brandy.

It now occurred to the wife to do what she had never dared, when B. was at home, to force on his perusal some tracts containing the most awful warnings against intemperance, and encouragements to the victim to struggle for recovery. He had no other books to beguile the time; he could not now as formerly, rail at or punish her, even had he any suspicion who she was; *what* might ensue if he read them? Her effort was crowned with success. Not a week had passed, when the abject entreaty for liquor, which had been urged night after night, was dropped, to be renewed no more. Jane's heart throbbed when she thought of this; but alas! even if he were really reformed, would he live to prove himself so?

Thus days rolled on, and the time for the trial arrived. The prisoner had communicated with his counsel; witnesses had been sent for; the principal lawyer engaged in the prosecution had unfolded the chain of evidence by which his guilt was to be proved; the court was to open next morning. The accused had received some of his former acquaintance during the day, and as night drew near he was alone. On his table lay a letter which he had just written; he was pacing the room, tranquil, but with mind filled with painful thoughts. The gaoler opened the door, announced a name, received the prisoner's startled ascent; and the next moment the long estranged husband and wife were together. B. did not stir; he was petrified by surprise; but Jane rushed to him; her arms were round his neck, and she wept aloud. Her husband was moved, but struggled apparently with his pride; he unclasped her arms, stepped back a little, and looked earnestly at her.

Sad, indeed, the contrast between the two; the man almost spectral in aspect, haggard, wan, emaciated—not even the shadow of his former self; the woman blooming in the freshness of almost maiden beauty: no unhallowed vigils, or excess, or evil passions, had stamped their traces on *her* brow, or marred the symmetry of her form, and the very purity and tenderness that shone in her expression, rebuked the conscious sinner as loudly as if an angel's tongue had proclaimed his degradation! As he shrank back, and stood thus silent, Jane stretched out her hands beseechingly; "Oh, Walter!" she cried, "have you not yet forgiven me?"

"Forgive you, Jane? Oh, Heaven! what a wretch am I!"

"I was wrong, Walter, to desert you, even at the worst; but oh! say you do not bear hard thoughts toward me!"

"Tell me, Jane, is it you who brought me these?" pointing to the books.

"Yes, Walter; for I thought you would read them now—and—-"

She was interrupted by the sobs of her husband; he sank on his knees as if to thank her, but to prevent that, she knelt with him, and prayed for him in the deep emotion of her heart.

When B. was sufficiently calm, he asked after his children, and, pointing to the table, said: "There, Jane, is a letter I had written you, in a better spirit, I trust, than the last. If it were God's will I should live longer, I might make a better husband and father; but I dare not think of that now."

Jane longed to ask one question, but her tongue refused to utter the words. Her husband seemed to read the meaning of her anxious look.

"Before high Heaven," said he, "I declare to you that I am innocent of the crime for which I shall be tried to-morrow."

A shriek of joy, scarce suppressed, burst from the wife; she clasped her hands and raised them upwards; gratitude denied her speech.

"Then you will live"—she gasped at length.

"No—Jane—I dare not hope it; and I deserve to die. I am guiltless of murder, but what have I been to you and my children? What have I been these last years? a reckless outcast—my own destroyer—the enemy of God! I tell you, Jane, I have long looked to the gallows as the end of my career, and I have come to it at last! But I have mastered the tyrant that brought me to this; yes, I have!" He laughed convulsively as he said this, and his wife turned pale. "Look here, Jane—look here!" and lifting up the coverlet of his bed, he produced several bottles of brandy and whiskey. They were *full*.

"I asked you to give me liquor," he continued, "and you would not; but others, less merciful, brought these to me! Do not shudder and grow so pale, Jane; I swear to you, I have not tasted one drop, though I have had them a fortnight! Those books saved me; for I read of even worse cases than mine. I took an oath, Jane, on the Bible you brought me the first night, my mother's Bible, that I would never taste liquor again. And I have these, to try if I *could* keep my resolution."

"Oh, Walter!" was all the sobbing wife could say; but her tears were those of joy.

"You know, Jane, I was always fond of books, and if I had not been a slave to drink, I [would] have been fit society even for the judges who are to try me to-morrow. Oh, if I could only live my life over! But it is too late now, yet it is something—is it not," and his pale face kindled, "to think that I *can*, that I *have* overcome the fiend at last! *That I shall not die a drunkard.* Remember that, and let everybody know it; I have it written here in your letter. God will remember it, will he not, when my soul stands before him in judgment."

"Oh, my husband, you shall not die!" cried the wife, as with streaming tears, she clasped him again to her arms.

"The will of God be done; and that I can say now sincerely; I am willing to go. The Bible says no drunkard shall enter His kingdom; but I am *not* a drunkard! I am a degraded wretch, an outcast of men, about to die a felon's death; but I feel a triumph, Jane, a joy unspeakable, that I have conquered my worst enemy. I thank God that he has supported me through the struggle. It was a terrible one!"

I need not at length record this interview; I need say no more than that, after weeks of the most agonizing suspense and anxiety, Jane had the happiness to hear that her husband was fully acquitted of the crime laid to his charge; to receive him once more and welcome him to a home.

For months he lay helpless, the victim of a wasting sickness; but his wife worked day and night to procure him comforts, and her children played round his bed, and in her was what the poet sweetly terms, "a hymn of thankfulness," never silent. When he recovered, he found it not hard to bear her company in her cheerful toil, and never would he suffer himself to be persuaded to touch what once had proved his bane, and so nearly brought him to an ignominious end.

It is not long since I heard an address of touching eloquence, on the subject of Temperance, delivered by Walter B. There was truth in every word of it, for he deeply felt what he uttered; and it came home to many a heart, and drew tears from many an eye. He told his own history, and described himself as once the most wretched and lost among the victims of that vice, and yet there had been others more lost than he, who recovered. It was this, he said, that first inspired him with hope for himself.

FRANCES DANA GAGE
1808–1880

This, the second of Gage's "Tales of Truth" (in *The Lily*, March 1852: 17–18) portrays the marriage of a beautiful and promising young woman and the subsequent decline of her marriage because of her husband's intemperance. Typical of many women's temperance stories, Polly appears destined for a bright and happy future, an unlikely candidate for the difficult life of an inebriate's wife. Unlike some stories and novels that stop with the depiction of hardships experienced by wife and children, however, Gage's tale suggests that women must finally take matters into their own hands. In her story, Gage highlights the problem with "treating," a custom that proliferated in nineteenth-century America. Social custom demanded that men "treat," or buy alcoholic drinks, for one another when meeting in public. Voters expected political candidates to "treat" them, as well, in order to assure their support.

(See additional biographical information on Gage in part 1.)

Tales of Truth (No. 2)

Polly Dean was as merry and rosy a blue-eyed belle as ever pulled flax upon a hillside, or flourished a home-made checked apron in a log cabin in the western clearings. Polly was a belle in more than one sense.—First, she was the prettiest girl in the diggins, (I am speaking after the manner of men you know, who always put beauty before all other considerations.) Second, she was the smartest, could get the best dinners, spin the most cuts of yarn in a week, pile brush the fastest at the chopping bees, and dance the lightest and gayest at the log rollings and quiltings; and what was more than all put together, she was the only daughter of Esq. Dean, the owner and proprietor of the large valley farm where the county seat had just been located, and where, already, ten log houses, a blacksmiths shop, a shoe makers stall, and a hewed log tavern stood up imposingly upon the banks of the stream and took upon themselves the sounding name of Deanville.

The whole people of the county that could be named, according to the Constitution of the state—that is, "the free white male inhabitants over twenty one," would not have numbered more than five hundred. But these "free white male inhabitants," had their counterparts in the shape of angels, who wore home made frocks and coarse calf skin shoes—did the washing, cooking, spinning, weaving, darning and mending; dropped the corn in the spring time and helped husk it in the winter; milked all the cows, (for that was work quite beneath the dignity of free white men in those days) took all the care of the children, and made home a sort of paradise by keeping up great fires and having plenty of roast turkeys and venison hams (roasted, you know, by hanging on a string before the fire) and corn cakes baked on a board, to cheer their lords and masters when they should return from the jolly wolf hunt, the shooting match, the general training, or such other chivalrous sports, which lightened the labors and cheered the toils of the backwoodsmen of Ohio forty years ago.

But I was talking about Polly Dean, wasn't I? Well, she was just the prettiest, smartest and richest girl in the county of ———— no matter what county. It was a way out west . . . forty years since, but now lies in the very heart of civilization, and the center of the United Sates—so it don't matter what county it was. And Polly was the belle of course.

Now I forgot to tell you that Deanville, being the county seat, had a court house in it, made of stout beach logs two feet through; and the court house had a jail of the same sort; and the jail would have prisoners now and then, and the prisoners must have a lawyer, and the lawyers as a matter of course, again—next to the proprietor of the town, would be the big man, or the beau, towards whom all the eyes of the unwedded angels in homespun in the county of ———— would turn. While his eyes would turn (as a matter of course again) to the belle and heiress of the village.

This was exactly the position of affairs, when Polly Dean met John Wells, the lawyer, at a husking frolic, given in honor of her birthday, one moonshiny night in October—when Polly had reached the sighed for era in every girl's life, eighteen—when the statute books proclaim her to be a free woman. That is, she is free to marry the man she chooses without asking her father. I never could see any other freedom it conferred, except it was the freedom of earning her own living—which, by the way, they most all have to do long before that time arrives.

John Wells was as big as a common giant; "right good lookin," (so the girls said,) and a very good specimen of a backwoods lawyer; for though the judges and jurors were not much afraid of the weight of his arguments, they had a high conception of the strength of his fists—of which they had felt the force in more than one instance, when not on the bench or box.

But, la! what a long story I am making! John Wells fell in love with Polly Dean at first sight—how could he help it? and she fell in love with him, and they were married and set up for themselves, and were the aristocracy of Deanville.

But bless your hearts! things ain't now as they used to was; Mrs. Lawyer Wells didn't think nothing of doing her own washing out under the shade of the great beach that stood by the spring right where every body could see her, nor of spinning tow all day on the front porch that had no other lattice to hide her from the villagers than the luxuriant gourd vine that grew gourds that would hold two gallons a piece. What nice wash ladles they did make! John Wells was a great man. The people liked him, and they liked his sensible wife too, and so they sent John twice to the Assembly and then they sent him twice to the Senate; and I don't know but they would have sent him twice to Congress if it hadn't been for Polly—at least the leading politicians said it was all her blame. May be it was. I'll tell you how it happened.

In those days it was thought a real disgrace to have a quilting, husking party, spinning bee, or any other gathering and not send round a glass of whiskey toddy once or twice of an evening—real good raw whiskey, sweetened up nice with home-made sugar or molasses; and the young men all tasted, and thought it quite *onjenteel* not to get a little bit mellow and warm on such occasions. (And to tell you the truth, Mrs. Bloomer, though I don't want you to tell it again, I have seen the girls' eyes sparkle late in the evening. But may be it was only because) well no matter—that ain't what I was going to tell you.

John Wells *would* have a "little something to take"—would be manly when he was out among folks; and Polly (wives are so apt to be suspicious) began to suspect that he did really sometimes take more of the "O be joyful" than he really needed to do him good—and she said so once or twice, *or near that often* right out;—for Polly was "a Woman's Right's man" and would speak her own mind.

But John insisted that it was not so. That a man needed something to keep him a going, and that with all his cares and anxieties, and the heavy pressure of "State affairs" harrowing his mind, the stimulus could not be dispensed with.

Polly did not think it any more necessary for John to have a dram every morning to help him to strength to talk politics at his office, or to lounge all day before the log tavern, than it was for her to have the same amount of stimulus to enable her to cook, wash, scrub, work the garden, sew, and take care of six children—for while we have been telling our story, the merry, bright eyed, nimble-footed girl has become the pale, dim-eyed, toiling, broken mother of six children; and worse than all, oh! worse than all—*a drunkard's daughter and a drunkard's wife.*

Polly's father, who at the time of her marriage was counted a rich man in his new world, had by the slow and sure wastage of intemperance lost all, or nearly all, of his substance; and the little that was left was no longer considered as the property *to be* of John Wells. For since the first year of his daughter's marriage, there had been a deadly feud between the father and his children. Old Esq. Dean was not the man to brook a rival in the affections of his people, and John Wells was the very man to fill a rival's place.— He was a jolly fellow, and shrewd withal, and made a pretty good living—that is, Polly managed to do pretty well for herself and children by the dint of spinning, weaving, making garden, raising a patch of corn and potatoes, and so on—up to the time about which we are just going to tell you.

Every additional public honor laid upon poor John's shoulders, seemed to require additional stimulus. When "the dear people" made him Prosecuting Attorney he drank one dram a day, and only got mellow upon occasion. When they sent him to the Legislature he took two, perchance four drams to strengthen his brains thro' the day, and got mellow in the evening only.—But when he went to the Senate his drams grew past counting; he kept mellow day and night.—And poor Polly could hardly recognize the proud, bold, manly man that she took for better or worse ten years before, in the blue-nosed, blur-eyed, bloated semblance of a man that returned to her after an absence of some three months.

Poor Polly! she wept, prayed, and remonstrated—toiled, struggled, and grew pale from day to day and from week to week; but no hope of amendment cheered her fainting heart.

She had never drank, never tasted, even, the fell beverage that had been the bane of her childish years and was now blighting all the joys of her matron life with its withering curse. John made out to keep about—never got so terribly drunk but that he could talk and discuss the nation's prosperity and safety; and never was he so staunch a patriot, never such an opposer of wrong and misrule, as when he had as big "a brick in his hat" as he could walk straight under.

And so his clique set him up for Congress. It was going to be a hard fought election—a terrible hard fought election—for John's antagonist was a sober farmer that would not stand a treat. He was "as mean as pusley,"—so said the Wellsites. So John got a whole barrel of liquor and set it on his porch, and treated every man that would drink. But unfortunately (nobody ever could guess how it happened) the plug got out of the half inch auger hole in the head of the barrel one night and the contents all ran out.

Polly said "may be her gown had loosened it switching back and forth"—for she had spun two days work the day before, and every thread she wound up, she had to brush right past the head of the whiskey barrel, and more than once her gown had caught on the same tap.

I said John was shrewd; so he was, and he looked right into Polly's eyes while she said that "may be," and ever after that he took his friends down to the hewed log tavern to drink with him for the nation's glory.

Things were growing no better, fast. Home was almost deserted; its comforts entirely neglected. Polly grew paler and weaker. A seventh member was about to call upon her for love and care. The wood pile was exhausted; the flour barrel empty; the pork barrel in sympathy with it; and trials more than woman ought to bear meekly, stared the poor wife in the face.

John had been three days, night and day, at the tavern, so beastly "blue," that he did not even make an attempt to get home. Polly grew desperate, and resolved to do something—to make one more effort to reclaim her husband—for he was still her husband, the man of her love, and the father of her children.

She knew that the most sensitive point in his character was pride; that he was proud of her and never so lost to himself and the deep tones of his own soul, but that an impropriety of hers would arouse him to all a husband's jealous care.

It was growing near nightfall the third day of his absence, Saturday eve, and three days before the election, which every one was sure would go in his favor. Half the village voters were gathered round the tavern to "cuss and discuss" the pending crisis of affairs.

John Wells had got out on the horse-block before the door, and with a face as red as a full blown peony, and a tongue as thick as— as a man's who is just as drunk as he can stand, was making a speech to a throng of "free white men," as sober and sensible as himself, when his wife appeared round the corner and walked straight up the steps into the bar-room.

"I want a half pint of whiskey, Mr. Smith," said Polly, and she threw down a sixpence upon the counter with the air of an old customer.

Mr. Smith handed her the liquor. She took the glass and walking to the door drank it down, smacked her lips with a seeming relish, and set herself down carelessly upon the door steps in plain sight of the speaker on the horse-block.

The whole crowd turned to look—the speech was wound up short. A murmur of derision ran through the assembled mass. John descended from his stand with a much steadier step than he ascended. The intensity of his feelings had sobered him. He walked up to his wife and with as kind a tone as he could command, said, "come Polly let's go home."

"Go home!" said Polly, "why John Wells, I just came from home, and it's a fool to this place. I knew you was taking real comfort down here, so I thought I'd come down too, and get away from them squalling young ones. I don't wonder you stay down here; Smith has first rate liquor, and I'm tired and hungry and need a stimulus to keep me a going. Give me a half pint more Mr. Smith— John and I. We don't often get to take a drink together now a days."

"Come Polly, go home with me this instant," said John in a tone of authority.

"Oh! the terrible sus; you think I am going right straight back 'fore I've fairly got there do you? Why John Wells, you ain't fair; you've been here three days and I think you might let me stay long enough to take the second drink! Come Smith, be in a hurry with that half pint."

Smith handed her the mug and with a "here's health to you, John," she was about to gulp it down, when John sprang forward, caught it from her hand and hurled it, glass and all, into the middle of the street. Then seizing his wife with the strength of a giant, he bore her away without uttering a word.

The bystanders were silent a moment also, and then muttering curses and remarks were heard, and one after another each shrank away to their homes.

John Wells did not pause till he reached his own door-sill with his now passive burthen.—They entered and he threw himself into a chair and burst into tears. His wife allowed him to weep in silence.

"Oh Polly," he at last exclaimed, "you have ruined me forever."

"I," said Polly, "no not I—but you have well nigh ruined yourself, John. If it is right for you to live at the tavern, it is right for me. If it is good for you to drink, it is good for me. What my husband can do without being disgraced, I can do without bringing disgrace upon him. And now, John, mark my words. The examples you expect me to follow, set for me.—The path in which you expect me to walk, must be first trodden by your own feet. I promised before God to forsake all others and cleave only unto you, and so help me heaven, *I will do it.*"

"Polly," said John, starting to his feet as her last words fell upon his ear.

"What, John?" she replied with her own soft voice.

"I will never, so help me heaven, drink another drop of ardent spirits."

Again he folded his wife in his arms, and wept over her. Who does not know how easily an inebriate will weep?

Polly went about her work joyfully; her plan had so far exceeded all her hopes. But let me whisper to you reader, *she had not drank a drop of whiskey nor did she intend to. Smith had only filled her glass with water.*

John got up the next morning duly sober; and what was more, did not go to the tavern that day; nor the next, nor the next, which was the election day; and when he went to the Court House he refused to treat, and so he lost his election.

There were a great many different opinions as to the propriety, or impropriety of Polly Wells' manoeuvers. The men, with few exceptions, condemning in her, even a semblance of their own every day habits; and the majority, I believe, of the women, stoutly maintained that men *must* have indulgences to sin, over and above their weaker companions. A few—a precious little few, insisted that she could not have done a wiser or a wittier thing. For say what they would about it, it had its effect, and John Wells had not been seen at the tavern since.

I am inclined to think it had its effect for good through the whole community, for a drinking candidate has never been popular since in the County of ———.

John Wells lived to a good old age, and he was often heard to say, that he believed solemnly, that if he had not been brought to feel the deep shame and humiliation in his own heart, which he had so often laid upon the heart of his good wife, he never should have had power to have resisted temptation, and up to his dying day, he stoutly maintained the doctrine that society would never be harmonious and beautiful until men learned to practice in heart and life, the same purity and virtue which they require at the hands of woman. And what was more, he insisted, "that so long as man claimed to be the superior of woman, mentally, educationally, physically and politically, it was his duty to stand as her superior *morally,* and to guide and guard her in her weakness, and keep her in his heart of hearts, free from all sorrow and wrong.

CAROLINE HYDE BUTLER (LAING)
1804–1892

Butler's "Amy" (*Sartain's,* January 1851) combines, as women's temperance fiction often does, more than one reform issue. Butler's Lydia Gales is the victim of an intemperate father. Both the women in her family and the women in Amy Chilson's family suffer from the unjust inequity in an economic system that restricts women's employment to difficult and low paying occupations, and women in both families are treated poorly because of their reduced economic circumstances. But Lydia's situation proves worse than Amy's because she is further victimized by a legal system that gives her alcoholic father all rights to her wages. (Mr. Gales's departure for the grocer does not suggest he will buy food. Grocers were the most common source for packaged liquor.) The piece speaks to the necessity that women not only join in resistance but also refuse to perpetuate the economic exploitation of other women. Mrs. Mayhew serves as a model for women because she "deal[s] mercifully and gently with the poor." But Mrs. Harris, Mrs. Frisbie, and Mrs. Dunn help to maintain a system that victimizes women.

(See additional biographical information on Butler in part 1.)

Amy

"I will a plain, unvarnished tale deliver."

—Shakespeare

"So you have changed your seamstress, I see," said Mrs. Mayhew to her fashionable friend, Mrs. Harris.

"O yes, and you cannot think what a difference it makes in our expenses; you know I paid Chilson half a dollar a day, and she only came at eight and worked till seven."

"That was reasonable, certainly," interrupted Mrs. Mayhew; "I am sure I don't see how any one could well work cheaper."

"You don't; well then, I only pay the girl I have now, two and sixpence, and she works an hour later, and sews beautifully; what do you think of that?" exclaimed Mrs. Harris, triumphantly.

"I think that it is not enough," answered her friend. "Only consider, my dear Mrs. Harris, twelve hours of steady labour, for the pitiful sum of two and sixpence; surely, it is hardly just!"

"If I pay the girl all she asks, I don't see why it is not just!" replied Mrs. Harris, reddening. "She is a better judge, probably, than either you or I, of what she can, or cannot afford; if she chooses

The plight of seamstresses. From Caroline H. Butler, "Amy," in *Sartain's.* January 1851, p. 19.

to do my sewing for two and sixpence, I don't know why I should offer her more."

"Poor girl; probably she is afraid to demand the price which is by justice hers, lest, from that grasping and overbearing spirit with which such demands are too often met, she would be refused all employment," said Mrs. Mayhew. "There is a pitiful oppression exercised toward this class of persons, Mrs. Harris; there are those, even among the most wealthy, who will bargain and chaffer with the poor seamstress, to gain a penny's advantage. What matters it that justice is on the side of the weak, so long as might supports the oppressor? And, therefore, they must either starve, or bend to the yoke."

"That may be the case with some persons, but not with me," replied Mrs. Harris. "No one is further from wishing to grind the poor than I am. I pay to those whom I employ all they ask, and no more; and that, Mrs. Mayhew, I consider to be right. 'Charity begins at home,' and I contend it is every wife's duty to use judgment and economy in the management of her household."

"Very true; but not at the expense of justice and humanity," said Mrs. Mayhew. "'Live and let live,' is an old adage, and one which I wish was imprinted in letters of gold upon every hearthstone. I simply plead for justice, not for charity; and, believe me, if the former were more frequently meted out, there would be less call for the latter! But, allow me to ask what has become of Miss Chilson? She appeared to be a very nice girl."

"Yes, I believe she was, and very faithful," answered Mrs. Harris. "But, somehow, I never exactly liked her—in fact, it is very annoying to see persons in her situation put on so many airs as she did—it is disagreeable."

"Every person should possess a proper self-respect," said Mrs. Mayhew.

"O yes, certainly, but, sometimes, Chilson had a way with her that was really quite provoking. Now, for instance, one day we had company to dinner, and, only an hour before the time, our waiter took a miff at something, and left the house; of course, it was then too late to procure another, and so I just simply proposed to Chilson to take her place, as it would accommodate me so much."

"Which, I presume, she would not do," said Mrs. Mayhew, smiling.

"Mercy, no indeed! Why she looked as indignant as any princess. I always thought it very ungrateful of her. Then, another time, when I was out of a chambermaid, I requested her as a favor to do the work just for one day, and, I declare, if I had not actually demeaned myself to apologize, I believe she would have left the house, and my children's dresses half finished. To be sure, she was quite kind when little John and Anne had the measles, and insisted upon sitting up with them two or three nights."

"And yet you dismissed her, Mrs. Harris, for no other reason than that you found a person who would work for you more reasonably?" said Mrs. Mayhew.

"For that only; but I consider it a duty to save every penny I can, for you know we have a large family, and our expenses are heavy; and, if I can hire my sewing for less than I have been paying for it, why I ought certainly to take advantage of the opportunity. But, I confess, I was sorry to tell Chilson she need not come any more."

"Did she seem disappointed?" inquired Mrs. Mayhew.

"You never saw any one so agitated as she was at first," replied Mrs. Harris. "And when I paid her what little money I was owing her, and told her I had no further use for her services, the tears stood in her eyes."

"Poor girl! I fear, my dear friend, you have unintentionally done a cruel deed!" said Mrs. Mayhew. "It is a very difficult thing for a poor young girl to obtain a new situation. Men can rough and battle with the world, but with the friendless female, it is different. Miss Chilson may have many dear ones—a father—a mother, dependent upon her exertions; even the little mite she earned from you, may have been of vital importance to them, and of which, my dear Mrs. Harris, you have thus thoughtlessly deprived them."

Mrs. Harris was now really angry, and answered accordingly. "Indeed, Mrs. Mayhew, I did not know that I was accountable to you for my actions; when I am, it will be time enough for you to assume the office of Mentor!"

"I am sorry to have offended you," said Mrs. Mayhew, rising calmly from her seat; "when we meet again, I trust all will be forgotten. One thing more; can you tell me where Miss Chilson lives?"

"No; for I never asked her," ungraciously replied Mrs. Harris; "but I believe somewhere in Third Street. I am sorry I cannot relieve your *benevolent* curiosity!" she added, ironically.

Mrs. Mayhew bowed, and left the house; while Mrs. Harris, in no very comfortable frame of mind, ascended to the nursery.

"How very disagreeable that woman is getting!" she muttered to herself; "I really believe I will cut her acquaintance—she is too much of the Fry school to suit me!"

In one corner of the nursery, a pale, sickly-looking girl sat, bending over her needle, surrounded by three or four noisy, quarrelsome children.

"Heavens, what an uproar!" exclaimed Mrs. Harris as she entered; "be still, all of you—you are enough to craze one! Have you finished the trimming to my cape?" she asked, turning to the sewing girl.

"Not quite, ma'am," she replied, without raising her eyes from her work.

"Not quite! Why it is more than an hour since you began it; you must sew very slowly, I am sure," said Mrs. Harris, snappishly.

The girl made no answer; but a tear rolled slowly down her pale cheek, and dropped upon the delicate silk in her hand. Mrs. Harris immediately observed the stain on the beautiful fabric, though not the cause.

"Why, what is this, Gales? See, you have spotted my cape, you careless creature; what is it? Is it grease, or what?" she exclaimed, angrily.

The colour rose to the cheek of the poor girl as she answered.

"No, ma'am, it is not grease, it is no stain; it is only—only water."

"Only water! Well, I must say, I think it is very careless in you not to put by your work when you drink! Have not you almost finished? For I have an engagement at one o'clock, and have set my heart upon wearing my new silk."

"It will very soon be completed, ma'am," was the reply.

"Ma, she don't sew half so fast as Chilson did," whispered little Fanny; "and has been doing nothing half the time, but just sitting with her handkerchief to her eyes; I don't like her a bit!"

Mrs. Harris turned slowly round. "I see you are very slow with your needle; my other girl, Chilson, would have done the work in half the time. I don't like eye-servants."

The poor girl sighed heavily.

"I am very sorry that I have not been able to do more this morning. I had a headache when I left home, and it has increased to such a degree, that I fear I must ask permission to return."

Mrs. Harris was somewhat touched by her sad tone and pallid looks.

"Well, I am sorry you are sick, Gales—perhaps you had better go up stairs into the chambermaid's room and lie down a little while—you do look pale. Remember, I never require any one to work for me unless they are able—and, by the way, are you subject to headaches, Gales?"

"I have suffered very much, ma'am, but somehow I believe I am getting used to them," answered the girl with a faint, sickly smile.

"Because," continued Mrs. Harris, "if you are not healthy, why of course I cannot consider my engagement with you binding; I have a great deal of sewing, and cannot afford to hire any one who is constantly putting it by on account of sickness."

Another tear stole down the cheek of the poor seamstress as she meekly folded her work.

"I should be very sorry to lose your patronage, Mrs. Harris," she answered, "and I hope you will try me a little longer—I will use every exertion to please you. If—if—I could have a room to myself I think I could do better."

"A room to yourself—nonsense—Chilson never thought of such a thing! Pray what objection have you to this?" exclaimed Mrs. Harris.

"I do not wish to complain, but sometimes the noise of the children makes my head whirl and ache very badly."

"That I can't help; if you sew for me, you must get used to the noise—that's all—Chilson did. I cannot have any other room but this littered up with work, and I choose the children to be kept here."

"Very well," said the girl with the same sad smile. "I dare say I shall get used to it. If you please, I think I will go home now—I am very sorry to have disappointed you today."

Mrs. Harris deigned no answer, and putting on her bonnet and shawl, the poor, young seamstress wearily threaded the gay, noisy streets to her own wretched abode.

Six months prior to the scenes just related, a small house, located in a quarter of the city densely packed with a hard-working, industrious class of citizens, had been rented by a family of the name of Chilson. The ground floor of the dwelling was disposed of to a bookbinder, only reserving for themselves two small rooms above, and a kitchen in the rear. They were strangers in the neighborhood; but from the fact that the father of the family was utterly helpless, from a paralysis which had destroyed both mind and body, they excited a lively interest and commiseration.

Mrs. Chilson was evidently an invalid, although she was never heard to complain: if she suffered, it was silently, and with quiet cheerfulness and resignation performed her heavy duties. Amy was the eldest, and had just entered her eighteenth year. Caroline was fourteen, and the little Nina a child of ten summers. Their united labours served to maintain them comfortably from day to day, and to meet the rent, &c., but it was done by constant, unremitting toil, and by using every penny with the most scrupulous economy, so that it was evident, should any untoward circumstances prevent the mutual aid by which their little fund accumulated, it would be severely felt by all.

Their path in life had not always been the humble one through which they now struggled, battling with disease and poverty; for at no very late period, though long enough to have escaped the memory of sunny friends, they had lived in affluence. But reverses came to them as to thousands of others, happily not always with such disastrous effects; for the sudden loss of his fortune so completely mastered the energies of Mr. Chilson, as brought him in the course of a few months to his present deplorable state—helpless— hopeless—a burthen to himself and family; but far were they from owning the burthen. It was a lovely sight, the devotion of mother and children to that poor, helpless, old man.

Upon Amy the hopes of this little family were placed. She was their support and comfort. Although, as I have said, born in affluence, Amy Chilson now followed the humble occupation of a seamstress. She considered herself fortunate to have obtained the patronage of three ladies of fashion, by whom she was kept constantly employed, and there is no need of saying that, on her part, Amy was faithful and unwearied in her efforts to please. Day after day, beneath the rays of a scorching sun or through drenching rains, did the young girl hie cheerfully to her toil—subjected through the day perhaps to supercilious looks, the sneer, the cutting reproach, the whims and caprices of her lady patronesses. But it was to earn bread for the loved ones at home, and so poor Amy submitted to all with a cheerful, happy spirit, reaping the harvest of contentment even for her own lowly lot, when placed in comparison with the hollow, frivolous scenes to which she was a daily witness. Mrs. Chilson folded books for the honest bookbinder occupying the lower story. It was but little she could earn, it is true, but every little is much to the poor. Caroline embroidered in worsteds, knit comforters, mittens, and children's jackets, while it was little Nina's province to help all, to amuse father, tidy up the room for mother, and assort the gay worsteds for her sister. Busy as a bee then was Nina from morning till night, and her voice, like the song of a young bird, brought gladness to the dwelling.

It was late in the afternoon of a cold, boisterous day in midwinter, one of those days when one appreciates a rest within doors, and a nook in the "ingle side." A cheerful fire was blazing from the grate, while drawn up closely in one corner of the fireplace, a large, old easy chair supported the helpless frame of Mr. Chilson. At his feet sat little Nina assorting her crewels, and spreading them as she did so over the knees of the old man, who, pleased as an infant at their rainbow shades, toyed and laughed as she playfully waved each skein before his eyes, ere placing it with the others. Seated near the only window in the room, that not a ray of precious daylight might be lost, sat Mrs. Chilson and Caroline, each busily engaged with their work. No carpet covered the floor—but it was admirably clean, and every little article of furniture—the few chairs, the table, the little bookshelf—were as neat as they could be. In one corner of the room a coarse muslin curtain concealed the bedstead, which turned up to the wall, after a fashion now superseded by the more graceful sofa-bed and other ingenious devices.

"Poor Amy will have a cold walk this bitter evening," said Mrs. Chilson, looking forth as she spoke upon the dreary scene. "See, Caroline, how every one hurries along, as if eager to reach their fireside;—God help those who have none to go to!" And with pious gratitude Mrs. Chilson mentally thanked her Maker for the comforts yet left them.

"I hope I shall soon be able to take Amy's place, mother," said Caroline; "it is hard she should always be the one to encounter such dreadful weather; next year, don't you think next year, mother, I can work for Mrs. Harris as well as Amy?"

"You are a good child!" said Mrs. Chilson, putting back the long golden ringlets, and kissing the fair young brow before her.

"Hark, how the wind blows!" exclaimed little Nina, listening to the gust which now swept around the dwelling. "How I wish we lived in Arch Street now; then dear sister could stay at home. Ah, I can just remember, mother, how, whenever it stormed, you always sent the carriage to bring Amy and Caroline from school."

"Carriage," mumbled the poor invalid; "car-riage—oh, yes, order the car-riage; and tell John to drive care-fully—care-fully—it is warm—very warm for the poor horses."

"Poor dear father!" sighed Caroline, "he little knows how hard his darling Amy toils for us; ah, she is coming,—yes, there she is just turning the corner; why how slow she walks!"

Amy. From Caroline H. Butler, "Amy," in *Sartain's*. January 1851, p. 28.

"The wind is very strong, and directly in her face, poor girl!" said Mrs. Chilson.

Nina in the meanwhile sprang from her seat, and ran fleetly down the stairs, to open the hall door for her sister.

Slowly, slowly Amy toiled up the narrow staircase, for grief made her footsteps heavy, and with a pale, sad countenance she entered the little chamber.

"Now God help us, dear mother!" she cried, falling on her mother's neck, and bursting into tears.

"Amy, my child, my darling, what is the matter?" exclaimed Mrs. Chilson.

"Sweet sister, dear Amy, what is it,—what has happened?" cried Caroline, hanging fondly over her, while little Nina, falling on her knees, threw her arms around both mother and sister, sobbing as if her dear little heart would break.

"Amy, tell me, I beseech you, what it is distresses you; has any one dared to insult my poor child?" cried Mrs. Chilson.

"Oh no, thank God not that, dear mother!" answered Amy, unloosing her arms from her mother's neck, and looking sadly in her face, "but I know not what is to become of us, nor where I shall find work for to-morrow, for, alas, dear mother, Mrs. Harris has told me I need not come to her again."

"Amy!"

"It is so, mother; and on calling at Mrs. Frisbie's and Mrs. Dunn's, I find through Mrs. Harris's recommendation they also have engaged another person to work for them."

"My poor children," said Mrs. Chilson, regarding the weeping group; "and what reason have they for dismissing you, Amy?"

"They give none, and I know of none, unless they may have found some one whom they can employ cheaper; but I should not mind it so much if I knew of any other situation where I might at once obtain employment, for I fear, dear mother, ere I am able to secure another situation, you will suffer for my little earnings."

"'God tempers the wind to the shorn lamb,' my love," answered Mrs. Chilson, kissing her. "Let us not forget that others must live as well as ourselves, and perhaps some one even more needy has obtained Mrs. Harris's patronage; let this thought reconcile us to a misfortune so unlooked for; we will place our trust in God, and look forward with hope to the future."

"Dear mother, you are always so cheerful and so resigned," said

Amy, "that it is a reproach for your children to give way one moment to despondency in your presence. Come, dear Caroline, dry
your eyes, and you too, darling Nina, let us follow our mother's
noble example,—yes, we *will* look to the future with hope. And
now, girls, let us get the supper ready, and then we will calmly consider what is best to be done in this emergency."

"Yes, sup-per, have sup-per," slowly articulated the old man;
"we'll have oys-ters, Mrs. Chilson, and cham-pagne: John, bring
in glass-es, wee'll have a glo-ri-ous supper!"

Amy bent over her poor old father, and kissed his cheek, tenderly smoothing his long silver hair.

"Thank God!" she whispered to Caroline, "our poor dear father does not realize our troubles."

When their frugal meal was prepared, Amy, kneeling on a low
footstool by the side of her decrepit parent, fed him as tenderly as
she would have done a babe, and then in a low, sweet voice sang a
pleasing lullaby, which soon closed the eyes of the weary old man
in sleep.

The evening was passed in forming hopes and plans for the
future, which the morning was doomed to dissipate.

For weeks poor Amy vainly sought employment,—occasionally
the sympathizing neighbours favoured her with some trifling work,
but this was at best precarious. Mrs. Chilson, too, became suddenly
ill—the father was daily growing more querulous and exacting—
their little money was gone—and with rigid economy their small
stock of fuel and groceries was rapidly diminishing. What wonder
that poor Amy almost despaired—for she saw only poverty and
wretchedness impending over those she loved.

Such was one result of Mrs. Harris's policy.

After an absence of six years, Leonard Darlington returned from
India. During this long separation from country and friends, he had
accumulated a handsome fortune, and had now come home, as he
expressly declared, to look out for a wife, and settle down into the
sober state of matrimony.

He was not yet six-and-twenty, fine-looking, graceful in his
manners, and agreeable in conversation. But what was far better,
he added to these outward gifts a noble, generous heart, and fine
talents, highly improved by education and travel.

The morning after his return, Leonard strolled into his sister's apartment, and throwing himself carelessly upon the lounge, proceeded to make inquiries about those of their friends with whom he was most intimate ere he went abroad.

"The Nixons, Ida, what has become of them?"

"Oh, they are immensely rich, and are living in splendid style. Cornelia—you remember Cornelia?—she is a sweet girl, I assure you, and quite a belle."

"Time does work wonders then!" answered her brother, laughing, "for I only recollect her as a little, freckled, awkward schoolgirl, with great gray eyes. Well, the Cassidys and the Derwents?"

"Very dashing, fashionable people, I assure you, Leonard," replied Ida. "To be sure, Mr. Cassidy failed a year or two since, and everybody thought they would go down, but it made no difference at all in their style;—they did, I believe, give up their carriage for a month or two, but they now sport one of the most elegant equipages in Chestnut Street."

"The Chilsons, Ida,—are they still living in Arch Street?" inquired Leonard.

"Oh no; their glory has departed, Leonard; indeed I know nothing about them. Mr. Chilson failed ever so many years ago,—just after you went away, I believe,—and they lived so shabbily, that of course ma could not think of visiting; afterwards I heard Mr. Chilson had a fit or something of the kind, and then they moved off I don't know where."

"You surprise me," said her brother, "when you and Amy were such intimate friends—surely the loss of property could not have affected your friendship!"

"Why you know, Leonard, people of our style cannot visit everybody;—Amy was a dear girl, and I am sure I almost cried my eyes out at first, because mamma would not let me visit her any longer; but I suppose it is all right; we must do as the rest of the world do."

"No, it is not right, Ida," answered her brother; "and who or what constitutes the world you speak of? A few people who live in fine houses, and ride in fine coaches! Fie, Ida; if upon such you pin your faith, if of such is your world, then break from its trammel at once and for ever, dear sister; such servility is unworthy of you."

"Nonsense; how you talk, Leonard!" exclaimed Ida. "What queer notions you have picked up—as odd as the people you have been among. Recollect, Mr. Leonard Darlington, we are ranked

among the *elite* of the city, and to extend our acquaintance to bank-
rupts and beggars, would be folly."

"Ida, my dear sister, if you are, as you say, among the *elite,* which,
I suppose means the most fashionable, then set a noble example, and
welcome the good and virtuous to your circle alike, whether they
come in ermined robe, or in the homely guise of poverty."

"Ridiculous, Leonard!" said Ida, turning pettishly away from
him.

"And listen, Ida," continued her brother; "suppose you in turn
should become poor, do you think *your* world would no longer
recognize Ida Darlington, the belle of W—— Square? No, Ida, you
would be forgotten in a week, and your dearest friends would pass
you unrecognized, or with a condescending bow, more cutting than
their neglect!"

"You talk so strangely," answered Ida; "as if *we* could ever
become poor! And if we did, I am sure the loss of wealth could never
alter *our* position in society!"

Leonard smiled: "Well, dear sister, I trust you may never be
made to acknowledge the fallacy of your present belief! Poor Amy
Chilson! Then you can tell me nothing of her?"

"Nothing, Leonard; why you look as forlorn as Don Quixote.
Ah, I had forgotten your boyish *penchant;* now I remember, you
used to call her your little wife. And so six years of absence has not
obliterated the impression the soft blue eyes of Amy made upon you
heart! Heigho, poor Leonard! But come with me, I will introduce
you to Cornelia Nixon; in her brilliant smiles you will soon forget
your old flame; come, Leonard."

"Ida, I will not rest until I find out what has become of Amy
Chilson," replied her brother; "and if I find her all I expect, and
her heart be free, it will go hard but my youthful dream shall be
realized. However, I have no objections to renewing my acquain-
tances with Miss Nixon. Ah, sister," he continued, kissing Ida's rosy
cheek, "the world has almost spoiled you, this little heart must beat
more healthfully ere we part again."

The reader will recollect Mrs. Mayhew, and the interest she expressed for Miss Chilson. She had been in the habit of seeing her
occasionally at Mrs. Harris's, when invited by that lady to the nursery, either to pass maternal criticism upon the swollen gums of
"baby," or to examine the "love of a silk or cashmere," just sent

home from Levy's. At these times she had been much struck by the modest and ladylike deportment of the young seamstress, and, upon learning her sudden dismissal from Mrs. Harris's, felt deeply interested for her. She resolved to find her, that if, as she feared, the selfishness of Mrs. Harris had been a cause of misfortune to the young girl, she might herself repair the evil.

Upon calling at Mrs. Frisbie's and Dunn's to ascertain the address of Amy, they professed the same ignorance as Mrs. Harris. So long as the needle plied faithfully, what interest had they in the machine by which it was wielded! Mrs. Mayhew, however, continued every possible measure she could devise to discover Amy's abode, but her efforts proved vain; when it happened one morning that her youngest child was seized with a sudden illness, which in a few moments brought the family physician to the bedside.

After administering proper remedies to the child, the Doctor sat down, and, turning to Mrs. Mayhew, said: "I have met with a very singular adventure, and found an old friend under the most painful circumstances. Last evening I was called in great haste to attend a person whom the messenger reported to be, as he feared, in the agonies of death. I lost no time; my gig was fortunately at the door, and, bidding the man get in with me, I drove as fast as possible to the house of the sick person, and hastened up the gloomy stairway, and into the room my conductor pointed out. Upon a low bed lay a woman, apparently nearly exhausted by a violent hemorrhage of the lungs. The blood was still oozing from her mouth and nostrils, and a cold, clammy sweat already bedewed her death-pale countenance. At the head of the bed sat a beautiful little girl, propping the pillow which supported her mother; while, kneeling on the floor, a young girl, with a face almost as deathly as the one over which she was bending, gently wiped the blood as it gushed forth, and tenderly chafed the brow and temples of the suffering woman. Never shall I forget her look of agony as she read the doubt which sat upon my countenance. I bade her take courage, that I hoped to save her mother. I soon stopped the bleeding, and applied proper restoratives to the almost inanimate form. Her pulse gradually strengthened, her breathing became more regular, and in a short time I had the satisfaction of seeing her open her eyes. There was something in her countenance which struck me from the first as being familiar. I could not help thinking I had seen it before; but when or where I could not remember. It appeared to me, also, that as the poor sick lady languidly opened her eyes, there was a ray of recognition as they met mine. The young girl beckoned me into an adjoining room, where another harrowing sight awaited me. An old man lay stretched upon the bed, as cold and senseless as the clods which must soon cover him. His eyes were open, but the film of death already hid the world from their sight. Painful was the heavy, laboured breathing which alone told he yet lived. Another fair girl, whom I had not seen before, sat by the bedside, and held one hand of the dying man clasped in hers.

"'Tell me, tell me, Doctor, will she live—will our dear mother live?' whispered the lovely girl whom I had first seen, catching my arm, and looking up, breathlessly, into my face.

"'I cannot answer for that even, my dear young lady,' I replied; 'yet, I assure you, from her present symptoms, I think I may safely bid you hope.'

"'Thank God!' exclaimed both sisters.

"I then inquired how long their mother had been ill.

"'For many weeks,' answered the elder; 'she has not been confined all the time to her bed, but has suffered greatly from debility and a heavy cough. We are too poor, as you see,' she added, glancing around the scantily furnished apartment, while a slight colour mantled her pale face, 'to call in medical aid, when it is possible, to dispense with it, and, therefore, our dear mother has been gradually getting weaker and weaker!' A tear rolled down her cheek as she drew me to the bedside of the old man. 'Look; our poor father has been for years but little better than you now see him—scarcely conscious of existence. About two hours since, I was preparing to go out for a few moments; my father was sitting, as usual, in his chair, and my dear mother had just thrown herself on the bed. I think my poor father must have had another fit, for he suddenly became convulsed, and fell forward upon the floor. My mother screamed, and sprang from the bed; but, alas, ruptured a blood-vessel in the attempt. The fright and exertion was too much for her, and she sank into the dying state in which you found her.'

"The poor girl could no longer suppress her tears, and, for a few moments, wept unrestrainedly. I told the unhappy young girls that their father would not, probably, survive until morning; and, recommending such measure as I deemed judicious, returned into the other room. As I approached the bedside of my patient, she opened her eyes, and made an effort to speak. Placing my finger on my lips, I entreated her not to make the exertion. She then smiled faintly, and extended her hand. Now the truth suddenly flashed upon me:

"'You are Mrs. Chilson!' I exclaimed, clasping her feeble hand in mine."

"Chilson—did you say Chilson?" eagerly demanded Mrs. Mayhew, for the first time interrupting the narrative.

"Yes, my dear Mrs. Mayhew. It is indeed too true; in that suffering family I recognized that of the once wealthy Richard Chilson."

The Doctor paused a moment to subdue his emotion, and then continued.

"In their days of prosperity I was their friend and physician, and now found myself again singularly brought to the bedside of the once beautiful Mrs. Chilson. But how great the contrast! When last I stood by her sick couch every luxury and comfort surrounded her, all the delicacies which wealth could furnish to tempt the appetite, the soothing kindness of friends, the most experienced and careful nurses—and now—But I cannot go on; you should witness their present misery to feel the force of what I would say! But to return. After a while, finding I had known them in their prosperous days, the young girls freely related their sad history. It seems the chief support for the family was dependent upon the eldest daughter—a beautiful, charming girl, Mrs. Mayhew—who for some time has followed the profession of a seamstress. A month or two since she was suddenly thrown out of work, and"—

"O, I know all the rest!" cried Mrs. Mayhew, bursting into tears. "Poor, poor girl! Thank God, I have at last found her!"

She then related to the sympathizing Doctor those events with which the reader is already acquainted. "And now, dear Doctor," she continued, "take me there at once—let us not lose a moment in going to the relief of this unhappy family!"

"God bless you, my dear woman!" exclaimed the Doctor, his honest countenance glowing with pleasure; "God bless you! You will cheat me of my prerogative of doing good if I don't take care!"

Let us now give a brief space to Mrs. Harris.

On the same evening when poor Amy Chilson was bending almost heart-broken over her suffering parent, she was dressing to attend a brilliant party given by the fashionable Mrs. ———. For more than a week the successor of Amy had been unremittingly tasked, in preparing the elegant costume in which Mrs. Harris chose to shine for that night, "and that night only." Another *chef-d'oeuvre* of this politic lady, was to put into the hands of her hired seamstress all the fine and difficult work, the embroidery, flouncing, and furbelowing, and the endless trimmings usually left to the expert dress-maker or milliner. But such a course saved her many a dollar, which she felt free, therefore, to expend upon some new and costly article of dress, in turn to be made up in the same cheap manner.

Patient and uncomplaining poor Lydia Gales sat at her task, but the fingers of the needle-slave moved slowly, for her strength was nearly exhausted, and a headache, as merciless as her employer tormented her. Now and then she raised her eyes timidly, and with a look of dread to the time-piece, for it only wanted half an hour to the time when the dress would be required, and, alas! There was yet much to be done to the beautiful robe, ere it could adorn the *well-made* figure of Mrs. Harris.

That lady, enveloped in a costly *negligee,* was under the hands of her hair-dresser, listening to choice bits of scandal, and trying to look grave at the gross flattery of her maid, whose chief business seemed to be in throwing herself into every possible attitude expressive of her admiration, like a dancing Jack set in motion by a string. Mrs. Harris, however, was not so absorbed as to forget her robe, and now and then broke out with,

"Pray, Gales, have not you almost finished? Do make haste! I never saw any one so tedious—there, as I live, you are placing that flower upside down!"

She might have seen that tears were blinding the eyes of poor Lydia, who, making no reply, meekly corrected her mistake. The obsequious hair-dresser gave the finishing touch, and taking a last look as he made his exit, pronounced the head *"magnifique,"* and the maid, giving a tragedy start, protested her mistress could not be more than sixteen.

But Mrs. Harris was growing impatient—it was getting late, so she hurried and scolded unmercifully, which, of course, only served to procrastinate. At length, however, the dress was pronounced finished, and so indeed was the poor seamstress; for, as she withdrew the last basting-thread, she fainted and fell to the floor, unfortunately crushing, as she did so, a splendid *bouquet,* which, at the price of five dollars had just been sent in from the florist's. Of course there was a great outcry in the dressing-room, shrill screams, and cries for hartshorn and cologne, and when, at length, the poor girl was restored to consciousness, her awakening senses were greeted with "Dear me, what a fright I have made of myself! And look at my dress! I declare the trimming is quite rumpled! So you have come to," continued Mrs. Harris, looking over one shoulder at Lydia. "Well, Gales, I may as well tell you, you need not come to me any more; I cannot have my nerves so dreadfully shattered—why it would kill me in a week, I have so much sensibility. Here is a *levy* for you; it is all I have convenient—there, you may go now; to-morrow you can call for the rest of your money. I hope you will get better, Gales, but you look dreadfully sick, and you must see the absurdity of my employing anybody who is too feeble to work. I told you so, you remember, when you first came to me, so you see you have no one to blame but yourself; you ought to exert your-self more—there, good night, Gales," and, turning to her mirror, Mrs. Harris coolly adjusted her ringlets, and admired the exquis-ite lace which draped her shoulders.

The poor girl staggered to the door, and was forced to lean for support against the banisters for some moments, ere she could trust herself to descend the stairs.

O, Mrs. Harris, could you have followed the tottering frame of that wretched girl to her miserable shelter—could you have en-tered with her into that low, damp cellar, where scarce a ray of sunshine ever breaks the desolate gloom—have listened to the cries of starving, ragged children for "Bread, bread!"—would not the blush of shame have outrivalled the *rouge* upon your cheek?

In one corner of this squalid abode sat a man, whose red and bloated countenance told too plainly the tale of his degradation—before him stood a small riband-loom, but the shuttle was idle, for the arms of the man hung sluggishly down, his head resting on his breast, while his heavy and muttered breathing showed him to be sleeping. In another corner a pale, haggard woman, her hair fall-ing matted and tangled from a dirty, torn cap, and her features ghastly with want and poverty, was striving to soothe the feeble wailing of a miserable little infant, which she held to her bosom.

Poor Lydia! What though her temples throb until the swollen veins seem bursting, and her trembling limbs can scarce bear her o'er the threshold, yet there is work, work to be done. No time for sickness have the poor—work—work—work; though the brain may whirl, and the heart sink, and the strained eyeballs fain court the darkness of the grave, yet hand and foot must to the task—work, work, or starve!

The step of Lydia, feeble as it was, aroused the sleeper. With a look of greedy joy he arose and staggered towards her.

"The money, the money, girl!" wrenching the work-bag from her hand, and eagerly rifling the little change it contained. "What, is this all?—curses on you!—now finish that job quick," jerking his head toward the loom; "quick, do you hear, it must go in the morning." And then, with savage brutality thrusting aside a little child, who, clinging to his knees, begged for something to eat, the miserable wretch slammed to the door, to spend at the next grocer's stand the little earnings of his *child!*

And there is no work for the morrow—there is no work for the day after—a week, and still no work—no employment. Alas poor Lydia! Who shall dare to judge thee?—Who shall dare to scorn thee, that, to save thy mother, and those helpless babes, thou hast parted with thine only jewel—thy *innocence*—

> "Thy good name,—the virgin's pure renown—
> Woman's white robe, and honour's starry crown,
> Lost, lost for ever!"

Better would it have been for thee, poor girl, to have died!

Such was the second result of Mrs. Harris's selfish policy. And would this were no common case. Yet could the secrets of all hearts be read, might not many of those whose sickly beat is beneath the gauds of vice and shame, betray that the hand of selfishness—the pitiful desire to make the most of a bargain—the power which wealth must ever possess over the needy and destitute, has thrust them thus piteously forth to live and die *outcast and degraded!*

Think of this, ye favoured sons and daughters of affluence, and deal mercifully and gently with the poor.

It is pleasant to look upon a brighter side of human nature than the last gloomy picture.

Under the unremitting and skillful care of Dr. M——, and the kindness of Mrs. Mayhew, which brought comforts and luxuries to the sick couch, to which the poor invalid had long been a stranger, Mrs. Chilson was soon able to be removed to a pleasant little dwelling hired by the good physician, and a nice Irish girl employed to assist in the work of the family. Caroline and Nina were placed at school, while the patronage of Mrs. Mayhew soon supplied Amy with constant employment, such, too, as she could do at home, without being forced to leave her mother, who was still in very delicate health.

One morning having finished a piece of work for which she knew Mrs. Mayhew was in a hurry, Amy put on her bonnet and carried it to her residence, which was only a few steps from her own. As she went through the hall, she met a gentleman apparently just leaving the house, who, as he passed the unassuming girl, politely raised his hat. Their eyes met, and, without knowing why, both parties involuntarily bowed;—although strangers, the thought for an instant glanced through the minds of each—*we have met before!*"

"Strange!" exclaimed Leonard Darlington, as he walked slowly down the street, "strange, how the countenance of that sweet girl perplexes me. I am sure I must have seen it before, but where I cannot remember,—heigh-ho!—only in my dreams, I fear."

"Why, Leonard, I have waited for you this half hour!" cried his pretty sister Ida, meeting him. "Do you forget, truant, that you engaged yourself to Cornelia and me for the morning? Fie, what an ungallant lover!"

"Pray, sister," retorted Leonard somewhat impatiently, "don't apply the title of lover to me quite yet, if you please. I have told you often that my heart can never belong to Miss Nixon,—but ah, Ida, such a sweet vision as just now met my eyes!—would that I could trace it!"

"And where, my very sensitive brother, did this same vision cross your path?" demanded Ida.

"In the vestibule at Mrs. Mayhew's. She was not a visiter, I should judge. I might perhaps, from her simple attire, conclude her to be some humble relative of the family."

"*Ha ha!* Poor Leonard!—now I'll bet your wedding gloves that you have lost your heart to Mrs. Mayhew's pretty chambermaid, or her dressmaker;—fickle, fickle fellow! And what becomes, pray, of your six years' fealty to poor Amy Chilson?" interrupted Ida, laughing merrily.

"*Amy Chilson!* mused Leonard; "*Amy*—by heavens! Her very eye; but no, it cannot be—yet how strangely her countenance brings up before me the beautiful features of Amy."

The same evening Leonard presented himself before Mrs. Mayhew, not a little to the surprise of the lady, for only that morning he had offered as an apology for not accepting some invitation she had for him, a previous engagement to the opera.

Leonard soon introduced the subject which brought him there by observing:

"As I left your house this morning, my dear madam, I passed a young lady in the hall whose countenance greatly interested me, and my desire to discover who she was, is the only apology I have to give for my apparent fickleness of purpose."

"This morning, Mr. Darlington? I believe I have had no visiters to-day but Miss Cassidy; you are acquainted with her, I think?"

"Oh no, it was not Miss Cassidy by any means," said Leonard, smiling. "The young lady I allude to was dressed in very simple mourning, and if I mistake not, she had a small paper parcel—"

"Oh, now I think I know—yes, she has a very sweet countenance indeed,—I don't wonder it struck you," cried Mrs. Mayhew.

"But, who—who is she?" impatiently demanded her visiter.

"It is Miss Chilson—Amy Chilson—a young lady who—"

Leonard waited to hear no further, but springing from the sofa, he seized the hand of Mrs. Mayhew, pressing and kissing it, as though the dainty little digits of Amy were already within his clasp.

"My dear, dear lady, you have made me the happiest of men!" he exclaimed. "You have restored to me her whom for months I have vainly sought;—where is she,—where may I find her, Mrs. Mayhew?"

"Not a thousand miles off!" she replied, smiling; "only up one flight of stairs—as the young lady happens at present moment to be engaged in a game of romps with little Miss Lilla and Master Harry,—you shall see her presently; only restrain your impatience, and hear me for a moment."

She then gave Leonard a brief sketch of her acquaintance with the Chilsons, to which you may be sure he listened with breathless interest.

We will not trace the path of our young heroine further—we found her in poverty, and we leave her in a state of affluence, which, as the wife of Leonard Darlington, she honours and adorns. With her, her mother and sisters find a happy home, and it is needless to say that she who could make so dutiful a child, cannot fail of being an exemplary wife.

As for Mrs. Harris, she was the first to call upon the once despised *Chilson*. But Amy shrank from her with abhorrence. Whenever she meets her, the memory of that bitter night when she was turned hopeless from her door—the image of that poor old man—of that suffering mother—come up before her, and she turns faint and shuddering away.

Let us hope, however, there are not many of my fair country-women who resemble Mrs. Harris in heart, although there may be those who are thoughtlessly pursuing the same destructive course, who sincerely think they are not only doing their duty to their families, but really take credit to themselves for the cheap rates which they pay the poor seamstress. This is not because they are hard-hearted, or would willingly impose upon those whom they employ—it is want of consideration—culpable, I allow, but not irreparable. There is room for a better state of things; and may the day soon come when the truth of Hood's touching appeal may no longer ring upon the conscience.

WORKS CITED

Blocker, Jack S., Jr. *American Temperance Movements: Cycles of Reform.* Boston: Twayne, 1989.

———. *"Give to the Winds Thy Fears": The Women's Temperance Crusade, 1873–1874.* Westport, CT: Greenwood, 1985.

Bloomer, Amelia. Rev. of "Ruling a Wife," by T. S. Arthur. *The Lily* 1 Nov. 1850: 86.

Bolton, Sarah Knowles. *The Present Problem.* New York: Putnam, 1874.

Boyd, Melba Joyce. *Discarded Legacy: Politics and Poetics in the Life of Frances E. W. Harper 1824–1911.* Detroit: Wayne State UP, 1994.

Chellis, Mary Dwinell. *Our Homes.* New York: National Temperance Society and Publication House, 1881.

Douglas, Ann. *The Feminization of American Culture.* New York: Knopf, 1977.

DuBois, Ellen Carol. *Elizabeth Cady Stanton, Susan B. Anthony, Correspondence, Writing, Speeches.* New York: Schocken, 1981.

Gage, Frances D. Letter. *The Lily* July 1854: 104.

Gordon, Linda. *Woman's Body, Woman's Right: Birth Control in America.* New York: Penguin, 1990.

Hale, Sarah Josepha. Preface. *My Cousin Mary: or The Inebriate.* By A Lady. Boston: Whipple and Damrell, 1839.

Hine, Darlene Clark, ed. *Black Women in America: An Historical Encyclopedia.* 2 vols. Brooklyn: Carlson, 1993.

Lender, Mark Edward. *Dictionary of American Temperance Biography: From Temperance Reform to Alcohol Research, the 1600s to the 1980s.* Westport, CT: Greenwood, 1984.

Mattingly, Carol. *Well-Tempered Women: Nineteenth-Century Temperance Rhetoric.* Carbondale: Southern Illinois UP, 1998.

Minutes of the Second Convention of the National Woman's Christian Temperance Union, 1875. Chicago: Woman's Temperance Publication Association, 1889.

Rorabaugh, W. J. *The Alcoholic Republic, an American Tradition.* New York: Oxford UP, 1979.

Sklar, Kathryn Kish. "Victorian Women and Domestic Life: Mary Todd Lincoln, Elizabeth Cady Stanton, and Harriet Beecher Stowe." *The Public and the Private Lincoln: Contemporary Perspectives.* Eds. Cullom Davis, Charles B. Stozier, Rebecca Monroe Beach, and Geoffrey C. Ward. Carbondale: Southern Illinois UP, 1979. 20–37.

Stewart, Eliza Daniel. *Memories of the Crusade.* 1889. New York: Arno, 1972.

Stowe, Harriet Beecher. *The May Flower, and Miscellaneous Writings.* 1855. Freeport, NY: Book for Libraries Press, 1972.

———. *Uncle Tom's Cabin.* 1853. Chicago: John E. Potter, 1897.

"$10 Premiums" (announcement). *The Lily* March 1854: 40.

Tyrell, Ian R. *Sobering Up: From Temperance to Prohibition in Antebellum America, Eighteen Hundred to Eighteen Sixty.* Westport, CT: Greenwood, 1979.

Willard, Frances E. "The Average Woman." In Amy R. Slagell, "A Good Woman Speaking Well: The Oratory of Frances E. Willard." Diss. U of Wisconsin–Madison, 1992. Ann Arbor, UMI, 1992. Part 2, 619–25.

Carol Mattingly is an associate professor of English and director of the University Writing Center at the University of Louisville. She has published another volume concerning temperance, *Well-Tempered Women: Nineteenth-Century Temperance Rhetoric,* which reexamines and revalues women who participated in temperance reform.